Policing THE Fringe: A YOUNG MOUNTIE'S STORY

WILLIAM KELLY
WITH
NORA HICKSON KELLY

Centax Books
Publishing Solutions/PW Group
Regina, Saskatchewan, Canada

Policing the Fringe: A Young Mountie's Story
by
William Kelly with Nora Hickson Kelly

First Printing – July 1999

**Co-published by RCMP Millenium Foundation
and by Publishing Solutions, PW Group**

Canadian Cataloguing in Publication Data

Kelly, William

Policing the fringe

Co-published by RCMP Millenium Projects.
ISBN 1-894022-30-0

1. Kelly, William, 1911- 2. Royal Canadian Mounted
Police--Biography. 3. Police--Saskatchewan--Biography.
I. Kelly, Nora (Nora Hickson). II. RCMP Millenium
Projects. III. Title.

FC3216.3.K45A3 1999   363.2'092   C99-920102-6
HV8158.7.R69K445 1999

Cover and page design by Brian Danchuk, Brian Danchuk Design
Page typesetting and formatting by Holly Sentz

**Designed, Printed, and Published in Canada by:
Centax Books/Publishing Solutions/PW Group**
Publishing Director – Margo Embury
1150 Eighth Avenue, Regina, Saskatchewan, Canada S4R 1C9
Telephone (306) 525-2304   Fax (306) 757-2439
Email: centax@printwest.com

Dedication

[handwritten: July 20/2001]

*[handwritten: To Bob + Pam
Best Wishes on the next
posting- Ft. Nelson! The 'N' is great!
Take Care,
The Tracks]*

This book is dedicated to the Non-Commissioned
Officers under whom I served.

[We] "lived in the southern fringe of the great
northern timber expanse . . ."

Frederick Phillip Grove
Over Prairie Trails

Foreword

William H. Kelly engaged in the Royal Canadian Mounted Police in 1933, just sixty years after the Force was founded. The North-West Mounted Police (NWMP) was formed in the third quarter of the nineteenth century to police the emerging frontier of the Canadian west. The organization of the NWMP was paramilitary with strict discipline, but the men were trained to perform the duties of a civil police force. Transportation, of course, was that of the period, horsepower. The police officers travelled on patrol by horseback, and moved themselves and their goods between divisional headquarters and outposts by horsedrawn vehicles.

Constable Kelly thought that he was joining a highly modern police organization when he reported to Depot Division for training. But he has since found parallels with his experience and the frontier Force. Paramilitary training was imposed right from the start, and he soon found himself cleaning stables, drilling and mastering intricacies of equitation with his troop of thirty-two hopeful recruits. This was an experience shared by all members of the RCMP in its entirety or in part. The stories of surviving the ordeal of recruit training are legion but not many members have felt compelled to share the details with the uninitiated. Mr. Kelly has done us this favour and most effectively.

But recruit training was not all drill and discipline. The men were expected to begin to learn the basics of the law which they were being sent forth to apply. But the months spent in recruit training were far from the end of their apprenticeship. Bill Kelly found out when he arrived "in the field" that his superiors, including the non-commissioned officers to whom he dedicates this book, had more instruction for him of both the theoretical and practical sides of law enforcement.

This for me was the most instructive part of the book. I learned something about how green constables won their spurs, from the moment when Kelly coped with his duties at the remote northern Saskatchewan detachment of Meadow Lake. Sergeant Combes levied a charge of three dollars on Kelly, for which he received a copy of *The Peace Officers' Manual*. It became Kelly's guide through the bewildering maze of duties and responsibilities of a police officer. Coping with this and the pile of forms and reports the RCMP demanded of its members was a rite of passage for these young men supervised by the sympathetic but exacting NCOs.

Kelly ended up serving six years at detachments in northern Saskatchewan during the dirty thirties. This was not the work for Sherlock Holmes. He was instead confronted with the petty crime and statute contravention which were the commonplace of prairie communities of the era. Stock theft and illegal moonshine were his biggest challenges. He learned a lot about human nature too, whom he could count on in tight situations, and how to cut a corner without restricting a suspect's rights.

Kelly found also that his mode of operation had much in common with the Frontier Force. A team of horses, hitched to a wagon or a sleigh, was often the only way to travel on the rudimentary roads and trails of Northern Saskatchewan. His story of his sleigh being chased by wild dogs on a frozen lake could be right out of Jack London. This book does credit to its author, and is a worthy commemoration of the 125th anniversary of the Royal Canadian Mounted Police.

Dr. William Beahen
RCMP Historian

William H. Kelly

Deputy Commissioner Kelly, RCMP (Retired), was born in Wales, and came to Canada in 1928 at the age of seventeen. In 1933 he joined the RCMP, trained in Regina for nine months, and served five and a half years on detachments in the North Battleford sub-division of "F" Division (Saskatchewan). He spent the next six years (mostly war years) in the Criminal Investigation Branch of the "O" Division (Western Ontario), with headquarters in Toronto, where he was employed on security, sabatoge and black market activities. By 1946 he had attained the rank of Sub-Inspector. He was then posted to Personnel duties at various times in nine divisions of the Force.

In 1951 he was appointed as a liaison officer, based in London, England, to Police, Security and Intelligence agencies in Europe, and was also Officer in Charge of Visa control, supervising RCMP members employed on Immigration security in Europe in cooperation with Canada Immigration Officers. In addition, in 1952 and 1953, he was the RCMP representative at Interpol.

On his return to Canada in 1954, he supervised the enforcement of federal statutes. In 1958 he became the Assistant Director of the RCMP Security and Intelligence Directorate and in 1964 its Director. In 1959 he became the RCMP representative on the NATO Security Committee, and in 1963 he became the chairman of that committee. In 1967 he was appointed Deputy Commissioner, Operations. He retired in 1970, having served nearly 37 years in the Force. He then lectured in Criminology for two years at Ottawa University.

Since his retirement he has lived in Ottawa and with his wife, Nora, has written several books on the RCMP and one on policing in general.

William H. Kelly & Nora Hickson Kelly

William Kelly is a former Deputy Commissioner and Director of Security and Intelligence of the RCMP. After almost forty years of service, he retired from the Force in 1970. Since his retirement he has been active as a consultant to police forces and government bodies, a university lecturer in Criminology and a writer.

Nora Kelly is a former teacher, and a noted historian of the RCMP. She is the author of *The Men of the Mounted*, and co-author, with her husband, of *The Royal Canadian Mounted Police: A Century of History*, and *Policing in Canada*. The Kellys live in Ottawa.

**Previous Books by William H. Kelly
and Nora Hickson Kelly**

- *The Men of the Mounted*, Nora Kelly

- *The Royal Canadian Mounted Police: A Century of History*, Nora and William Kelly

- *Policing in Canada*, William and Nora Kelly

- *The Horses of the Royal Canadian Mounted Police: A Pictorial History*, William and Nora Kelly

- *The Mounties: As They Saw Themselves*, William Kelly

- *The Queen's Horse: Gift of the Mounties*, Nora Hickson Kelly

- *The Musical Ride of the Royal Canadian Mounted Police*, William Kelly and Nora Hickson Kelly

The Kelly Trilogy

A personal and private look at the men in the RCMP, their training and their service, and the women who support, put up with and love them; Bill and Nora Kelly's stories are revealing and fascinating. This exceptional couple are superb examples of the men and women who helped shape both the Force and the country.

POLICING THE FRINGE: A YOUNG MOUNTIE'S STORY

From 1933 to 1939, Bill Kelly trained and was stationed with the RCMP in Saskatchewan. During frontier postings, with patrols on horseback and no telephone, he dealt with bootleggers, illicit stills, cattle and horse theft and insanity. He patrolled on horseback, by democrat, canoe, snowshoes, police car and float plane. Hardship and adventure, life in a pioneer land – the daily routine of a frontier RCMP constable, the specific and absorbing details of Bill and Nora Kelly's fine book brings this time period alive.

POLICING IN WARTIME: ONE MOUNTIE'S STORY

While Canadian service personnel made heroic sacrifices battling the Nazis, other Canadians on the home front were sabotaging the war effort. Bill Kelly, as part of the RCMP Black Market Squad in Toronto, investigated and prosecuted black market activity and security risks in southern Ontario during World War II. Bill Kelly, Former Deputy Commissioner and Director of Security and Intelligence of the RCMP, and co-author Nora Kelly's accurate account of this time period deals with blackmail, fraud, spies, sabotage, illegal gold exports, foreign exchange, gasoline and other rationing abuses. These offences and subsequent RCMP investigations were repeated throughout Canada during the war.

MY MOUNTIE AND ME: A TRUE STORY

Nora Hickson Kelly married a man, not the Force – or so she thought! At times the RCMP became a demanding third partner in the Kelly marriage. One woman's story, Nora Kelly's book details the experiences of many RCMP wives. A determined and talented writer, Nora became a freelance journalist. Her inside knowledge of the RCMP made her the ideal author and co-author of several books on the Force. Her keen observations and astonishing memory make her writing true and vital. This important book provides a glimpse into the lives of the Kellys and of many wives and their mounties.

ONE

In the Fall of 1932, I was employed as herdsman to 100 Jersey cows on a farm on the outskirts of Woodstock, New Brunswick. My boss, an Aberdonian who had come to Canada some fifty years before, was a good man to work for. He expected a hard day's work for what he considered a fair day's pay. We four employees did not always agree with him on the latter, but on the whole he was reasonable. Nevertheless, he lowered my pay from forty-five dollars a month (and keep) to thirty-five dollars. But I appreciated the problems he faced in those early depression days, and it was easy for me to decide to stay with him. There were no other jobs to be found.

It so happened that about the time he again reduced my pay to thirty dollars a month, I saw for the first time a member of the Royal Canadian Mounted Police in full dress which included Stetson and red serge. As he marched down the street swinging his riding crop, all eyes were on him until he turned a corner. He was a new addition to the local RCMP detachment. On April 1, 1932, the RCMP had taken over the provincial policing from the New Brunswick Provincial Police. The Woodstock *Sentinel* reported that the constable I saw that day had just arrived from "Depot" Division in Regina, Saskatchewan. Seeing this constable made me think that I might consider the RCMP as a career. Within a couple of months I had made application at the local detachment for engagement in the Force, had written an educational test and had been accepted, provided I was able to pass the required physical examination.

After some delay I passed the physical examination and was sent to Ottawa. Another physical examination, then I was "sworn in" as a Probationary Third Class constable in the RCMP on July 6, 1933, along with two other recruits. RCMP headquarters was on the second floor of the Larocque department store on Rideau Street in downtown Ottawa. It was not at all impressive. The offices were piled high with cartons. Where there was room, men sat at desks typing. The three of us were "sworn in" before Inspector Patterson in a hallway, and we signed documents which had been placed before us on the top of some stationery cartons.

We were given transport requisitions which would enable us to get train tickets and sleeping berths to Regina, and nine dollars to pay for our meals on the train. I felt elated. Not only was the $1.50 a day and all found better than my pay on the farm, but I had now embarked on a career with steady pay and a pension at the end of my service. But first it would be necessary to satisfactorily serve the probationary period of six months.

We three very green recruits from Ottawa arrived in Regina at 4 a.m. on the morning of July 10, wondering what lay ahead of us. A police car met us and whisked us through the old prairie city before it was awake. Then we drove out to the "barracks", on the western outskirts, where we reported to the guardroom of "Depot" – the training Division.

Our driver deposited us in front of a barrack building where we waited for a night guard to give us further instructions. When he came he led us to an empty barrack room containing eleven single beds with a thin mattress rolled up on each. He told us to choose a bed and wait for a breakfast call. In the meantime "make yourselves at home". We did. Each of us unrolled a mattress, and lay on it until we heard men beginning to assemble on the broad sidewalk outside the window.

We saw that they wore brown denims and blue woollen toques and were forming up in two ranks. They looked a little bit like prisoners in a jail. Each carried a small cotton bag under his left arm. A man in a regular uniform appeared and someone called the roll, to which each man answered a clipped "here". Then they marched away. We had just seen something with which we would soon become closely associated – the morning stable parade.

We returned to our beds until a corporal came and told us to go to the main mess hall for breakfast. We stood in line to get our meal through the window-like openings between the mess hall and the kitchen. As we waited, the men we had seen parade earlier that morning came in, bringing with them the obvious odour of stables. Later, when we became a part of the stable parades, that odour became so familiar that we did not even notice it.

Back in the barrack room the corporal told us that we were the first of thirty men to be known as "F" Squad, which would begin training in a week's time. In the meantime we would act as orderlies according to the duties listed each evening on a notice board in the main hallway of the barrack block. Such duties were called "orderly" duties, but we soon learned that amongst ourselves a mess orderly was referred to as a "mess bitch", a stable orderly as a "stable bitch", and so on. We might be called to clean the halls of the barrack buildings, to help haul hay for the horses, or to do any other work required. After supper that first night, the corporal said, we should report to the barber in the RCMP canteen (dry) for a regimental haircut.

For the rest of the day, the corporal continued, we should visit the quartermaster stores to get our uniforms and other equipment. After several trips to the stores we had an unbelievable amount of kit and equipment. We wondered how we could possibly stow it away so that our barrack room would look as neat and tidy as those we had glimpsed as we passed in and out of the barrack block. It took a day or two, but eventually we managed it.

Kit and equipment were in two categories, loan issue and personal issue. Loan issue consisted of uniforms (but no red serge), boots, blankets, sheets, rifle, Sam Browne equipment with a .455 Colt revolver and twelve rounds of ammunition, several bags for carrying kit and equipment, and several other things, among which was a grooming kit in a cotton bag. When we had organized our kit and equipment, under and above our beds according to standing orders, the grooming kits had prominent and permanent homes on well-polished heavy black leather harness bags lying under the foot of each bed. When loan issues wore out, they could be replaced. The red serge, we were informed, would only be issued if we satisfactorily concluded our probationary training.

Personal issues included shirts, socks, winter woollen stockings, underwear (summer and winter), ties, tooth brushes, hand and bath towels, braces, etc., all issued annually, whether we required them or not. Extra articles of this issue could be purchased on repayment, that is, taken off one's monthly cheque.

The corporal spent most of that first day helping us get settled. We learned that he was a substitute drill and physical training (PT) instructor. The first thing he did was show us how to make our beds, regimental style. It was important, he said, to ensure that the sheet corners were folded correctly. We had been issued two grey woollen blankets and a brown one of better quality. One grey blanket was placed next to the sheets, and the brown one on top of that. The second grey blanket was rolled and placed on top of the pillow, covered with a laundered face towel. To assist us the corporal showed us a drawing of what the bed and equipment looked like when everything was in place.

All personal belongings had to be kept out of sight in the trunks we had brought with us and kept under our beds. It was advisable, the corporal said, for the bed to be made before the first morning parade. This would be the stable parade for which we would be dressed in our new fatigues.

After breakfast we would normally change into uniform, but until it was fitted by the Force tailor we would wear fatigues. We would be allowed fifteen minutes between each parade throughout the day. Every activity was a parade. The squad would "fall in" and we would answer a roll call, even if the activity simply meant going to a nearby classroom. We would simply answer "here", but if an officer was supervising the parade, even though a corporal called the names, we answered "here, sir".

Dust storms on the prairie were frequent, said our helpful corporal, and the loose barrack windows allowed the dust to seep into the barrack room. Each member, in turn, would have a daily responsibility of sweeping the barrack room floor. Slackness in this regard would result in it easily coming to the attention of the sergeant major when he made his daily inspection of the barrack rooms. As for the rest of the room's occupants, keeping their bedding and equipment free of dust was a daily chore. It was easy to find out if the top blanket was free of dust, he said. All the sergeant major had to do was hit it with his riding crop. This was also done by the Commanding Officer when he hit one bed on Saturday morning inspections.

On certain days, the corporal continued, our revolvers were to be placed on the beds for inspection. At other times the revolver would remain in its holster, attached to the Sam Browne equipment hanging on the wall above the head of the bed, under the shelf on which our well-polished riding boots stood like sentinels. One thing the corporal didn't know was why, east of Manitoba, members of the Force were issued with a .45 calibre revolver and, west of Manitoba, with a .455 calibre. Men were tougher out west, said our western roommates.

The corporal conveyed so much information to us during the day that we wondered if we could remember it all. Fortunately, what one recruit forgot, another remembered.

We did not forget the corporal's advice to get a haircut that first evening, so three still very green recruits made their way from our room in "B" block to the basement of "C" block. No one needed to ask if we were new recruits. Our hair showed that we were. The barber, a regular member of the Force, solicitously asked what kind of a haircut we wanted. We had seen the haircuts of other recruits, but as he had asked us we thought we might be treated differently. But it was a joke he played on new recruits. We received the same kind of haircut as the others – clippers all over the head, leaving only a short forelock. That haircut more than anything else that day made us realize that we were indeed members of the Royal Canadian Mounted Police. The barber had put the mark of the Force on us as surely as if he had branded us with a hot iron. We did not appreciate it at the time, but for the sixty-odd years since then I have never had my hair cut completely "civilian" style.

During the next few nights, senior recruits taught us how to "bone" the leather of our hat bands and Sam Brownes so that they would take a shine. We also learned how to put four "dimples" in our Stetsons by soaking the crown in water, and how to get the heavy patina off the uniform buttons by burning it off with matches. We spent the first week doing bitch duties and spending every evening getting our equipment in shape. We even ordered one of two pairs of riding boots to be "blocked" by a local shoemaker. This meant an added thickness of leather in the legs so that they would not wrinkle, and at the same time take a high polish. Meanwhile new recruits were arriving to whom we passed on our new-found knowledge about leather, Stetsons and buttons.

New recruits found saluting an immediate problem. We had been told to salute all officers, but the problem was in knowing who were officers among the uniformed men we met as we worked around the barrack buildings. The NCOs appeared so well dressed that surely they should be saluted. When we did so they corrected us, often with a look of disgust. We soon learned the difference between commissioned and non-commissioned officers. Another difficulty arose. At what distance from an officer was a recruit not required to salute? Slowly we came to judge this distance. When an officer did not return a salute, we knew he was too far away to receive one. Also, it was reasonable for us not to recognize his rank.

The salute we gave was far from regulation, and must have created great amusement among those members watching from the administration building which also housed the headquarters of the Saskatchewan RCMP police division, designated as "F" Division. In saluting when marching, movements of the arm are made in concert with the movement of the left leg. This rule was roundly abused until we knew better. One thing we learned quickly was to "sir" a commissioned officer, and the sergeant major. But at first we "sir'd" just about everybody senior to ourselves.

We checked the notice board every evening to learn our next day's "bitch" jobs, and any other information the notice imparted. In this way I learned my regimental number. The item read:

"Reg. No. 12001 3/Cst. Kelly, W.H.
engaged at Ottawa, Ontario. July 6/33,
and posted to Depot Division."

Whatever else one might forget in life, a member of the RCMP never forgets his regimental number any more than he forgets his name. When two or more constables of equal service are on duty, the one with the lowest regimental number is officially the senior member. There was some grumbling from those recruits from western Canada. They often were engaged days before those engaged in eastern Canada. But they didn't receive a regimental number until their documents arrived in Ottawa several days later. So they had a few days more service, but according to the rules, they were junior to men with less service. It rarely happened that there was any need to distinguish the seniority of constables, but our regimental numbers always made us aware of the seniority of each member.

On my first Saturday in Regina I found myself without a bitch job. So with one of my fellow recruits, Bob Lough of Vancouver, I went to see the RCMP Musical Ride perform in the Regina Exhibition grounds, where the World Grain Show was being held. We had seen the Musical Ride in training at the barracks, now we were going to see the performance that had helped to make the RCMP known all over the world.

The performance was in full swing when a very fast aeroplane flew low over the field, scattering the frightened horses, and throwing most of the their riders to the ground. But only one was unable to catch his horse, mount, and continue in the performance. His horse refused to be caught. When the riderless horse took his place in the ride, it continued to go through the movements. The disconsolate constable went to the sidelines until the end of the first half of the performance. Then he was able to remount as the Ride performed the stationary lance drill. The crowd was highly amused at the rider's inability to catch his horse, and clapped enthusiastically.

Lough and I were just as amused, but not to the extent that we joined in the clapping. Even as new recruits we somehow felt that the rider's embarrassment reflected on us. What we did not know at the time was that an American flyer, Frank Hawks, had just broken a flight record between New York and Los Angeles. The Exhibition authorities had invited him to fly over the World Grain Show on his return flight to New York. No one gave any thought to its possible effect on the performing Musical Ride.

Meanwhile, we recruits had learned from the notice board that "F" Squad had now been officially formed. We would begin training on Monday morning.

1931, Woodstock, New Brunswick.
On the farm.

1932, Woodstock, New Brunswick. On the dairy farm where I worked before joining the RCMP, I am second from the left.

July 1, 1933, Woodstock N.B. On the Kelly farm with my sisters and brother the day I left to join the RCMP.

July 1, 1933, Woodstock, N.B. On the Kelly farm the day I left home to join the RCMP.

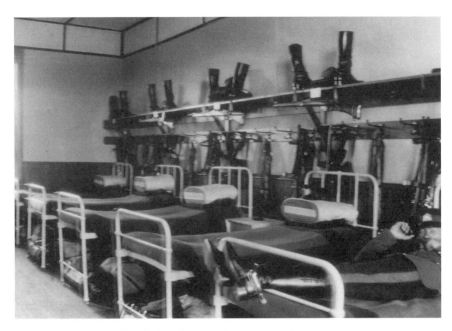

1933, Regina. RCMP Barrack room,
my bed is third from the right.

1933, Regina. Waiting for a singing lesson
in Professor John Henry's waiting room.

TWO

The thirty men of "F" squad were a mixed lot. Most were over six feet in height, and although the minimum was five feet eight inches, two recruits left us wondering if the examining doctor had overlooked this requirement. I was five feet eleven inches, but it still placed me among the shortest men in the squad. Some men, like me, came from the farm. The others included ranchers from Alberta, clerks from British Columbia, a couple of Cape Breton coal miners, and several who had left university to join the Force. The latter seemed to think that RCMP training was just an extension of their college days. They paid as much attention to their social life as to their studies, and sometimes more. One member had left a seminary to become a policeman, but he left at the conclusion of his training.

It was soon apparent that considerable study would be required if we were to pass the written examinations at the end of three months, the end of Part I training. I had been out of school for several years and it took some time for me, as for some others, to get into a studying routine. But passing Part I meant we went into Part II, whereas failing could mean returning to "civvy" street, where jobs were few and far between.

By the time we began our training, we knew whom we should salute and whom we should call "sir". We had to "sir" Sergeant Major E.O. Taylor, even though he was not a commissioned officer, but we rarely had to talk to him. He was the opposite of what we had expected, a middle-aged man, very dignified, who never spoke above a conversational tone. When S/M Taylor attended a parade he walked quietly up and down the ranks without saying a word, adjusting a belt here and a jacket there. We respected him completely.

The S/M lived in a house on the "Square", with his wife and two late-teenage daughters. Even the threats of punishment by the drill instructor could not prevent heads from turning whenever the girls passed a recruit squad in training on the barrack square.

Our regular drill instructor was Corporal George Griffiths; we referred to him as "Griff" behind his back. Formerly of the Welsh Guards, he had lost most of his Welsh "lilt", but his rolling r's came pouring out with great vigour during his frequent criticism of an individual or the squad in general.

Corporal Griffiths was about five feet ten inches in height, but his slim build, emphasized by his riding boots and highly "pegged" breeches, made him seem taller. He walked like a rooster, throwing out his chest with each step. Sometimes when giving instructions he seemed to snarl, and at other times his remarks were pregnant with sarcasm and profanity. I learned some time later that, the previous year, orders had been given not to use profane speech on drill parades. "Griff" was as tough as we had expected. For punishment he sometimes kept us repeating a new movement until the whole squad did it correctly. The many mistakes of one or the other of us resulted in repetition after repetition. Then he would say in a mild voice, "Don't blame me, blame that dunderhead who can't put one foot in front of the other." Other punishment included his ordering a man to run around the football-drill field up to ten times.

Most of us in "F" squad knew nothing about military drill, and we had the hard time we expected from the instructor. Even so, we had no reason to envy the recruits with military experience. On an early parade these men were asked to step forward, and Griff put them through some basic drill movements. Unlike the rest of us, they knew what the instructor's commands meant. But from Griff's remarks they were somewhat short on execution. Instead of showing how things should be done, they showed how things should not be done. "Deplorable" was one of his polite remarks.

We were entertained, but only briefly, by Griff's scathing remarks and his demonstrations of how he saw the militia types carry out his instructions. In an exaggerated way he showed us how they shuffled their feet as they came to a halt; how they swung their arms across their bodies instead of straight forward and back; and how they waddled when marching. Then he had them repeat those movements so that the rest of us could see what he meant, much to their embarrassment.

But nothing, however, evoked as much criticism as the way the "militia" saluted. The RCMP salute should be done in one movement. The right arm at the side should make one movement in an arc to the side. It should stop with the forefinger just above the right eye, nearly touching the headgear – forage cap or Stetson. The arm should remain still. This should leave only one angle in the arm – at the elbow. Then the hand should be returned to the right side, sharply and by the "shortest route".

We guffawed at Griff's demonstrations. His right arm started from his side with a wiggle. The hand went out somewhere in front, reaching the cap by the shortest route. There it continued to flutter instead of remaining perfectly still. Now there were two angles in the arm, one at the elbow and the other at the wrist. Then on the downward motion of the arm, "it was thrown somewhere to the winds", as Griff put it.

We had laughed as though we knew how things should be done and, what's more, were able to do them. But when our turn came to perform, we received equal abuse. However, when at last we learned to do a thing we did it in proper RCMP fashion, whereas the militia types found it difficult to overcome their faults, and in some cases they never did.

We frequently heard from Griff that he had been "blessed with the awkward squad". But life was made bearable by the humour that our mistakes created. We laughed at one another's faults in spite of the punishment of running several laps on the football field. We were thankful for the short rest periods when the instructor had to spend some time on individual instruction for the more awkward ones, especially the recruit with two university degrees, whom we sometimes called the "brain". One day Griff yelled at him, "If there are any more at home like you, tell them not to join the RCMP until I have gone to pension." We couldn't have imagined that in due course he would become a senior officer of the Force.

Some of the most difficult things we had to learn were the movements required when we received our pay cheques on a "pay parade". The squad was drawn up in two lines and told to "stand at ease" facing an officer sitting at a table several yards away. When a man heard his name called, he had to come to attention, march to the table and halt with his arms to his sides, salute, and reach out for his cheque. Holding the cheque in his right hand he should bring his arm back to his side. Next, he should pass the cheque to his left hand and bring his arms to his sides again. He should then step back one pace, salute the officer, make an "about turn", and walk back to his place in the ranks. After another "about turn" to face the officer he stood "at ease".

No one did all the steps correctly, but the militia types came closest. One or another of us did everything wrong, from forgetting to salute, to keeping the cheque in the right hand when saluting after receiving it. Some, knowing that they had made mistakes, tried to correct them, making matters much worse. A common mistake was forgetting to salute after receiving the cheque, before making an "about turn" to return to places in the ranks. Any mistake resulted in the instructor making sarcastic remarks. After our first pay parade we practiced in our barrack rooms to avoid a repetition of our mistakes. On the next parade we made a much better showing, but it took several pay parades before we were all perfect. Then we wondered how we could have been so stupid on the first parade.

I was neither the best nor the worst man at foot drill, so I was not surprised when on an early drill parade I heard Griff shout at me.

"Kelly, pick your feet up!"

His crisp command came four beats to the bar. But I could see I was picking up my feet as high as the others. Then another shout, "Kelly, keep your head up!" But I believed I was doing just that.

"Kelly, swing those arms!"

I felt sure the instructor was picking on me. It amused the rest of the squad that the drill instructor seemed to have a one-man drill squad – Kelly. After more such orders Griff brought the squad to a halt. Angrily he shouted, "Kelly, take one pace forward."

As I stepped forward I had visions of running around the field for the rest of the drill period. Griff rushed toward me. He put his nose close to mine, yelling, "And who the hell told you to step out of line?"

"My name is Kelly, Corporal," I said meekly.

"Get back into line," he growled as he turned to the man he had been calling by my name.

"And what name do you go under?" he barked. When told, he shouted, "You are the man I've been shouting at all morning. Ten laps around the field!"

It was no surprise to anyone in the squad that this man had actually been the culprit. He was indeed the most uncoordinated person I had ever encountered. Whether in drill, physical training or equitation, he seemed to have more difficulty than all the rest of the squad put together. Even in lectures he always waited until time had expired before he started to ask a question, lessening the fifteen minutes we were allowed to get ready for the next parade or lecture. But eventually he made a success of his career in the Force. He was not the recruit we called the "Brain".

The drill instructor spoke no word of apology for the embarrassment he had created for me. But I sensed that for a while afterwards he did not criticize my mistakes, even when I thought he could rightly have done so.

Occasionally the other drill instructor would exchange squads with Griff. Corporal Robertson, an ex-member of a Scottish regiment, was sometimes even more sarcastic than Griff. According to "Robbie" we could do nothing right. In his strong Scottish accent he kept repeating that he was glad he wasn't responsible for our drill performance at the passing out parade. Or he shook his head and said, "and I thought my squad was bloody awful." It seemed to us that the purpose of changing squads was to make us believe that the regular instructor was not such a bad fellow after all. After one such parade we knew we were right. On our way to the mess hall a few of us saw Griff and Robbie nearly bursting their sides with laughter, probably telling each other of the abuse that had been heaped on their respective squads. We realised it was a game they played with every squad, probably to enliven their own monotonous duties.

At last "F" squad became very proficient in this drill. Even Griff had become mellow, and rarely criticized us. By that time we ourselves were our keenest critics. After a drill parade we heaped scorn on anyone making a mistake. This was far more effective than the invective thrown at him by the instructor. And it hurt the offender most when the whole squad happened to be punished for his mistake.

As our drill instructor mellowed, it occurred to us that his attitude in the early parades had been an act he put on for new recruits. But on further reflection we admitted that it seemed any instructor dealing with a squad of new recruits was bound to become extremely frustrated. In any case, we continued to have less frequent drill parades. They had become relatively pleasant interludes in our general training.

Meanwhile, after about six weeks of training we had developed both physically and mentally. In addition to foot drill we had daily physical training. The physical training instructor, Corporal Sykes, inevitably referred to as "Bill", was a mild-mannered man who got the best out of us without the histrionics of the drill instructors. The classroom lectures, which involved the study of various criminal statutes and police procedures, had enhanced our mental alertness.

Our "bitch" jobs went on as usual. We disliked stable orderly duty the most, especially as our Part I training did not include equitation. In each one of the three wooden stables an orderly went on duty each day from 6:30 a.m. to 6:30 p.m. Twenty horses stood in each stable, ten on each side of a twelve-foot walkway, rear end to rear end. The regular stable parades came to each stable during the three mealtimes to groom and feed the horses, during which the stable orderly went to the mess for his meals.

During the day the orderly had nothing to do but keep an eye on the horses, and keep the stable clean and tidy. This meant keeping the walkway clear of straw and the inevitable horse droppings. In order to break the monotony, the orderlies turned this task into a game of trying to catch the droppings before they reached the floor. When a horse raised his tail, the orderly would run to him with the shovel extended in his hands. If he was not too far from the horse he reached it in time. It is impossible for anyone without this experience to know with what satisfaction the results were dumped in the ever-present wheelbarrow.

Sometimes, however, to the disgust of the orderly, his rush to a raised tail was met only by a gust of malodorous air. Unfortunately, one raised tail often encouraged other horses to do the same and, of course, the orderly could not attend adequately to all of them. This usually happened about one hour after the horses' mealtimes. Orderlies were most perturbed when, just after tails had returned to their normal position, the riding master or the veterinary inspector paid his daily visit to the stables. The visitors were as aware of the habits of horses as we were, but their grumbling made it seem that an unclean stable was the fault of the orderly. By 6:30 p.m. each orderly had put in a long and tedious day, and he thankfully left his duties for a necessary hot shower.

From 6:30 p.m. to 6:30 a.m. the stables were under the supervision of a visiting night guard who came and went periodically throughout the night. His job was to see that the horses remained properly tied up, that no horse required veterinary attention, and as the stables were made of wood, to see that no fire hazard existed.

In my experience as night guard (another "bitch" job), there was only one occasion which required more than the usual routine attention. One night I was about to switch on the lights in a stable when I heard the patter of feet. The patter appeared to come toward me, then go away. After hearing several "comings and goings" I switched on the light. I saw a constable of the Force, wearing beaded moccasins, and with an oats measure in his hand, leave the stall of a horse named "Broncho". The man, one of a number of "northern" men who had arrived at Depot some months earlier, was obviously giving Broncho an extra ration of oats. Rumour had it that this man, on being transferred from the north, had travelled on top of the train from Edmonton to Regina.

I walked up to him and asked him what he was doing. As I asked, I saw quite clearly what he had done. He had half-filled Broncho's manger with oats. I persuaded him to empty the manger and return the oats to the bin in the feed room. Then I took him to the guardroom and turned him over to the man in charge.

Broncho is a story in himself. How he came into the RCMP stables I never found out. He was a very dark bay with a large and ugly head. His hip bones protruded, and his ribs were clearly visible. There was no doubt that he needed nourishment, but all sympathy for him vanished when anyone tried to treat him in the normal way.

If ever a horse could be called a brute, Broncho certainly could. He was naturally bad tempered. He had to be fed and groomed from adjoining stalls, so that there was a large four-by-four wooden bar between him and the man who groomed him. He would try to bite anyone who placed hay and oats in his manger, and attempt to kick those grooming him. It took several men to saddle him, and he bucked viciously when anyone tried to ride him. He was not only a nuisance, but also dangerous. But amazingly, the man from the north could walk into his stall and give Broncho a slap on the rump, and he would act as a normal horse. Similarly, for the same man, grooming, even saddling and riding him proved to be no problem. So, of course, this particular constable was given Broncho to care for. Broncho was completely unsuited for equitation training. So while others were training, Broncho and his friend went off across the prairies and back at a slow walk. Recruits were glad that this strange companionship had developed. A few days after the "oats" incident, the constable was escorted to Ontario to undergo mental treatment. Soon after this, to everyone's relief, Broncho left the stables.

About this time "F" squad's Part I training came to an end. By then we had acquired the required proficiency in drill and P.T. But we still had to pass written examinations in such things as detachment adminstration, criminal law and police procedures. I was somewhat apprehensive, but I needn't have worried. I received a better than average mark.

I now had confidence that I would find the second part of training much easier. Foot drill and physical training had become routine. But equitation would have the same importance in Part II training as foot drill had in Part I. This held no fears for me even though the only experience I had in riding was on farm horses, bareback. But I had handled horses for a number of years. I looked forward to Part II training.

1933, Regina. A picture to send home.

1933, Regina. Corporal George Griffiths, "Griff", our Welsh drill instructor.

THREE

After our first three months at "Depot" Division the much vaunted RCMP training held no fears for us. We accepted such rules as not being allowed to remain out of barracks without a pass after 10:30 p.m. We knew that if we wanted it we could get a pass allowing us to remain away from barracks until midnight or later. We accepted rising at 6 a.m. reveille and lights out at 10:45 p.m. We knew when and whom to salute, and we marched smartly whenever we were on the barracks square, all of which we did without a second thought.

We recruits even became proud of our haircuts. They were as surely badges of the Force as the brass badges worn on the forage caps. By now it had been impressed on us that, although we were part of a quasi-military organization, the whole purpose of our training was to prepare us for the civilian job ahead – enforcing the law in a democratic society in which the police were servants of the public. Nothing in our training destroyed the initiative we would need when we went to "the field". We had learned much about administering a detachment and enforcing the law. It was later, after leaving the training division, that we discovered how much more there was to learn.

In our Part II training we delved more deeply into federal statutes, particularly the Criminal Code, the Juvenile Delinquents Act and the Railway Act, which all provincial police forces in Canada enforced. The RCMP was under contract to all provinces, except

Ontario and Quebec, to act as their provincial police. We were not taught anything about provincial statutes, because, we were told, we would learn about them in whatever province we happened to be stationed.

Every recruit was expected to be able to drive a car. We were taught the principles of a four-cycle combustion engine, although we were not being trained as mechanics. That knowledge didn't help us drive cars any better, and those of us who had seldom driven a car, would have appreciated practical instruction. Part II training included instruction in rifle and revolver drill, as well as in the practical use of both weapons at the nearby rifle range. We progressed to *jiu-jitsu* in the physical training class.

Everything was a parade. Even before a lecture we were lined up in two ranks for a roll call before marching off to the lecture hall, usually only a few yards away. Between subjects we were allowed a fifteen-minute break, during which we sometimes had to change from one uniform to another. In lectures there was no time to ask questions after the period expired. One member, the uncoordinated one, repeatedly did this, making us wait for the class to be dismissed. We came very close to carrying out the many threats to throw him into the horses' drinking trough. When we complained to the lecturer about him, the only answer we received was, "There's one in every squad."

After three months we had developed sufficiently to undertake the more serious "bitch" job of Prisoners Escort. Normally, this meant escorting prisoners brought from Regina jail each day as they did chores of one kind or another around the barracks, until they left for the jail in midafternoon. This procedure seemed to be mostly a matter of training for the escort.

Occasionally a member of the Force would be sentenced to a term of imprisonment "in the Regina guardroom" pending his dismissal from the Force. The penalty in such cases was usually thirty days in jail, for an offence against rules and regulations. In the daytime he was supervised by an escort as he went about the barracks doing odd jobs. Mostly, such men were only waiting to hear the commissioner's decision on an appeal they had submitted against a recommendation of the trial officer that they be dismissed from the Force. When an appeal was dismissed, as it usually was, the convicted member was given his discharge immediately. We wondered what offence he had committed, but we didn't have to wonder very long. Soon the offence and punishment, along with the commissioner's decision on any appeal, would be published in the weekly General Orders. G.O.s were one way in which the commissioner in

Ottawa corresponded with the members of the Force. They contained special orders to the field, such as raises in pay, promotions, men and horses being taken on or struck off the rolls, detachments being closed or opened, and the punishment meted out in Orderly Rooms throughout the Force.

One item in our training never changed – the Saturday morning C.O.'s inspection. We began to prepare for it on Friday evening by scrubbing the barrack room floor and dusting every nook and cranny. There was never a shortage of dust in that time of the great prairie drought. The ever-blowing prairie wind forced dust through the loose window frames into our rooms and into our blankets. In summer, when we kept the windows open, it was even worse. We polished and shined our equipment, oiled our rifles and revolvers, and washed our lanyards. On Saturday morning, before the eleven o'clock inspection, we put clean sheets on our beds, and with a partner we each took our blankets outside to shake the dust out of them. Each recruit feared that it would be his bed the C.O. would hit with his riding crop to see if any dust remained in the blankets. We always made sure that the length of our hair was acceptable, that is, severely clipped.

On Saturday morning we had the usual before-breakfast stable parade. After breakfast we returned to the stables to scrub them down, groom the horses and clean the saddlery until 10 a.m. Then we returned to the barrack rooms to prepare for inspection, and make sure everything was shipshape, according to local orders. Rifles and revolvers were placed on the beds in approved fashion, together with the ammunition which had been issued to each man. Each trunk was safely stored beneath the bed, along with a canvas kit bag and a highly polished black leather saddlery bag. There they could be easily checked, along with the polished black stable boots and grooming kits which had been placed on them. A highly polished Sam Browne hung on a peg on the wall above the head of each bed. A rolled-up blanket was put on the shelf above the Sam Browne, with the Stetson on it. On each side of the blanket there was a well-polished riding boot with toes pointing to the wall.

The inspection began precisely at 11 a.m. The C.O.'s retinue included the sergeant major and the Division Orderly, and sometimes an officer or two who happened to be taking a training course at "Depot". The Officers wore "blues", and the NCOs wore their red serges. The C.O. would first visit the stables and the "artisan" shops, those of the blacksmith, the armourer and the saddler. One member in each room kept an eye on the inspection party so that it would not arrive at the barrack room unexpectedly.

The Division Orderly led the inspection party into the barrack room, and called us to attention as we stood "at ease" at the foot and at the right front corner of our beds. As the C.O. inspected each recruit he asked, "Any complaints?" The answer was always "None, sir." We had been taught that "None, sir" was the proper answer. No one had even suggested that if indeed we did have complaints we should answer, "Yes, sir." The C.O. would pick up a rifle here and a revolver there, and look through the barrels. Then he would bring his crop down on a bed to see if the dust had been shaken out of it. From his house, if he had wanted to do so, he could have seen this being done the night before. With these things done, he would glance around the room and quickly depart, leaving us standing at attention.

When the C.O. had completed his inspection of all the barrack rooms, we were allowed to go to the mess hall even though it had not yet been inspected. The mess staff, including the mess "bitches", had been preparing for inspection since early morning. They had scrubbed and polished everything in sight, including the kitchen sinks. For the inspection the cooks were dressed in their uniforms; newly laundered white jackets, pants and tall white hats. When the C.O. arrived, the room was called to attention for him to ask in a loud voice as he passed toward the kitchen, "Any complaints?" He walked on not waiting for an answer, but it came usually from an NCO who would answer "None, Sir". I often wondered if someone unexpectedly stood up and answered "Yes, Sir", what the reaction would be.

In the kitchen the C.O. spoke briefly with the cook and sipped a little soup. Then, with his retinue following behind according to rank, he led the march back through the mess hall. Lunch on Saturday was the best meal of the week, but all meals were good. Some of us, including myself, had never eaten so well. I was sure the C.O. knew that the Saturday meals were exceptional, we did not eat as well on other days.

One week we had no butter with the noon meal for several days. There was much grumbling, but no one thought of making a complaint. But at the next monthly mess meeting, which was another parade we all had to attend, by arrangement we all refused to vote that the mess bills be paid. The chairman, the sergeant major, was nonplussed for a moment. Then in his quiet way he said it made no difference. The bills would be paid anyway. We had expected that they would be, but recruits were never invited to another mess meeting.

We blamed the mess secretary, a regular member of the Force, for the butter incident. It was his job to purchase supplies for the mess after discussing the daily menus with the cook. We failed to appreciate the difficulties of feeding a large body of men on thirty cents a day per man, or ten cents a meal, according to rules and regulations. We thought that perhaps he had run short of funds, hence the butter incident.

Some time later the Force celebrated its 60th anniversary, its Diamond Jubilee, with a sumptuous Christmas dinner in the mess hall at 3 p.m. on Christmas day. The division's commissioned officers and NCOs sat among the men, and in front of each of us lay an orange-coloured two-page menu. I have it before me as I write. The meal consisted of tomato juice cocktail, lobster salad, tomato and oyster soups, relishes, baked ham with champagne sauce, turkey and cranberry sauce, and five vegetables, including candied yams. For dessert there were English plum pudding, hot mince pie, Christmas cake, fresh fruits, nuts, tea, coffee, "aerated waters", beer and wine. With the good fellowship that prevailed it was indeed a meal to remember.

Saturated, we returned to our barrack rooms to rest up for further celebrations that evening with our friends in Regina. As I and my roommates lay on our beds discussing the splendid meal, the best we had ever had, the matter of the absent butter came up. Someone said he suspected that the mess secretary had been saving up to pay for the Christmas dinner. We wondered how much he had scrimped on other items to pay for the meal, which undoubtedly cost more than regulations allowed. We had no way of knowing that, probably, headquarters in Ottawa had given the division a grant to pay for it. In any event we were prepared to forgive the mess secretary for anything he had done.

By Christmas "F" squad was well along in its equitation course. We considered it just another phase of our training. None of us thought that we might be sent to one of the six or seven mounted riot squads stationed across the country, available at the request of local authorities to deal with strikes or disturbances by groups of unemployed people. Nor did we anticipate that anyone in the squad would be sent to one of the twenty-three field detachments that still used horses – thirty-seven in all – instead of to one of the other 417 detachments in Canada that used only mechanized transportation. No one had advanced any reason why we should think in this way, but we did.

The philosophy behind RCMP recruit equitation seemed to be that the outside of a horse was good for the inside of a man. One of our riding instructors in 1933, Staff Sergeant Cecil Walker, in writing about equitation in the RCMP *Quarterly* a few years later, put it this way:

The mounted police horse is the equine detector of courage, or lack of it, in police candidates. Skilled tuition in equitation will replace timidity with boldness and develop a disregard for the inevitable body bruises which even the most proficient must experience. Handling of horse promotes mental alertness and rapid acceleration of muscular reflexes . . .

No doubt equitation does all the things the Staff Sergeant claimed for it, and it certainly helped to mature youthful recruits. But he overlooked the fact that most policemen in the world had acquired desirable police qualities without ever having been near a horse.

Recruit equitation had been part of the RCMP training since its inception in 1873. But for a number of years before 1933, some members believed that it was not an essential part of police training. Still others believed that whatever the value of equitation, every man who belonged to a "mounted" organization should be trained to ride a horse. We in "F" Squad, who wanted nothing to do with horses after leaving the training depot, disagreed heartily with Walker.

The matter of such training did not come to a head until 33 years later. In the summer of 1966, the federal Treasury Board ordered the RCMP to discontinue recruit equitation training. The Force would, however, retain the horses of the Musical Ride, and those required to teach equitation to future members, who would not receive it as part of their basic training. This change, however, did not to take place until after the large majority of 1933 recruits had completed lengthy service and had gone to pension.

*1933, Regina, Sask. Recruits waiting for transfer to the field,
I am in the centre in the front row.*

FOUR

At Depot Division in 1933 equitation horses were a mixed lot. The thirty-six Musical Ride light bay horses were well standardized in conformation, size and colour. Not all the equitation horses, however, conformed to the required standard of between fifteen and sixteen hands in height. They ranged all the way from fourteen to seventeen hands, and a few were even taller. Indeed, the RCMP found it difficult to obtain suitable horses and had to overlook set standards, just as they had done since the inception of the North-West Mounted Police in 1873.The colour of the equitation horses included all shades of bay, some chestnut and a few blacks. They ranged in age from the recently trained three-and four-year-old remounts to the sixteen to eighteen year olds that had been used for many years in the training of recruits. The older horses, at the beginning of an equitation course, understood the instructors' commands much better than did the recruits.

The difficulty in getting suitable horses arose from the fact that western ranches no longer raised saddle horses, as they had done before the automobile came into common use, when light horses were in demand by professional people and even farmers. During the 1930s, the Force searched constantly for three year olds that would make good saddle horses. After about six months training they were considered suitable for recruits to ride.

We of "F" squad approached equitation with great enthusiasm. We felt ready to mount our horses and gallop across the open prairie to the west of the barracks. We soon realised that our training did not include such a wild idea. We didn't even get astride a horse in the first several lessons. In the first lesson we simply listened to the instructor describe the anatomy of the horse, and give us some rules about how a horse should be handled. He also ordered that we must leave our spurs in the barrack room until further notice.

In the second lesson we learned how to put a saddle blanket on a horse. We tried it and by the time the instructor examined our efforts, the lesson was over. The next lesson taught us how to saddle a horse properly. We had to show that we remembered the lesson about the blanket. Then we were shown how to tighten the saddle girth properly, so that proper tightening would offset the natural tendency of a horse to expand its own girth. Proper tightening would also ensure that the saddle would not slip when a recruit mounted.

Still, the time had not come when a recruit could actually ride a horse. The next two lessons taught us how to "stand to" our horses, "prepare to mount" and be ready for instructions to mount. Equally important, we learned how to hold the double reins in our left hands. After doing these things and being checked individually by the instructor, we were ready to mount "by numbers". But that was to be the next lesson.

On one – put the left foot in the left stirrup; two – heave the body into a standing position, aided by placing the right hand on the back of the saddle. The left hand, now holding the reins, rested on the pommel. Being careful not to dig the toe of the left boot into the horse's ribs, three – throw your right leg over the horse's back, and settle into the saddle. Then put the right foot into the right stirrup without looking down to see where it is. Then we learned how to dismount by taking the lead from the rider on the extreme right. When he nodded his head we stood up in the left stirrup, now holding the saddle as before to steady ourselves. Another nod and we dropped to the ground. Then a "stand to your horses", and "make much of your horses", which meant patting them and saying nice things.

We received all this instruction in the riding school into which we had walked leading our horses in single file. At the end of each lesson we returned to the stables, about two hundred yards away, in the same way – without having ridden a horse one yard. Frustrated, we grumbled among ourselves. Surely, we thought, during the next lesson we would actually ride. During most of the next lesson, however, it seemed we were wrong. After we had mounted to the instructor's satisfaction, he chastised some recruits for pulling on the bits as they mounted. Then he checked our posture, the position of our hands, legs, feet and upper body. Again and again he shouted,

"Sit upright – heels down – toes up – soles out," and explained how the proper position of legs and feet helped the rider control the horse.

At last, minutes before the lesson ended, he allowed us to move our horses around the riding school in single file – at a slow walk. Then we dismounted and led our horses back to the stable. Again we thought that in the next lesson our training would speed up. It did, but not as we had expected. After mounting we were told to cross our stirrups, tie the reins around the horses' necks and fold our arms. Then we rode around the school several times at a walk. Even so, we were surprised when the instructor ordered us to trot our horses at a slow pace, and to take the bumps. Which meant not to "post" to avoid them. We continued walking and trotting for several lessons, discovering muscles we never knew existed, and acquiring raw patches on our posteriors, some of which required the attention of the RCMP doctor.

During this period we were allowed to use the stirrups and reins. But the instructor reverted to their non-use when he wanted to punish us for errors such as pulling on the bits unnecessarily. This always brought forth a burst of colourful language from Corporal Anderson (Andy to us), who shouted, "Good horses are hard to find, but men are a dime a dozen." We didn't know at that time the difficulty in finding suitable horses. But we did know in those depression days that men were plentiful, and that we were fortunate to have been engaged. Many years later I learned that in the eighteen months ending March 31, 1934, the period in which I joined the Force, 6,554 men had applied for engagement, but only 336 had been taken on.

Our two-hour equitation periods took place from Monday to Friday, morning or afternoon. Our instructor continuously repeated his earlier commands "Heels down, toes up, soles out." It seemed that this was the riding instructor's equivalent to the foot drill instructor's "Left, right, left, right." Then came some new orders – "Heads up, elbows in, backs straight."

Eventually we became proficient at trotting and could "post" to avoid taking the bumps. We felt it was a great step forward when we were ordered to jump a few low poles, with the reins tied up, stirrups crossed and arms folded. But being told to lean forward as the horse raised itself to take the jumps didn't ensure that everyone landed safely on the other side. Some recruits found themselves on the tanbark-covered floor, while their horses bounded away to line up behind the previous jumpers. Others remained on their horses but landed with their arms around the horses' necks.

The notably uncoordinated recruit finished the one jump astride his horse's neck. The frightened horse raced around the riding school as the instructor shouted in his loudest voice, "Stop that little horse! Stop that little horse!" As the recruit's horse carried him past the instructor, he yelled back, "This is no time for fooling, corporal." The horse continued for another turn around the school before its rider slid to the tanbark. The squad's grins turned to outright laughter at the recruit's remarks. Even the instructor could not avoid smiling.

Eventually we were allowed to wear our spurs. Slow walks vanished from our training. We trotted and cantered frequently, but never did we gallop. Later we learned to perform the basics of cavalry drill, moving our horses from single file at the trot and canter, into half sections (twos) and sections (fours). We wheeled right and left in columns and crossed back and forth across the riding school between oncoming horses. Soon we were doing some of the movements of the famous musical ride. We began to realize we might be called upon to replace men on the current musical ride. Few of us wanted to join the ride, but we knew we could be ordered to do so. But if that was our fate, then that was our fate.

In good summer weather, meaning no dust storms, we trained on the open prairie. In winter we took long rides if the weather was at all reasonable, anything less than twenty-five or thirty degrees below zero. On such rides we wore long woollen underwear, a shirt and sweater under the brown jacket, and heavy blue breeches. We wore one pair of lightweight woollen socks, next to the feet, long woollen stockings over the lower legs of the breeches, and still a third pair of heavy woollen socks rolled over horsehide moccasins. Over all we wore a three-quarter buffalo coat, and a muskrat hat, usually with earflaps tied under the chin. We also made use of the blue woollen toques that had been issued as headwear for stable parades. Each of us placed the toque inside our breeches, over our private parts, to keep them from freezing.

In the winter of 1933-34 the prairie drought was at its worst. Dust created great discomfort. Sometimes we could not see through the blowing dust any farther than a couple of horses ahead. Our feet almost froze in the stirrups. We drew our large buffalo coat collars up around our heads as protection against the wind. But as we breathed, solid ice built up around our faces. Our horses suffered, too. Icicles several inches long hung from their nostrils, and their frozen breath formed lace-like white sheets over their breasts and sides. Except for our extremities we recruits were quite warm. As we rode over the prairie we thought of the member who always had an orgasm on such rides. He was the butt of many comments, which stopped only when our instructor, riding ahead of the squad, shouted, "Quiet, back there."

We learned to drill with a carbine – a short cavalry rifle – and with a long truncheon that mounted police carried during certain kinds of crowd control. This reminded us of the riot squads to which we might be sent, although we tried to bury such thoughts in the deeper recesses of our minds.

Toward the end of our equitation course, the sergeant major/riding master, who had paid us infrequent visits over the training period, paid a longer visit than usual. Our instructor put us through all the exercises we had learned. This must have been our passing out parade in equitation, because we never had a more formal one. By this time even the uncoordinated member rode reasonably well, except that he never looked comfortable on his horse.

Throughout Part II we had periodic parades of foot drill and physical training, and the usual classroom lectures. When we had completed equitation, it was time for written examinations. This meant more concentrated study. For many nights recruits sat around the barrack room, studying together. When the examinations were over, I found I had done exceedingly well. Later I came to regret it for a time. But now there was no danger of returning to "civvy" street.

With the examinations over, and what we took to be a pass-out parade before the riding master, our probationary training period ended. About a week later, as if to confirm this, we were ordered to go to the quartermaster stores to be issued with our "red serges", and we went from there to the tailor shop to have them fitted properly. We had them in sufficient time to wear them when "F" squad escorted the Lieutenant-Governor of Saskatchewan when he opened the legislature in February 1934. On such parades the escort trots all the way from the official residence to the legislative building, and as no posting is allowed the riders must take the bumps. My partner and I were in the half section at the rear of the escort, far from prying eyes, so we thought we might post in safety. But by then we were so imbued with RCMP discipline that we continued to take the bumps. We couldn't let "F" squad down.

While we waited to be transferred to the field, we spent most of our time attending stable parades and exercising the horses. Occasionally we had foot drill and physical training parades just to help keep us in shape. We attended court in the city of Regina, and began a course in touch typing. But generally we put in time, waiting for the day when we would leave the training depot. We couldn't understand the reasons for the delay. Later, however, I learned that it was because the provinces in which the RCMP acted as provincial police, "purchased" members of the Force according to their police budgets, which were not always ready at the time recruits graduated at the training depot.

Not all the men who started training in "F" squad finished the course. One man dropped out because of ill health. Another left because he wasn't suited to the Force's discipline. One, whose parents had forced him to join so that "it would make a man out of him", was unsuited to RCMP discipline. He purchased his discharge. Another dropout, the son of wealthy Quebec City parents, constantly appealed to them for money. Once he wanted it so that he could buy a new saddle, although the RCMP provided saddles.

The training division was indeed a melting pot of men with different backgrounds, and with levels of education ranging from grade school to university. Some had been earning their living for years, while others had never worked a day. Some had been employed on manual labour, or as clerks in banks and various offices, or on farms, as I had been.

Although RCMP training left its members with their own individual characteristics, it had brought about a standardization that fitted them well for the job they were hired to do – enforce the laws in a democratic society. Probably the most important thing they had learned was that when they went into the field they would take the same standards of service to wherever the RCMP enforced the law in Canada.

It was not the fault of the RCMP if a recruit left the training depot without appreciating what was meant by the "good name" of the Force. Lectures in its history emphasized the service that members had given to Canada since its inception in 1873. Recruits and serving members were never told that the RCMP was different from any other kind of police force. But after learning of its past they were bound to think so. Later I found that the general public differentiated between the terms "policeman" and "mountie", a term derided by members of the Force.

The public is inclined to believe that military or quasi-military training, as in the RCMP, turns men into robots capable only of following rules and regulations strictly to the letter. They believe that such training leaves no place for initiative and imagination in their work. On the contrary, these latter qualities are especially required of policemen involved in dealing with the public in the investigation of crime, even the less serious provincial statute offences.

Our physical training was purely military, but this was balanced by lectures on the police work the Force was required to do. While rules and regulations provided some behavioural constraints, they did not hinder the development of desirable qualities.

1934, Regina. Barrack square, my first Red Serge picture.

1934, Regina. Myself during the training period at "Depot" Division.

FIVE

For nearly two months after completing our training we waited for our transfers. Our main interest was getting a transfer that would take us out of Saskatchewan, a place we associated with dust, drought, wind and "baldheaded prairie". The only members of "F" squad who wanted to stay were the few whose homes were in the province. Recruits from British Columbia wanted to return there, but they knew that the policy of the RCMP was to send men to provinces other than those from which they came. The rest of us didn't mind where we went, as long as it wasn't Saskatchewan

At one point during the two-month waiting period I came down with the "flu". Although I felt ill enough to go to the post hospital, I chose to remain in my barrack room bed. A roommate, George Woodward, whom I always referred to as "Stormy Weather" because he was always singing, humming or whistling it, on leaving for town one evening suggested that he bring back some brandy for me. He thought that was just what I needed. I agreed. On his return he gave me two four-ounce bottles of Monet brandy. I had never had a drink of hard liquor before, and I thought that if one bottle was good, two bottles would be twice as good.

The next morning at reveille I felt well enough to go on stable parade, but before doing so, plagued with an unusual thirst, I drank two or three glasses of water. Then I stood in line in the cold morning prairie air awaiting the roll call. As we marched off to the stables

I thought I was mentally alert, but I knew I was physically intoxicated. By the time I reached my horse's stall I could only lean against his ribs with bowed head.

"What's wrong?" asked the corporal in charge, also the NCO in charge of my barrack room. I was sure that not only was I in trouble for being intoxicated, and "importing" liquor into barracks, but so was "Stormy Weather". I decided to confess my offences but not to say how I had got the brandy. After telling the corporal how I became drunk, he got another man to take me back to the barrack room and bed.

I stayed in bed for two more days without hearing anything official about my misdeeds. But my roommates teased me about my "booze-up" and "secret drinking". The corporal inquired several times about how I felt. I was sure he was just waiting for me to get well before lowering the boom, after which I would be taken to orderly room to answer the several charges to be laid against me. When I did get well, nothing happened. Some time later the corporal told me that Stormy Weather had told him how I got the brandy. I never knew if the corporal kept the incident to himself or if he had gone to the sergeant major and they decided not to charge me. In any event I was grateful.

Strangely enough, I became intoxicated again soon afterwards. A friend and I were leaving the barracks on a very cold winter night, for an evening downtown. As the two of us passed the assistant commissioner's house at one corner of the barrack square, he came out and asked us if we could spare a few minutes to help the post carpenter repair some damage to the roof caused by a recent wind. We could hardly refuse. He said the carpenter required someone to hold a roof manhole cover in place for a few minutes.

He led us up two flights of stairs to the attic. I leaned through the manhole, helping the carpenter finish the job. On returning downstairs, we found the assistant commissioner standing by a small table on which were two glasses and a bottle of whiskey.

"You'd like a drink," he said, and then left us.

We didn't want to drink but thought it discourteous to refuse. Not knowing much about liquor, we obviously filled the glasses too full. We walked across the field to where we could catch the streetcar. But by the time we arrived there we were so intoxicated that we decided to return to barracks and bed.

I thought then, and have often thought since, "Why did the assistant commissioner not help the carpenter himself? Was it beneath his dignity?" If so I said to myself "some dignity". I was to serve under this officer for a number of years at two places in Canada, but I could never forget that while he had lacked nothing in hospitality, he had not seen fit to assist a carpenter on a cold winter night when all he would have had to do was what I did.

During the whole of my training period I had taken weekly vocal lessons from Professor John Henry, a well-known vocal teacher. Under his direction in late winter of 1933-34, the Regina Rotary Club put on a Minstrel show titled *Racey Daze*. Appropriately dressed in fox hunting garb, borrowed from the Sifton family, well known in Regina for their interest in horses, I took part in the show. By this time my interest in singing was also well known, if only from the noises that came from the shower each day, which, surprisingly, often encouraged others to join in.

Racey Daze performed for a week in Regina's Darke Hall, and was a great success. Recruits and their girl friends, the instructors, and commissioned officers and their wives attended. After all, it was the only show in town. It occurred to me that now the instructors' positions and mine were reversed. They had to sit quietly and listen to me. What's more, they had to pay for the privilege.

Professor Henry had a program on the Canadian Broadcasting System (later CBC), featuring a male quartet. Even after I left Regina I returned occasionally to take a solo part in his program. My interest in singing continued, and eventually played a decisive part in my career in the RCMP.

As we waited for our transfers to be announced, we could talk of little else. When would orders come out? Where would we be sent? Members themselves started rumours about transfers, pretending that they had confidential sources of information among the instructors or those employed in the Orderly Room. If we wanted to pick on an individual we would start a rumour that he was being transferred to a place we knew he didn't want to go to. Members from British Columbia were rumoured to be going to the Maritimes, or worse still, they were staying in Saskatchewan. Someone would "confirm" the transfer from a "reliable" source. So it went on from week to week.

We knew little about "F" Division, which did the police work in Saskatchewan. But we did know that a large part of it covered territory similar to that around Regina, with dust, wind and drought, summer and winter, and temperatures more extreme than we had formerly been used to. This made most of us want to be transferred away from the prairies. It also disturbed us when one recruit, with a relative serving in Saskatchewan, reported that "F" Division was nothing more than an extension of the training division. Then one night in early March 1934, a recruit dashed breathlessly into the barrack room, shouting that a transfer list had been posted. We rushed to the notice board in the main hall and learned that those listed were to parade before the C.O. the following morning in "Review Order". This meant breeches and boots, Stetson and red serge. For the rest of the evening we eight polished buttons and shined Sam Brownes.

We envisioned transfers to every place in Canada except Saskatchewan. But one recruit, whose name was not on the list, said he had heard that they needed replacements for the riot squad then on strike duty in the Crow's Nest Pass. We didn't believe him. We were being transferred to detachments, we joked, not at all sure that there wasn't some truth to the story about replacements for the riot squad. After all we eight named in the notice had headed the examination lists. The RCMP wouldn't send their best recruits to ride horses. In fact, we persisted, we had been chosen for our unusual ability for very special work. If they wanted replacements for strike duties, surely the men lowest on the examination lists would have been chosen. But still in the back of our minds we wondered if we had been chosen for riot squad duty.

With great anticipation we paraded before the C.O. next morning. He congratulated us on being the first of our squad to be transferred to the field. But our high spirits quickly vanished as he told us to proceed down the hall to the office of the Commanding Officer of "F" Division, Assistant Commissioner Stuart Taylor Wood. It was clear we were not leaving Saskatchewan.

With our hearts deep in our shining riding boots we stood before the desk of our new C.O., listening to his words of welcome. There was plenty of experience to be gained in "F" Division, he said. One only had to apply himself to his work to succeed. Then he asked each individual if he intended to make the Force his career. All but one said yes. "Ducky" Pond, a forestry graduate from the University of New Brunswick, said, "Oh, no sir, only until I can get something better." By now we were well acquainted with Ducky's lack of tact. Incidentally, a few years later he obtained a job with the Saskatchewan Department of Natural Resources.

After an awkward silence the C.O. began to tell each man his destination, some of which I had never heard of. When he came to the last two men, Constable Hervey and me, he said we were going to Regina Town Station in the city. My God, I thought, disappointment compounded. I was not even going to leave Regina.

After we left the C.O.'s office, a corporal told us to turn in certain equipment to the Quartermaster's stores, and be smart about it. A truck would soon be ready to take us and our baggage downtown.

As we got our equipment together, one of us suggested that being among the top men on the examination list had ensured our transfer to "F" Division. The C.O.s of "F" Division and the training division were in collusion. The C.O. of "F" Division, when authorized by Ottawa to take a number of recruits, looked over the examination list and chose the top men. It was then I thought that doing so well in the examination had not worked to my advantage. I wished I had been lower on the list.

Soon Hervey and I found ourselves unpacking beside two empty beds in a room in Regina Town Station. We had finished when Hervey said it was time for lunch. I realized I had been waiting for a trumpet call to announce mealtime. Soon we marched jauntily down the street in our brown jackets, Stetsons, breeches and boots, swinging our riding crops (without which we would have felt undressed), and with our spurs jingling. It was not much more than a year earlier that I had seen my first member of the RCMP in uniform, walking in a similar fashion down the street in Woodstock, New Brunswick. As we went to a Chinese restaurant nearby, I was conscious that the streets of Regina presented a more pleasant sight than the bald prairie around the training division, just a few miles away on the edge of the city.

That afternoon we paraded before Sergeant "Dolly" Roberts, the NCO in charge. He told Hervey and me to spend the rest of the day settling in, which we had already done, and to be ready for work the next morning. He then suggested that we read Local Orders so that we would have some idea about how the detachment operated. After that we should read Standing Orders, which were of a more general nature. If we had any time left, we could read the *Criminal Investigation Branch Instruction Book*, which covered many of the practical aspects of RCMP police responsibility. We had heard very little about such orders and instructions in our training. Hervey facetiously commented that perhaps the sergeant had forgotten to tell us about the hundreds of rules and regulations, and the sixty-five provincial statutes about which we knew nothing. And of course there was always the Criminal Code of Canada and dozens of federal statutes.

When the sergeant had finished with us, we knew there was much more to learn before we became practical policemen. We began to wonder if at the training depot we had learned anything at all.

Our reading in the office that afternoon was interrupted by our watching what went on there. We were as interested in what was taking place as if we were civilians. A member brought in a prisoner, fingerprinted him, filled out some forms, and took him down to the cells in the basement. We eavesdropped as men answered telephones. Others came in off patrol and spoke about what they had been doing. After supper we returned in time to see a night guard burden himself with magazines, the Criminal Code and his Sam Browne. The latter contained his Colt .455, which he loaded right there in the office. None of this nonsense of loading under supervision any more.

We stayed in the office all evening, listening to the others as they sat at their typewriters pounding out reports and talking about what they were reporting. One of them had returned after taking a prisoner to the penitentiary, another had attended court and so on. About nine o'clock one of the men asked Hervey and me if we would like to put on sweaters and "do the town".

We went to the Chinese restaurant, where we sat in a booth drinking coffee, listening to our friend talk about police work, Sergeant Roberts, more police work and more Sergeant Roberts, for whom he had great respect. As we returned to the detachment we knew what "doing the town" meant.

We had also learned that enforcing the Criminal Code and certain provincial statutes made up most of the work being done at Town Station. We realized it was true that we would learn about provincial statutes after our arrival in the field. Our instructors there would be our fellow workers.

I had found the activities that afternoon and evening so interesting that I had forgotten my disappointment at being transferred to "F" Division, and the even greater disappointment of not leaving Regina. It also occurred to me that throughout the day I had not heard anyone complain about having to do police work in Saskatchewan.

1934, Regina. The first draft of "F" Squad being "trucked" from "Depot" Division en route to their various postings.

SIX

ossip at the training division had led Hervey and me to
believe that detachment men would tell us to forget all
that we had learned there. But Sergeant Roberts only
said that we would find considerable difference between theory and
practice. The next morning he emphasized the importance of studying various "orders" and those statutes which the RCMP enforced in
Saskatchewan. He said the Criminal Code was the most important,
and we must appear knowledgeable when the Regina Sub/Division
C.O., Inspector William Schutz, conducted his weekly inspection on
Saturday mornings.

The C.O. was a bit of a crank on the Criminal Code, the sergeant
said, and examined the men on their knowledge of it, so we must be
prepared to answer his questions. I had presumed on leaving training that examinations were a thing of the past but apparently only
the form was different. I had begun to learn that, to progress in the
RCMP, a member should constantly study.

The sergeant had other things on his mind. He told me to get
ready to accompany a constable who was going on a mental patient
case. Before I left him, he mentioned that I could expect night guard
duty fairly often, and I should watch for my turn on the daily notice-
board. I knew my turn would soon come because Hervey would be
on night guard duty that evening. The interview ended when the
sergeant told me to get into civilian clothes as mental cases were
dealt with in this way. Soon I was on my way out of Regina, heading

southeast, in a police car driven by Constable Jim Benson. We were going to a farm about twenty-five miles from Regina, where the farmer was sufficiently ill to warrant his being committed to the Weyburn Mental Hospital.

Jim wanted to know all about my past, and I, his. He was an Albertan and glad to be stationed so close to home, some 600 miles away in northern Alberta. But he was unhappy about being stationed in Regina, where he had been since leaving training, about eighteen months before. He didn't get along with the sergeant, who seemed to think that his detachment was an extension of the training depot. The sergeant was a strict disciplinarian, Jim said, and he had decided to get away from Regina by applying to go "north" for three years.

I knew the "north" meant the Yukon or the Northwest Territories, which included the Arctic regions. If he were transferred, Jim continued, it would mean that he could save some money, but in any event he had to wait another five years before he could get permission to marry. His fiancée didn't like the idea. But he had submitted his application. I found it difficult to believe that "Dolly" Roberts was a harsh disciplinarian. What interested me most, however, was Jim's method of getting away from a posting he did not like.

I learned from him that the police handled most of the mental cases. Two doctors could commit a patient to a mental hospital without police involvement, or a mental patient could ask to be admitted. But most people asked for RCMP assistance. This required someone to lay a charge under the Mental Diseases Act and have the patient appear in court for a hearing. The evidence of a doctor was necessary. The court was usually presided over by a Justice of the Peace, who would, if necessary, issue a warrant to a member of the RCMP, authorizing him to escort the patient to a mental hospital.

At the farm the elder of the farmer's two sons met us in the yard. His father, he said, had had a mental breakdown some time before, brought on by several years of crop failure. At first, he, his brother and mother had been able to deal with his father without any trouble. But recently his father's behaviour had become so erratic that they could no longer handle him. One of his peculiarities was loading the farm truck with machinery of all kinds, preparatory to making a journey of about 300 miles to his imaginary homestead in the Carrot River country in northeastern Saskatchewan. His father had never been to Carrot River, but had heard of people homesteading there.

The son agreed that the case should proceed before a J.P. in a village a few miles away, with the family physician as the medical witness. We went into the farmhouse and made the arrangements by telephone. The patient, for that's what he was, gave us no trouble in getting ready for the trip. As his sons helped him, Jim Benson spoke to the farmer's wife, who had been sitting in a corner of the kitchen, silently weeping. She confirmed what her son had told us and agreed that her husband's committal was best for everyone.

The two sons took their father in the farm truck to the J.P.'s home and we followed behind. The elder son swore to a written complaint before the J.P. and court was opened. The son told his story and of his father's mental condition which was confirmed by the physician. The J.P. then committed him to the Weyburn Mental Hospital, some distance farther along the highway we had travelled from Regina.

Father and sons continued to the hospital in the truck, and we followed behind in the police car. The sons accompanied their father inside. Until now they had shown little emotion, but as they saw an attendant taking their father away, they burst into tears and hurriedly left the building.

This was the first of many such dramas I experienced over the next few years. They often included poignant scenes of a weeping wife watching her husband being taken to hospital, and her pitiful unacknowledged wave of goodbye. That first of many cases remains clearly in my mind. Jim Benson and I arrived back at Town Station about suppertime. We both went to the notice board to see who was detailed for what duty the next day. I read:

Night Guard: Thursday March --
Reg. No. 12001, 3rd/Cst. Kelly, W.H.

I became familiar with the duties of a night guard when I read the local orders that evening as Jim made out his "237", the general report of the RCMP. When he finished he handed it to me to read. I saw my name in it as the one who had accompanied him. I had done nothing but watch what went on, but I took some satisfaction from seeing my name in an official RCMP report for the first time. I knew then that, if necessary, I could perform such a duty alone. This, I thought, was real on-the-job training.

The next morning I accompanied another constable on a patrol to serve summonses, and to interview people about the character of a neighbour who had applied for naturalization. I spent the afternoon in the office rereading local orders on the duties of a night guard.

At 6:30 p.m. I went down to the basement for my first glimpse of the fifteen-foot-high, white painted, brilliantly lit guardroom. I had with me my Sam Browne, equipped with a .455 Colt revolver that I had loaded for the first time without supervision. I also had the

Criminal Code, in view of the impending Saturday morning inspection and examination.

The six cells standing in a row along one wall held four prisoners, two of them Indians. The day guard had me sign a book, showed me the warrants which authorized the prisoners' detention, then gave me the keys to the cells. The prisoners had been served their suppers, he said, and would not be served breakfast until after I went off duty at 6 a.m. All I had to do, he continued, was stay awake until relieved, then he left. I was handling my first duty alone. I settled in a chair before a small desk.

I read the Criminal Code until I was tired of it. But as the Criminal Code contained more than 1,100 sections, my reading did little to prepare me for the inspector's questions.

On Saturday morning I stood in line for inspection with seven constables of the detachment. The sergeant called us to attention. The C.O., a slightly built man in blue uniform, with his forage cap cocked to one side, although we had been taught to wear ours straight on, walked in front and behind us inspecting our dress. No comment, and the sergeant stood us at ease.

Then the inspector in a quiet but deliberate tone explained the importance of studying the Criminal Code. It was the most important tool of our trade. Without knowledge of the Criminal Code one would never make an efficient policeman. His soft-spoken words made me think of those of the sergeant major at Depot Division and Sergeant Roberts. Were all senior members of the Force soft spoken? Just then the inspector said that what we had learned in training was a mere pinprick of Criminal Code knowledge. After my reading in the guard-room I was prepared to believe that even a "pinprick" was an exaggeration.

I stood at the extreme left of the line. If anyone to my right failed to answer a question correctly, he moved to my left. This method allowed the men who answered the most questions correctly to progress toward the top of the line. The inspector made no comment on anyone's failure to answer correctly, but I was sure that Sergeant Roberts, standing to one side, must have noticed that I answered no questions correctly and remained at the foot of the line. During the next couple of weeks I studied the Code diligently, only to suffer the same fate the next two Saturday mornings. It seemed the inspector always asked someone else the questions I could have answered. I took some consolation from this. Hervey, who answered most of his questions, always ended up near the head of the line.

I continued to go on patrol with other members to watch and learn. On one occasion I accompanied members of the Liquor Squad to search a farm for a suspected illicit still. We searched for a couple of hours without finding any incriminating evidence, something I was often to experience when later I was on a detachment of my own. But I thoroughly enjoyed wandering over the farmland, and through what little bush existed, during the search.

My turn at night duties came my way more frequently than I believed it should. But I realized that as a junior constable I could expect it, seeing it was the only job that I was allowed to do alone. Even those who got the duty less frequently than I complained about it. It was clearly not a popular duty. On one occasion I had just settled down for another weary night when the door to the guardroom opened. Down the stairs came an Indian youth carrying a small pack, followed by a burly member of the RCMP wearing a buffalo coat and a muskrat fur hat. The weather for such dress had long passed in Regina.

He handed me a warrant which showed the youth was being escorted to the juvenile jail at Moosomin, some miles east of Regina near the Manitoba border. I learned that they came from Goodsoil detachment in the North Battleford sub/division, in northwestern Saskatchewan, the most northerly detachment in the province that could be reached by summer trail. It was seventy miles north of the nearest railroad, had no telephone or telegraph, and there wasn't one yard of graded road in the 4,000 square miles of his detachment area. It was settled on the southern fringe by homesteaders from the drought-ridden areas of southern Saskatchewan. Except for his private car, which he used rarely in the summer, but more often when things "froze up" in the wintertime, his main means of transportation were a police team and democrat, a large version of a buggy.

This convinced me that I never wanted to be stationed at Goodsoil detachment, but what intrigued me about his story was when he described a world which I thought could not possibly exist in Saskatchewan – a world of forests, large rivers and lakes full of fish. Some lakes contained so many fish, he said, that there was a winter and summer commercial fishing season. I found this hard to believe. I had lived in Saskatchewan for nine months, and all I had experienced were wind, dust and baldheaded prairie. But when he showed me the location of Goodsoil on a nearby wall map, I could see it well marked with rivers and lakes but no roads of any kind. He was enthusiastic about the fact that Goodsoil was only about thirty miles north of the end of a graded gravel road at Loon Lake, but had little to say in favour of the trail from there to Goodsoil, full of large mudholes and hummocks. He brightened when he told me that cars could be used in the wintertime, when everything was frozen over and snow softened the "rough spots".

I would have liked to listen to him all night, but he left after telling me that Goodsoil consisted of the detachment building, two general stores, a blacksmith shop and a log community hall, all built in a small cluster alongside the trail. The original settler lived in a log farmhouse nearby. After all my hopes when in training, I found myself in a Division which had horse detachments. Regina was much too close to them for my liking.

A few days later Hervey and I were called to the sergeant's office. He told us we had been transferred to North Battleford sub/division and we should pay any outstanding meal and laundry bills, and be prepared to leave the next morning. I could only think of the man in the buffalo coat who had told me that in that sub/division there were three detachments that used horses.

I had told Hervey about Goodsoil detachment and, of course, coming from Alberta he was not at all surprised. Only a few weeks before I would have been glad to leave Regina for any place in the province, but in the light of the transfer, even Regina looked good. Anyway, I thought, I did not have to make an application to go "north" like Jim Benson, to get away from Regina. I had begun to think that my poor performance at the Saturday morning Criminal Code examinations had something to do with my being transferred, but I felt better when it occurred to me that Hervey had done exceedingly well on them.

At first the train rolled northwest over the dull brown, undulating and treeless prairie with which I had become familiar. Farmers were working on the land, hoping the seed they would plant would remain in the ground and not blow away as most of it had done for several years. I had begun to understand why people referred to this part of the prairie as "next year country". Looking at the farms I found it difficult to believe that Hervey and I were heading for a land of lakes, rivers and forests.

But in an hour or so, green patches of winter wheat appeared, giving the prairie an appearance of some life. Then bluffs of poplars and white birch began to dot large areas of prairie. By the time the train had crossed the large South Saskatchewan river at Saskatoon, the bluffs were larger, the fields were greener, and we saw a much more pleasant landscape. As we continued our journey to North Battleford, we saw larger areas of trees and young green grain crops. It was then that I realized how drab the southern prairies had been.

A constable with a police car met us at the station, and soon we had unpacked our kit and made our beds in a room on the second floor of the two-story brick detachment building. It also housed the headquarters of the sub/division which had an inspector in charge. We hoped he was not a Criminal Code crank like Inspector Schutz. We need not have worried. The detachment was inspected every three months and there were no examinations.

Our first impressions were favourable. Instead of being in a large barrack room we found ourselves in a two-bed room. We had not had supper and we were advised to go to the Dominion Cafe, operated by Chinese, where most of the men ate their meals. We found out why. The food was good and we could buy a meal ticket for five dollars which allowed the purchaser to eat 21 thirty-five-cent meals, a saving of $2.35, no small amount in those days, and more than a day's pay. We didn't use the meal ticket for meals that cost less than thirty-five cents. Our breakfasts were usually twenty-five cents and these we paid in cash, as using the ticket for any meal less than thirty-five cents would have wasted part of the value of the ticket.

As we prepared for bed, Hervey and I agreed it was good to be about 200 miles from Regina, although we knew we were still in "F" Division, "an extension of the training depot". I was having a hot shower and singing loudly when I heard someone say, "What the hell's that?" I didn't say a word, but thought if I stayed around long enough he might get used to it.

As I lay in bed, appreciating the comforts of the accommodation, my mind turned to the constable at Goodsoil, just 170 miles away, who had neither running water nor electricity, and whose toilet was somewhere back of the detachment building – among the trees.

1934, North Battleford. RCMP sub/division headquarters and detachment offices.

SEVEN

The next morning Hervey and I met Corporal Bill McRae, the NCO in charge of North Battleford detachment. He was big, rawboned, mild mannered and fatherly, and needed nothing more than his size to enforce discipline. We were not surprised, after our Regina experience, when the Corporal said that Hervey and I would be on night guard duty oftener than we would like. As he explained, the cells in the basement housed not only the detachment's own prisoners but also, frequently, prisoners from other detachments en route to the Prince Albert common jail or penitentiary. He didn't need to explain that we would have extra guard duties because we were junior to the other eight constables on the detachment.

Corporal McRae's advice about work and study were similar to Sergeant Roberts' in Regina, but he added two important points. Young constables in North Battleford, he said, were very popular with the girls, some of whom hung around the Dominion Cafe where we were to eat our meals. We must be extremely careful to avoid "girls of the wrong kind". He also warned us about the abuse of liquor, especially as the RCMP enforced the Saskatchewan liquor laws.

"And now," he said, as Hervey and I prepared to leave, "you two had better get into fatigues. Police cars out back need washing. After that you can whitewash the stones around the parking lot."

He had already told us that there was plenty of work on the

detachment, but we had foolishly thought he had meant police work. We spent the next two days washing cars and whitewashing stones. Our manual labours were not a complete loss, however. We learned to recognize Inspector Fowell, the C.O. of the sub/division. We practiced our saluting whenever he walked from the office to his car in the parking lot. Hervey, my senior by a couple of regimental numbers, did most of the saluting. I saluted only when Hervey did not notice the C.O. It comforted us somewhat that, as members recently from the training depot, the one thing we could do well was to salute.

As we had done in Regina, we accompanied other members on patrol. At least, the corporal said, it would help prepare us for the time when we would patrol alone. I wondered if that day would ever come.

At last it came, unexpectedly. One morning the corporal, as usual, came out of his small inner office and saw that all other members had left on patrol and that I was alone. He looked through the office windows to the parking lot, and instead of telling me who I should accompany on patrol, he merely said, "All the police cars are gone. You'll have to take my private car."

He handed me the keys to his cherished coupé, and I realized he was sending me out alone.

I also realized that he assumed I could drive. I had driven a few times before I joined the Force, but only enough to support the statement I had made on my application that I could drive a car. Besides, driving a gearshift car in those days was much more difficult than driving today's cars with automatic gearshifts. At that moment I remembered receiving full marks at "Depot" for describing in detail the principles of a four-cycle combustion engine. But I knew that would not have impressed the corporal.

Silently I took his keys, and he gave me the details of the first case on which I was to work. A taxi from Meadow Lake, a village 110 miles straight north, was on its way to North Battleford. The driver was suspected of carrying furs stolen earlier from the warehouse of a store in the village.

His briefing concluded, the corporal gave me a piece of paper containing the license number of the taxi and the name of the driver.

"If you find any furs when you search the car, bring them with the driver to the office," he said. Then, as an afterthought, "and anyone else with him."

It took me some time to figure out how to start the motor, and just as long to puzzle out the movements of the gearshift. By trial and error I found the reverse gear. At last, and very very slowly, I backed the car onto the street. There was more delay as I made sure I had the car in first gear before I moved forward, away from the detachment.

By that time it must have been obvious to the corporal that my driving experience was extremely limited, and he must have regretted allowing me to drive his personal car. I almost expected him to dash out to the street and retrieve it. I felt sure that if he could have left the detachment with someone more experienced than me, he would have made the patrol himself. But he made no move in my direction, and I drove at a snail's pace to Number 4 highway, which led north to Meadow Lake.

About a mile beyond the town limits I stopped the car at a place on the highway from which I could see an oncoming car from a long distance. I was not, on this my first police patrol alone, in a panic, but I certainly was apprehensive. I knew what I had to do but I doubted my ability to do it. Should I keep the car headed toward the north? Or should I turn it around to face town? In the latter case I wouldn't waste time turning around if the driver refused to acknowledge my signal to stop and I had to give chase. With my lack of driving experience I shuddered at the thought of using the corporal's private car for any kind of chase.

Other questions arose. Should I keep the motor running so that I could get away more quickly if there was a chase? Should I go farther north where I could see the taxi coming from a still greater distance? How close should I allow the taxi to come before I stepped out to signal the driver to stop? If too soon, I thought, he might turn around and race back north, throwing the furs out of the car before I could stop him. And if the worst possible thing happened, how could I go back to the corporal and tell him I had failed to stop the taxi? Finally, I decided to turn the car around to face town, and I turned off the motor. I felt reassured as I considered my own advantage; no one would think there was a policeman in the corporal's coupé.

I waited for about two hours without seeing a car come from the north. Now other fears began to arise. Had the suspect gone into North Battleford by another route? Had he perhaps taken a turn to the east, some forty miles back, on the road to Prince Albert? Even if I had been in a police car, in those days it would not have had a radio. Should I return to the detachment for further instructions? Then I took comfort from the thought that, if the corporal wondered if anything was wrong, he could come and find me.

After I had waited about three hours, a car came along with nothing to identify it as a taxi. But its mud-splattered condition indicated that it had come a long distance. When it was about 100 yards away I got out and waved it down. To my relief the driver pulled in behind the coupé. As I watched him do so, I noticed his car's license plate was the same as the one I had read a hundred times on the corporal's piece of paper.

The car had no trunk in which to hide stolen goods, so I checked the back seat. There I saw two bulging gunny sacks. I looked into one and saw it contained furs. I had no idea what kind of furs they were, not having seen any such things before. I placed the bags in the corporal's car, and told the driver to drive slowly ahead of me to the detachment. I felt smug because after checking his driver's license I had kept it. When we arrived at the detachment I felt sure the corporal was happier to see his car safely returned than he was to see the taxi driver and the furs.

"Hm, hm, muskrats, eh!" he said as he looked inside the sacks, "take him down to the cells. I'll phone Meadow Lake and have them send a man down for him."

Only then did I realize that I had made my first seizure of stolen goods and had made my first arrest. There had been no formal arrest as I had been taught in training. I had not placed my hand on the man's shoulder and said, "I arrest you in the name of the King." Practice was indeed different from theory, at least for me who had never seen anyone placed under arrest.

I checked the prisoner in with the day guard and returned to the office. The corporal told me that Meadow Lake was sending a man down for him. I then began to wonder what my authority had been for arresting this man. If anyone asked me I could only answer that the corporal had told me to do it. Actually, as I learned later, finding a person in possession of stolen goods was sufficient authority.

Next, the corporal told me to submit a report on what had taken place, and get it ready in time for a copy to be given to the man from Meadow Lake when he arrived. Also, I must mention the use of his private car, so that he could charge the RCMP seven cents a mile on his twice-monthly expense account. I obtained a copy of an old case report and followed it as closely as I could, changing the words where necessary. I asked the corporal what I should say where concluding remarks were called for. "Handed over to Meadow Lake detachment," he said. That seemed logical enough for me.

I left the report, and five carbon copies, in the typewriter. After space left for my signature, the corporal typed a "forwarding minute" to the NCO i/c Meadow Lake detachment. "Please let me know if and when Const. Kelly is required as a witness in this case." This procedure was foreign to me but I was to get used to it. It seemed that one could hardly turn around in the RCMP without being required to submit a report in six or more copies.

That evening I was assigned to night guard duty, the only prisoner being the man I had arrested that morning. He seemed a likeable enough fellow. We talked about Meadow Lake, and what it was like to live in that village on the edge of the "great northern timber expanse" as the Canadian author Frederick Philip Grove described such areas. Later that evening Constable Alex Lilley arrived from Meadow Lake, looking every bit as youthful as myself. As we talked about his being stationed there the name of Goodsoil detachment came up. I remembered my talk with the constable in charge of that detachment, in the Regina guardroom, and asked Lilley what he thought of the place.

"That God-forsaken place! I never want to be within 1,000 miles of it," he answered with some heat. "But I don't have to worry about being transferred there, or even staying in Meadow Lake. They want men to train as dog masters and I've put in an application. I've also applied for a transfer to a detachment where I can train for a pilot's license. One or the other is bound to come through."

My mind went back to Jim Benson who had applied to "go north" to get away from Regina. Apparently there were several ways to get away from a detachment one didn't like.

Lilley told me he liked the sergeant in charge at Meadow Lake, and he liked Meadow Lake itself. But the police work there was not his "cup of tea". He was sometimes left alone when the sergeant, acting in his patrol sergeant capacity, left Meadow Lake once a month for several days to inspect two other detachments. Meadow Lake sounded like a nice place. Then I realized that the "God-forsaken place", Goodsoil, was only seventy miles farther away to the northwest. As Lilley and the prisoner prepared to leave, he turned around and said, "So long! If I get a transfer someone will have to replace me, and it might even be you."

"God forbid!" I thought.

A few days later I accompanied the corporal on a patrol in answer to a call from a farmer who lived near the place where I had arrested the taxi driver. The farmer told us that the farm across the road was owned by two middle-aged sisters and, lately, they had been acting strangely. They had always been considered "light-headed", but now they were running around the yard in the nude. He had seen them running about nude only a few minutes before he called the detachment.

We drove to the farm and the corporal knocked on the front door of the farmhouse, but received no answer. As I waited in the car

I saw a head poke out from behind one of the barns. I yelled to the corporal and got out of the car. The two of us rushed to the barn. By now the sisters, both nude, were running away as fast as they could, into a field. In spite of our calls they kept on running.

The corporal decided he had no time to deal with them. He would pass the case to a constable. It would probably end with the women being committed to the North Battleford Mental Hospital. This reminded me of my visit with Jim Benson to the Weyburn Mental Hospital with a demented farmer. I thought I might have been given this case, in light of that experience, but obviously the corporal thought otherwise.

Several years later, after I had been stationed at several other places, I was back at North Battleford detachment. Corporal McRae had gone to pension and a Corporal Bovan had taken his place. He gave me a letter the RCMP had received from a California lawyer. He wanted to know if two sisters, committed to the local mental hospital a few years before, were still alive. He expressly asked that a member of the Force should actually see the sisters. I checked the police files and discovered we had a file on the two sisters, and that they were the same women Corporal McRae and I had seen running nude in a field several years before.

At the hospital, Dr. Nelson, the director, told me that the sisters were still there. "You'll be lucky if you see them," he said with a laugh. "Whenever a stranger enters the ward they draw their blankets over their heads. They don't take them off until they consider it safe to do so, sometimes an hour or so after the stranger has left."

Dr. Nelson led me to a verandah ward with a row of twelve beds facing the windows. Before we entered, he explained that the sisters were in beds alongside each other, about halfway down the row, and that they were the only two white-haired women next to each other. When he opened the door, I stepped quickly inside and caught a glimpse of two white heads and a flurry of blankets in beds about halfway down the row. This, plus a check of the hospital records, enabled me to make a satisfactory report to the California lawyer.

EIGHT

A t North Battleford detachment, from time to time I did office duty from 6 p.m. until midnight, and then I was on call until morning. One night I was on office duty when a sergeant came in escorting a prisoner on his way to jail. The prisoner was the taxi driver I had arrested with furs stolen in Meadow Lake. He must have pleaded guilty because I had not been called as a witness. His escort must be the sergeant, "Scroggy" Coombes, about whom Lilley had told me. After the sergeant took his prisoner down to the basement cells, he came back to the office and asked me to call up the C.O. on the telephone. When the C.O. came on the line, the sergeant said to me, "Tell him to go to hell." I pleaded with him to take the phone. When at last he did so, he said, "Hello, Turkey! I just wanted to say hello."

After a brief conversation he hung up.

"I've known the old buzzard for many years," he said, "we were on detachment together." Then, with a chuckle, he went upstairs to the bed available for such visitors.

I knew the C.O. had the nickname "Turkey" because of his surname Fowell. I presumed he'd had it since early in his service, but I never thought I would hear anyone, certainly not an NCO, call him that to his face. Later, after I had known Sergeant Coombes for several years, I'd never heard anyone call him "Scroggy" to his face, nor did I find out how he came by it.

I closed the office at midnight and went upstairs to bed, but was awakened at 2 a.m. by the loud honking of a car horn. The C.O. was calling for me, the office duty man, to drive him to his home a few blocks away, and to drive the car back to the police garage. It was a habit for which the C.O. was well known.

The next morning, I was following the sergeant downstairs when the side door at the foot of the stairs opened, and in walked the C.O., smartly dressed in his "blues". Sergeant Coombes stopped on the bottom step to let him pass.

"Good morning, Sir," he said sharply.

"Good morning, sergeant! I trust you had a good night's sleep!" The C.O.'s reply was equally sharp.

"I did until some damn fool sat on his car horn in the middle of the night," snapped Coombes, who knew of the C.O.'s nocturnal habit, "I would sure tell him a thing or two if I knew who it was."

I waited for the C.O.'s reply. He hesitated, coughed, and then walked quickly down the hall to his office. The sergeant looked back at me and gave me a big wink and a nod of his head, as if to say, "That'll fix the old buzzard." According to Lilley's description this was vintage "Scroggy" Coombes. Even so, like Lilley, I came to admire him.

Sudden deaths were a common occurrence on the prairies. Then, as now, the police were usually the first to be informed. Before I had any experience with such deaths, I wondered how I would react to seeing and handling dead bodies. I had never even seen one, except that of my maternal grandmother many years before.

A few weeks after arriving at North Battleford, I accompanied a senior constable when he investigated the death of a woman in childbirth. We drove to a cabin on the Red Pheasant Indian Reserve, a few miles south of old Battleford, a small town across the Battle River from North Battleford. The coroner, Dr. Nunn of Battleford, met us at the cabin. The three of us entered the rather dark dwelling together, and we went into a small bedroom. There lay the dead woman! The doctor pulled back the blanket covering her. Beside her we saw her dead newly born baby.

I was watching the doctor when I heard a thump behind me. I turned to see my companion slumped to the floor in a dead faint. I dragged his 200 pounds outdoors and he soon revived. Meanwhile, Dr. Nunn had questioned the husband and satisfied himself there was no reason for any police action. The woman had failed to survive what was obviously a most difficult childbirth.

On the way back to North Battleford my companion told me that he fainted every time he saw a dead body, and that he couldn't do anything about it. I smiled to myself. The senior constable was a bit of a "health nut". He lived mostly on dates and nuts, and had several kinds of physical training equipment under his bed. As for me, I knew now that I needn't worry about any adverse reaction to dead bodies.

After I had been in North Battleford about a month, I had quite recovered from my disappointment at not being transferred out of Saskatchewan from the training depot. I was looking forward to spending a pleasant summer in this very pleasant small city. Corporal McRae had begun giving me cases to handle on my own. They were not very important, only minor thefts and assaults, but through them I learned to prosecute. Also, my car driving ability had improved through my practice in driving police cars.

One morning the corporal told me to make sure my boots and buttons were well shined, because at 10 a.m., precisely, he would parade me before the C.O. He didn't say why, but I presumed the C.O. wanted to give a new member of the sub/division the usual lecture on the dangers of liquor, of getting involved with the wrong girls, and neglecting my study of the Criminal Code and other statutes.

At exactly 10 a.m., the corporal snapped, "Kelly, let's go." I marched the twenty paces down the hall to the door of the C.O.'s office. The corporal opened the door and, with a "right turn, quick march, halt, left turn," placed me facing the C.O.'s desk. He was reading something, and for a moment or two I wondered if he knew the corporal and I were there. I stood at attention, staring over his head at the wall.

"So you are Constable Kelly," he said rather brusquely, looking up at last. "I don't believe in lecturing my men, but I tell them two things – leave liquor alone (do what I say and not what I do, I thought) and have nothing to do with any girl you wouldn't be proud to take home to your mother." I waited for the corporal's instructions to leave the almighty presence, but the real reason for being paraded was yet to come.

"We need a constable at Meadow Lake detachment," the C.O. said, "and you have been chosen. You will be replacing a constable who is going to train as a dog master." So Lilley had been successful, and he might even train as a pilot, if his dog training post took him near an airport.

"Lilley will be coming in later today to pick you up," the C.O. continued. "That is all, Corporal." After a "left turn, quick march, left turn" I found myself back in the detachment office. The corporal had known all along why I was being paraded, but hadn't said a word about it. I was sure that when he had been asked by the C.O. whom he thought should replace Lilley, he had recommended me. I wondered why he had not chosen Hervey. As we reached the office, he said, "Don't forget to pay your meal and laundry bills." After doing as he said, I spent the rest of the day making out reports on my uncompleted cases, and packing.

I kept thinking that the transfer, like the one from Regina, had come "out of the blue". This one placed me much closer to the Goodsoil detachment which Lilley had referred to as that "God-forsaken place". I, too, thought of it as such, always with foreboding, and now with apprehension, since Meadow Lake was within seventy miles of Goodsoil, and it was within Sergeant Coombes' patrol area. I was now going to a field detachment, away from a sub/division headquarters detachment, and where, unfortunately, there was a team of horses. Lilley had told me about them, but the only detail I remembered was that "they could jump like kangaroos".

This transfer broke the string that tied me to the training depot through my friend Hervey, who I was leaving behind. In late afternoon in heavy rain, Alex Lilley arrived from Meadow Lake. After supper we loaded my kit and trunk into the police car, Code No. 1092, a 1929 Ford Sedan, and set out on the 110-mile drive in a steady and heavy rain.

The journey took six weary hours. We travelled, after the first twenty miles, due north over the rutted and muddy, supposedly gravelled, Number 4 highway. To break the monotony Lilley and I discussed everything we could think of, including people I would meet in my work, the way the sergeant dealt with "his constable", and the sergeant's wife. She was a motherly type, Lilley said, and she tried to make sure that "her constable" ate well and kept the right female company. But, emphasized Lilley, if I wanted to keep my reputation, I should stay away from the girls Mrs. Coombes recommended. They were not the little angels she thought, although they went to her church. He obviously spoke from experience.

The sergeant refused to exercise the horses, although he helped to feed them, Lilley said. Also, he often cleaned the stable, even before the constable was out of bed, because he was an early riser, though he made it clear that cleaning the stable was the constable's responsibility. He was an experienced policeman and had great patience with a young constable trying to learn what policing was all about. When I mentioned that Sergeant Coombes had called the C.O. "Turkey" on the telephone, Lilley said that was typical. He also said the sergeant had acquired the reputation of being a practical joker, mostly deserved, but he was mellowing somewhat of late.

We drove the last seventy miles through densely wooded country. The woods, the heavy rain, the gloomy darkness, and the constant swish of the windshield wipers made me think we might end up in a witch's cauldron.

"Twenty miles to go," muttered Lilley, "we just passed the height of land."

For about fifty miles we had been travelling on an uphill grade. Now we started downhill, as the rain still fell in torrents. How much the farmers in the dried-out south would appreciate such a rain, if only it would fall on them, I thought. By this time I was bitterly cold and sleepy, but the chill of the car kept me awake. The RCMP did not issue car heaters. It would still be some years before they did so on a regular basis.

At last, as the car began to slide from one side of the road to the other, Lilley announced we had arrived within the confines of Meadow Lake village, where there were only mud roads. In the gloomy darkness we passed many low buildings, with not a light to be seen. Soon we pulled up alongside a raised wooden sidewalk.

"This is it," said Lilley. Stiffly we got out. Through the gloom I could faintly see the sergeant's light-coloured bungalow, the detachment office (my home to be) and the stable.

Helped by the reflection of the light that Lilley had switched on in the office, I unloaded my kit in the still-falling rain. The bedroom, off the office, was just big enough for two single beds, with a trunk at the foot of each, and a washstand. There was a strong smell of cedar oil and I wondered where it came from. "Don't worry, you'll get used to it," said Lilley, "oiling the office floor with cedar oil is the sergeant's favourite pastime." With this in mind I went through the routine of untying my bedroll to get at my blankets and pillow, taking some sheets from my trunk and making my bed.

I got into bed, thinking that if I were at North Battleford I'd have a hot shower. But now I was in a place with no running water. Some time ago I had sympathized with the Goodsoil constable for having an outhouse back among the trees. Now I had one just behind the stables.

Only that morning I had got out of bed in a pleasant place, with hot and cold running water and excellent accommodation. Now I was on a rural detachment on the edge of civilization. Just a few miles to the north, there were only forests, lakes and rivers stretching into the treeline in the Northwest Territories. It seemed identical with the description of Goodsoil that Constable Bill Marshall had given me in the guardroom in the Regina Town Station detachment. Making matters worse, I had two horses to take care of. How my training companions would laugh when they knew I had been transferred to Meadow Lake. During my training period in Regina I had longed for a transfer out of Saskatchewan, and for a detachment where there were no horses. Now I was still in Saskatchewan, with horses, and Goodsoil, only seventy miles away by trail, hung over my head like the sword of Damocles.

As I lay in bed I kept thinking of things Lilley had told me on the way north. Since about 1790, Meadow Lake had been a trading post for Indians, trappers and hunters. Now the village had grown to about 1,000 persons, not including the Indians on a nearby reserve. For the past several decades the Meadow Lake area had been ranching country. Then homesteaders from the south began to settle there. What I learned from Lilley about the area made me think it was little different than what I had heard about the Goodsoil country, except that Meadow Lake had a telephone system, electric light and a highway to civilization.

I lay awake thinking of what the future might bring. I was not sure that I would like living under such conditions. It was little more than ten months since I had left farming in New Brunswick to join the RCMP. Would I be putting in for a transfer to go "north" like Jim Benson, or to train to be a dog master or a pilot like Lilley.

I looked over at Lilley, fast asleep and perhaps dreaming of the place he was going to the next day. I put out the light by pulling the string over my head, and fell asleep wondering how long I would remain in Meadow Lake, and to what detachment I would be transferred next. Goodsoil, perhaps?

After Lilley left the next morning, driving his own small car loaded down with kit and equipment, I never saw him again. He must have trained as a pilot and left the Force. In any case, he became well known in Canadian commercial aviation. In general orders a few weeks after Lilley left, I read where Jim Benson had been transferred from "F" Division (Saskatchewan) to "G" Division – the north.

1934, Meadow Lake. The "new" constable in front of Sergeant C.A. Combes' bungalow.

1936, November 11, Pierceland, Sask. On the only street in the Goodsoil detachment area after attending an Armistice Day service. Reverend Frank Myers on far left.

NINE

W hen I awoke next morning a faint stable odour mingled with that of the sergeant's cedar oil. I noticed
Lilley had already fed the horses and cleaned out the
stable. "I enjoyed fixing the horses this last time," he said. "But now
it's your turn. Remember to water them after we come back from
breakfast." Just as we were leaving for breakfast the sergeant came
into the office with a cheery "good morning". His appearance impressed me. His high boots were polished and his jacket buttons
shined. I was to learn that he expected his constable to pay as much
attention to his own appearance.

As we set out for the Chinese restaurant two blocks away, I saw
beds of flowers around the police buildings, "a hobby of the
sergeant's," said Lilley. The water in the ditches and the mud on the
street reminded me of our arrival the night before. As we turned a
corner to walk a second block, at the far end I saw a railway station,
which surprised me. Lilley explained that there was only a once-a-
week train from Prince Albert, arriving Monday evenings and leaving early Tuesday mornings. The police rarely used it, even though
their prisoners had to go to the common jail or the penitentiary at
Prince Albert. Taking prisoners on the Tuesday morning train meant
returning by way of North Battleford, a tiresome day's train journey,
plus another day-long 110 miles by police car relay to get home to
Meadow Lake. On the other hand, prisoners escorted to North
Battleford by police car could usually be left there to be taken to

Prince Albert by other escorts. Nevertheless, seeing the railroad station lessened the sense of isolation that I was experiencing. Lilley wasted no time leaving Meadow Lake after breakfast, driving his own car. For the first time since leaving training I was the sole constable on a detachment.

Now I had no one to talk "shop" with except the sergeant, and it didn't seem the same. I soon found, however, that I could discuss police work with him and get some good advice in return. On his instructions I got into fatigues and groomed the horses, Kit and Bess. Their bay colour and four white hairy feet showed clearly their Clydesdale blood lines. But their size, however, showed their smaller standardbred bloodlines as well. They were alert and in excellent condition, all in all a fine driving team. I was willing to believe, as Lilley had said, that they could "jump like kangaroos".

So at Meadow Lake I started out grooming horses instead of washing cars and whitewashing stones, as I did at North Battleford. While I groomed my new charges I could only wonder why I, rather than Hervey, had been sent to Meadow Lake. When I went back to the office the sergeant was bemoaning the loss of Lilley.

"A damn fine constable," he said. I began to think that my efficiency would always be compared to Lilley's. I needn't have worried. I soon learned that, with a few exceptions, every constable stationed with Sergeant Coombes was "the best damn constable in the Force". Granted he had some good ones stationed with him, but he had some that could hardly fit this description.

He did not lecture me about women or liquor or anything else regarding the behaviour he expected, and he encouraged me to ask anything I needed to know about the work. In any case, he was sure that between us we could handle the work of the detachment. A psychologist, no less, I thought. But, he added that the responsibility for the horses was mine alone. This included feeding and grooming them, cleaning the stable and exercising them in my spare time. I was surprised therefore when he gave the horses their noon meal, and later, when my early rising sergeant often fed the horses and cleaned out the stable before I got up.

He told me that he would be away from Meadow Lake for several days each month, inspecting as many as four detachments in his capacity as a patrol sergeant. He was sure I could handle things in his absence. Either he had more confidence in my ability than I had or it was his way of instilling confidence in his junior man. It didn't help at all when I heard that when he went to Loon Lake, forty miles to the west, and to Goodsoil, some thirty miles north of it, there was no way I could get in touch with him. There were no such frills as telegraph or telephones in these places, and hardly a navigable trail from Loon Lake to Goodsoil. I asked him about Goodsoil. "A great place to be stationed," he said with some enthusiasm. "There are no roads to patrol to enforce the Motor Vehicles Act and mail arrives only once a week, if the condition of the trail permits a truck to bring it in from Loon Lake."

There was no telephone system so there was no easy way for people to make complaints, or for the C.O. at North Battleford to get in touch with the Goodsoil constable. In fact, the constable could patrol for days or weeks on end, completely out of touch with the rest of the Force. Nothing the sergeant said changed my mind about Goodsoil being the "God-forsaken place" that so many others had called it.

I exercised Kit and Bess every day, sometimes saddling one and leading the other for about three miles, out past the Indian reserve. Then I released the one I was leading and raced it back to the stable. I never won. At other times I took each in turn to the stampede grounds to run around the "race" track and jump the fences. This kept the horses and me in good shape, and I came to enjoy working with them.

Police work around Meadow Lake did not include "big crime", but mostly minor Criminal Code offences such as thefts, assaults, vagrancy, offences under the provincial Motor Vehicles and Liquor Acts, and under the federal Excise and Indian Acts. Homesteaders frequently visited the detachment to make complaints, or to ask for advice about such things as line fencing laws or the Stray Animals Act. We handled cases concerning mental patients and accidental deaths, and occasionally searched for persons lost in the bush. We also made numerous character enquiries about persons who had applied for naturalization. We dealt with illicit distillation by way of the Excise Act, mostly through informants anxious for the reward if their information resulted in a conviction.

The policy of the federal National Revenue department, for whom the RCMP enforced the Excise Act, was to pay an informant, giving information which led to a conviction, twenty-five per cent of any fine imposed, whether it was paid or not. With this as an incentive, some homesteaders were always on the lookout for the illicit manufacture of alcohol so that they could collect the "moiety". This did not always work out, and I got used to submitting reports on "non-resultant searches". Occasionally we were successful. But even the finding of illicit alcohol or fermenting mash rather than an illicit still, resulted for a first offence in the mandatory $100 fine, a large sum in those far-off depression days. Usually it went unpaid, and the convicted person went to jail for the mandatory jail term – three months.

The fact that there was no liquor store closer than North Battleford, 110 miles to the south, encouraged illicit distillation of alcohol in the Meadow Lake area. This situation also gave rise to the bootlegging of legal liquor as well. There were two known bootleggers, one who sold only hard liquor, the other liquor and beer. Both sold it by the drink on their premises and in bottles to take away. One of the less reputable storekeepers was known to sell lemon extract and wood alcohol, especially to the Indians, and this resulted in a few prosecutions.

The sergeant had found that the best way to deal with the local bootleggers was to have undercover policemen come periodically from Regina. They would pose as travellers and purchase liquor. The first we would know of their presence in Meadow Lake was when they arrived at the detachment with the bootlegger, and sometimes a customer or two, along with their purchases, so that the detachment could deal with bail and the resultant prosecutions.

We enforced the Indian Act more frequently than the Excise Act. It was an offence in the 1930s, and for decades before, for an Indian to be drunk, or found in possession of intoxicants at any time, even in his own house on the reserve. We had a reserve within a couple of miles of the village. All Indian prosecutions were summary conviction cases with fines, and jail in default of payment. Rarely did an Indian have enough money to pay the fine, which meant that he had to be escorted the 110 miles to North Battleford, to be left there for another escort, or sometimes taken directly to Prince Albert jail. I soon learned that taking Indians to jail appeared to be a waste of time.

Through no fault of their own they had no gainful employment, and their lifestyle encouraged laziness and drunkenness. White men would have behaved similarly, or perhaps worse, under the same conditions. At least Indians seldom turned to crime.

Another federal statute which created a considerable amount of work, which had nothing to do with arrests, fines or jail, was the Naturalization Act. After an immigrant (other than British) had been in Canada for five years he could apply for naturalization to the Department of the Secretary of State, which then asked the RCMP to make a "character" investigation, and report the results on special forms provided by the department. Our instructions were not to incur expenses on such cases and to deal with them when in the district on other matters. The number of "Nat" files, as we called them, outnumbered the others in our briefcases.

I accompanied the sergeant on every patrol. This continued until he felt I could deal with matters on my own. When with him, I would write out any statements required from persons being interviewed. The sergeant allowed them to read their statements, and make any desired changes before they signed their names. The sergeant and I witnessed the signatures. We took statements, not only from those liable to prosecution, but from those who might be called as witnesses, also from those giving information required by other detachments or government departments.

After such patrols I typed the reports and the sergeant signed them. In this way I learned quickly the "art" of report writing, RCMP style. We never "went" anywhere. We always "proceeded". Never by car, but always by Police car, Code No. 1092, and so on. At the foot of the report the status of the matter being reported upon was shown in upper case letters, such as HANDED OVER TO GOODSOIL DETACHMENT, or STILL UNDER INVESTIGATION, or COMPLAINT UNFOUNDED, or PROSECUTION ENTERED. It was rumoured that one constable concluded a report with "Concluded for Want of Investigation".

Everyone also had to conclude each report with reference to expenses incurred, such as – "No Expense Incurred" or "Expenses Incurred – Shown on F.93 [Expense sheet] for the period January 1-15, 1937." All these things had been taught us at the training depot, but they didn't seem nearly as important then as when I submitted a "real" report and expense sheet.

I began to realize that "F" division was indeed an extension of the training division. Insignificant mistakes in a report often resulted in the sub/division headquarters sending it back, along with caustic remarks about resubmitting it correctly.

A month or two after my arrival at Meadow Lake the sergeant demanded that I give him three dollars. When I asked why he wanted it, in his flippant way he said, "Mind your own business." I knew he wanted it for some good reason and gave it to him. I didn't know then that it would be the most important three dollars I had ever spent. A couple of weeks later a parcel arrived. The sergeant opened it and handed me a small red book called *The Peace Officers Manual* by Rogers and Magone, two lawyers in the provincial Attorney General's office at Queen's Park in Toronto. As he handed it to me he said that he could do no more for a young policeman than to see he received this book.

I soon appreciated its value, not only to young policemen but also to all policemen involved in the investigation and prosecution of offences under the Criminal Code. It outlined the policeman's power of arrest in each criminal offence; whether a warrant was required or not; the amount of evidence required to form the basis of a *prima facie* case against an accused; whether offences were triable by way of indictment or by summary conviction; and even the wording of the charge. Such a book was of immense value to all policemen, but especially to those in isolated places far from legal advice. I often wondered why the RCMP did not issue such a book to all recruits leaving the training division. The *Constables Manual* it issued dealt with many things of great assistance to the young policeman concerning his general duties, but nothing at all which dealt specifically with criminal offences as Rogers and Magone did.

The item on what evidence was required was a guide to a criminal investigator when collecting evidence with a view to prosecution. Later on I began to use the book in a way for which it was not intended. When making a report on a case, and detailing the evidence on which I was basing a prosecution, I borrowed liberally from my little red book, often quoting verbatim without saying that my source was Rogers and Magone. In future years, each time I used this book I gave silent thanks to Sergeant Coombes.

The sergeant also taught me the value of a police notebook. It could be used for such things as descriptions of wanted persons, of licenses or cars owned by those suspected of doing something illegal, or oral statements made by persons being interviewed, and many other things. Some such notes could be used to refresh one's memory when giving evidence in court. "Be sure to make the notes immediately after or even during an event," said the sergeant.

As prosecutors, members of the RCMP required some guidance when they produced evidence in court. Sergeant Coombes insisted that I make out a "brief" even in the most simple cases. This listed the witnesses to be called, together with the evidence they were to give and, equally important, the exhibits they were to produce. From these and many other lessons I began to feel fortunate to be on detachment with Sergeant Coombes. I appreciated him even more when other young constables told me about their on-the-job training with other NCOs.

I had only been in Meadow Lake a short time when we prosecuted an Indian for being drunk. It was a simple case. Sergeant Coombes, on returning to the detachment from a patrol, found the Indian lying on the road – dead drunk. A prosecution ensued. Sergeant Coombes as the only witness described the circumstances under which he had arrested the accused. The Indian had a defence counsel, a rare thing in Indian cases, and when he addressed the court, he called Coombes a "common cop". This angered the sergeant who immediately asked for an adjournment for a few minutes. As we had just had an adjournment, the J.P., himself a Metis, agreed to it reluctantly.

I went into the constable's room to wait it out, only to be followed by the sergeant and the lawyer. The sergeant turned to face the lawyer and, putting his right forefinger under the lawyer's nose, very aggressively said, "Another crack like that from you, and I'll break your goddamned neck." When court resumed the accused was found guilty and assessed a fine or thirty days in jail in default. Unlike most Indians convicted of petty offences he had money enough to pay the fine. This meant that I would not have to make the wearisome patrol of 220 dreary miles to North Battleford and return.

That case had shown me for the first time that the sergeant had a temper. The lawyer and I sang in the United Church choir and the next time we met, he said, "Your sergeant has a temper, eh?"

Since its inception as the North-West Mounted Police in 1873, the Force had prosecuted most of its own cases. The exceptions wcre those taken to the higher courts to be tried by judges sitting alone or with a jury. Usually, members of the Force prosecuted all cases triable within the jurisdiction of Police Magistrates and Justices of the Peace, which in the 1930s caused members of the Saskatchewan Bar to criticize the practice. The lawyers did not criticize the efficiency of the Force, but they were having as much difficulty in making a living during the depression as other people. Having the RCMP handle prosecutions saved the impoverished provincial government a great deal of money, by not having to hire prosecutors, as the lawyers thought it should. RCMP members handled prosecutions quite well, even when accused persons were defended by counsel of the status of John Diefenbaker. I soon learned that not even a good defence counsel could succeed in a case in which ample evidence had been collected.

My experience as a prosecutor had begun at North Battleford, with pleas of guilty in minor cases. Now at Meadow Lake I graduated to more serious ones, at first under the watchful eye of the sergeant, in cases tried before Justices of the Peace. He handled cases prosecuted before the Police Magistrate. At first I had no desire to do so. But I watched him very carefully as he prepared his cases and the way he dealt with them in court. It wasn't any different than cases before Justices of the Peace.

I had to learn many things other than those related to practical police work. For instance, I needed to know how to administer a detachment. In Regina and North Battleford the senior NCO handled adminstration, but at outlying detachments with limited manpower, as at Meadow Lake, even the youngest constable was expected to take part in it. Although it was not so stated in the *Constables Manual* issued to me, later issues contained the following:

> A detachment member's ability to perform administrative duties is equally as important to the successful operation of the Force as is a well found knowledge of criminal investigation.

The Force had a meticulous monthly accounting system to deal with accounts for consumable goods such as coal, wood, soap, cleaning materials, and the cedar oil at Meadow Lake. Any detachment that had police horses had to process bills for veterinary work, oats and hay, and shoeing. The supplier of goods and services had to certify each bill, and then we attached it to a special RCMP form on which the member in charge of the detachment had to certify that such goods or services had been purchased solely for use by the RCMP. A daily record was kept to show the miles travelled by police car and police team. At the end of the month the record of the car was transferred to a special monthly return form. It showed the amount of gasoline purchased, car repairs, the average mileage per gallon of gasoline, and the total expenses for the car operation each month.

We dealt with the team mileage differently. Our daily diary recorded not only that mileage, but the activity of each member on the detachment. It included the areas patrolled, cases employed on, and mileage travelled by car or team. The diary was submitted semi-monthly. A daily record showed the purchase and use of such consumable goods as hay, oats, coal, wood and cleaning materials (including the sergeant's cedar oil), so that they could be included in the monthly returns. If none was used, such as coal in the summer-time, a "nil" return was required. Semi-monthly returns were required for such things as bank drafts, payable to the Receiver General of Canada, covering monies collected on behalf of the federal government, and semi-monthly expense statements for each member's expenses.

We were not paid straight salaries, but so much per day as pay and one dollar per day meal allowance. If we spent fifty cents for a meal on patrol, on our expense sheet we would charge the total amount, but then deduct thirty-three cents each for the number of meals taken. Thus the member collected only seventeen cents for each meal on patrol.

Monthly returns took up a great deal of our time, and often we had to work on them during the evening hours, due to the pressure of police work. If there was any delay in their submission, criticism arrived, disregarding the probability that the delay was caused by emergency police work.

In addition to making us account for operation expenses and other things, the administrative system contained subtle controls and supervision. At sub/division headquarters expenses could be checked against the work shown in the daily diary. Reports on the work done could be checked to see if the time spent on investigations was commensurate with their importance, and if the mileage referred to corresponded with that in the monthly car return form. By the time the inspecting officer arrived he was ready to inquire into anything his staff had cause to suspect. When he arrived, about once every three months, he made a point of checking the consumable goods records with the amounts remaining on hand. He closely checked the complaint book to see what investigations were outstanding, and to see that the reason for too many outstanding cases was not the "in office" item in the daily diary. Whether supervision came from the Inspector's visits, or long distance by his staff, there was plenty of it.

1934, Meadow Lake, Sask. Outside detachment.

TEN

W hat I disliked most about being stationed at Meadow Lake was the escorting of prisoners the 110 miles to North Battleford, not only in the heat of summer but in the much-below-zero temperatures of winter, without a car heater. The first seventy miles was through heavy bush country without any habitation. There was always a fear that the nearly worn-out police car, "old 1092" as we referred to it, would break down far from any place where mechanical repairs could be obtained.

No matter what I was employed on, it had to stop in order to get a prisoner to jail as quickly as possible. Most of them were Indians who went to jail instead of paying their fines. Although this was part of my duties, I considered such travel a disruption of more important matters that should be investigated.

During that first spring in Meadow Lake, 1934, when escorting prisoners to North Battleford, there were always farmers from the drought-stricken areas of the south making their way to the "promised land" of Meadow Lake. The same thing was happening on the roads to the Carrot River country in northeastern Saskatchewan, and on the roads in the Peace River country of northwestern Alberta. Early homesteaders had begun to settle in the Meadow Lake area before the turn of the century. But only in the late 1920s and early 1930s, as a result of the drought on the southern prairies, did droves of new homesteaders begin to settle there.

On the highway leading north to Meadow Lake I often met

newcomers driving a team and wagon, loaded with all their worldly possessions, either travelling slowly northward or camped alongside the highway. Some had a cow tied on behind. Mothers and babies rode on the wagon while men and older children walked. Occasionally a truck similarly loaded passed them by. Lack of rain had driven these people from their long-established homes. In Meadow Lake they would have plenty of rain, but also many years of back-breaking toil before they were free from government relief, and could live off the farm they carved out of virgin bush.

Most of the trees in the area were species of poplar, white birch and evergreens. When I lived in New Brunswick, woodsmen had told me that land on which these trees grew was not as good for farming as land on which the hardest deciduous trees grew. The latter included maple, beech, yellow birch and elm. No such trees grew wild in northern Saskatchewan.

The would-be homesteaders I met on the highway all wanted to know how much farther it was to Meadow Lake. I told them the distance to the village, but said that they would have to travel much farther to get to the homesteads they had filed on. The land south and east of Meadow Lake was considered unsuitable for homesteading. More suitable lands, within ten miles north and many more miles to the west and northwest, had been settled by 1934. New homesteads could be settled only on the periphery of those areas.

Lucky were the homesteaders who, upon arrival, found the place where they wanted to build a cabin or start a garden free of trees. Many, who had not had cabins built preparatory to their arrival, lived in tents while they built cabins for themselves. Before winter they built log sheds for their animals. One of the greatest difficulties arose from their inability to get sufficient hay to feed their animals over the winter. The lucky ones, whose homesteads contained sloughs, were able to cut wild hay. But that meant they would have less arable land when and if they cleared their homesteads of trees. As a result, the number of animals the homesteaders could bring north was limited.

Each homesteader had to do a certain amount of work on the homestead for each of several years, then he received his "patent", which meant ownership of a quarter section of land – 160 acres. Any adult sons in a family could also file on homesteads. In this way some families eventually owned large areas of land. Not all people who filed on homesteads remained long enough to finally own them. Probably many who stayed would have returned to the south, with all its difficulties, if they had realized what years of toil lay ahead of them.

Homesteaders had to clear their land with horses and manual labour since the cost of machines was prohibitive. Indeed, the only tractor I ever saw clearing land was a huge old-fashioned wood-burning steam tractor, with a large flywheel on the side. Many years later I visited these homesteads and found some of the best farmland in western Canada. Large wheat fields flourished, and also thousands of acres of yellow Canola, then called rapeseed.

Anytime I escorted a prisoner to North Battleford I found the journey monotonous. The first seventy miles of the 110-mile journey took us through heavy bush, often with very bad road conditions. I was lucky if the low-powered four-cylinder police car averaged twenty miles an hour.

On one such escort trip I used my revolver for the first time on duty. My prisoner was a young Indian on his way to Prince Albert jail. The previous day's rain had left the road covered with several inches of mud, in spite of its reputation as a good gravelled highway. About forty miles south of Meadow Lake, we had nearly reached the top of a hill when mud under the fenders built up so much that the car came to a staggering stop. I got out and cleared the fenders, but to make sure we would get to the top of the hill I asked the prisoner to help by pushing the car. As the car moved forward, I presumed he was helping me and I silently thanked him.

I looked back through the rear-view mirror and saw him walking back toward Meadow Lake. Stopping the car I got out and shouted for him to return. Without looking back he continued walking. I was afraid that at any moment he would run into the heavy bush on either side of the road and I would never see him again. I also envisioned myself facing a charge in RCMP Orderly Room for the serious "crime" of allowing a prisoner to escape.

When he continued to walk, despite further commands to return, I drew my .455 Colt revolver and, after he ignored still another command, without warning I fired a shot in the air. In the silence of the woods the shot rang out as though it came from a cannon. The prisoner stopped so suddenly, I thought for a moment that I had hit him.

He stood there petrified, as though I had aimed at him the first time, missed, and was about to fire again. When I called for him to come back, he turned slowly and came to the car. I put handcuffs on him and we went on to North Battleford without further incident.

I could have charged him with attempting to escape from custody, but I was so glad of his coming back that I decided to forget the incident and not tell anyone about it. In making this decision I rationalized that going to jail for thirty days, just for being drunk, was enough punishment to include that of trying to escape. If he had really intended to escape, I reasoned, he would have dashed into the bush. Also, if I charged him, it meant returning to Meadow Lake and having to repeat this journey a few days later. This was hardly the proper use of police discretion, but that was the way I saw it.

Driving problems in Saskatchewan in wintertime arose not only from snowdrifts, but also from the intense cold. Especially when driving in RCMP cars not equipped with heaters. Many people who owned cars simply put them up on blocks for the winter season. The police couldn't do that. To keep the windshield clear one could purchase a plastic gadget equipped with vacuum cups to hold it on the windshield. A series of wires in it were connected to the battery, which, when turned on, prevented the windshield from frosting. To help keep the windshield from frosting inside the car, the side windows were lowered a few inches so that cold air could flow through. Whether lowered or fully closed, the side windows usually froze in place, which necessitated the use of the "Winnipeg" signal. This was a quick opening and closing of the door on the driver's side. This signal warned drivers behind that the car was going to turn either left or right. In those days cars had no built-in signals.

One interesting feature about Meadow Lake was that quite often we received visitors at the detachment from places outside the area – trappers from the north, commercial travellers and others from the south. One day a man burst into the office and yelled, "Hello, you old-son-of-a-bitch."

The sergeant got up from his desk and, with his hand outstretched, moved to greet the visitor. In a flash they were wrestling on the office floor. It took a moment or two for me to realize it was all in fun. The visitor was George Revell, a member of the Saskatchewan Natural Resources Department who had just been transferred to Meadow Lake. Revell was an ex-member of the RCMP, and he and the sergeant were old friends. In earlier days in training wrestling each other had been their favourite pastime.

I came to know Revell very well in the next few years and made many patrols with him in areas north and northwest of Meadow Lake. He told me that Sergeant Coombes had always had the reputation of being a practical joker. Sometimes he was blamed unfairly, as when someone tied a can to the tail of the C.O.'s dog and set it howling across the barrack square at Prince Albert. Revell had done it knowing that Coombes would be blamed.

One day Coombes and Revell were the last half section (two riders) on an exercise ride through the streets of Prince Albert. Revell dared Coombes to tell the sergeant major, who was riding behind them, what they thought he looked like on the back of horse – a bag of manure, but in cruder terms. Coombes halted his horse, and as the sergeant major came abreast of him Revell heard Coombes say:

"Sergeant major, do you know what you look like when riding a horse?"

Revell held his breath.

"No, I don't. What do I look like?"

"I think you look like Jesus Christ entering Jerusalem on an ass," Coombes said, deviating from what he had agreed with Revell to say. Coombes rode back into line and nothing more was said until they returned to barracks. Then the sergeant major, accompanied by a corporal, came to where Coombes was cleaning off his horse. Coombes knew the corporal was there to witness anything he might say.

"Constable," said the sergeant major, "what did you tell me I looked like when riding a horse?" Coombes looked surprised. "I didn't say you looked like anything, sir," he answered.

The sergeant major made no response and walked away. But a few days later Coombes was transferred to a distant detachment, which had all the earmarks of punishment. The corporal in charge had the reputation of being difficult to get along with, and a number of constables had asked to be transferred away from him. The problem lay in the corporal's wife, who insisted that the constables help with the household chores. But to everyone's surprise, Coombes remained there quite happily for a long period.

When he first visited Prince Albert barracks after his transfer, Revell asked him how he liked his new posting. Coombes explained that when he arrived there he had a chat with the corporal. Coombes told him that the C.O. had let him know, if obliquely, about the corporal's difficulty in retaining constables. If he, Coombes, asked for a transfer, the C.O. would consider moving the corporal to a place where he would no longer be in charge of men. Revell knew that the C.O. had told Coombes no such thing, but knowing Coombes so well he was quite willing to believe that he had told the fabricated story to the corporal. In any event, the corporal's wife did not ask Coombes to help out with the chores, and Coombes and the corporal remained friends long after they left that detachment.

"Who was the corporal?" I asked Revell.

"Your present C.O. at North Battleford," he said.

I now understood why Coombes had spoken to the C.O. with such familiarity the night he had me call the C.O. for him on the office telephone, when he called him by his nickname "Turkey".

1934, Meadow Lake, Sask. Kit, one of the police team.

1934. Bess, the other member of the police team.

ELEVEN

A few weeks after my arrival at Meadow Lake I had the most embarrassing experience of my life. I was returning to the detachment along the wooden sidewalk, after eating lunch at the Chinese cafe. The sidewalk was about a foot above the road level and I saw a man lying on his side in the ditch. At first I thought he was ill and hurried to see what was wrong with him.

As I came closer I could see he was an Indian, and closer still I could smell that he was drunk. Then I saw his fly was open, and his private parts indicated that he was having an amorous dream. This made it impossible for me to make him presentable for our journey to the detachment cell about 400 yards away. My activity awakened him and he began to object to my "interference". By now a number of people had gathered on the sidewalk, among them giggling girls, and men making rude remarks.

I decided that there was no hope of him walking to the detachment, so I lifted him to his feet, and with a choke hold I heaved him over my hip, leaving his face, open fly and private parts pointing to the sky. The laughing crowd followed me to the detachment where the sergeant stood at the outer wicket gate, as amused as anyone in the crowd. As I held on to the prisoner, the sergeant was in no hurry to open the gate. I yelled at him to do so, and then he helped take the Indian up the office steps and into the cell. I laid a charge of drunkenness, leaving another possible offence aside. After his plea of guilty I had to make another 220-mile tiresome escort patrol to North Battleford.

For weeks my friends and acquaintances reminded me of the Indian's arrest. It seemed everyone in the village had heard about the arrest of the "romantic Indian", as he was euphemistically referred to. Even the Anglican minister, Roy Durnford, delicately referred to it when he visited the detachment, as he frequently did in his unsuccessful efforts to get the sergeant to go to church with his wife. One positive thing arose from the arrest – I became the best-known constable, in the shortest time, of any constable ever stationed at Meadow Lake.

One day toward the end of June, after I had given the horses their noon meal, I went back to the office just in time to hear the sergeant say on the telephone:

"Yes, sir, Kelly can handle it. I'm sure he can, I'll attend to it."

He hung up the receiver on the wall telephone, swivelled his chair around to his desk, and continued to do what he had been doing when the telephone rang.

"What can Kelly handle, Sarge?" I inquired.

Without looking up he said "Loon Lake detachment of course."

I stood there in amazement. Surely I was not being transferred again, and so soon. This would mean my fourth transfer in as many months. This one like the last two had come "out of the blue".

"What kind of a man is Gillis to work for?" I asked rather apprehensively, naming the constable I knew to be in charge at Loon Lake. Without raising his head the sergeant said, "You won't be working with Gillis. You'll be alone while he spends six weeks leave in Nova Scotia."

I was relieved because this meant that my stay at Loon Lake would be temporary. Still, I felt that I was being thrown to the wolves. I was only a second class constable, just four months out of training, with little experience in practical police work.

"Surely, my experience doesn't warrant that kind of responsibility," I said.

"I agree," said the sergeant, looking up with a grin, "but I'm sure you can handle it." He was obviously enjoying my discomfort. "You can get on your horse and come to Meadow Lake for advice any time you like. It's only forty miles away. By the way, you are expected in Loon Lake early Sunday morning. I'll take you there in the police car."

As he spoke, I realized there was no telephone at Loon Lake, and that the police transport there was just a team of horses. Sunday was only three days away. On Saturday as I packed I suggested to the sergeant that I leave some of my kit at Meadow Lake.

"Take it all with you," he said, "you never know what is going to happen next in this outfit." Did the sergeant know something he wasn't telling me? At any rate I was not so sure any more that I would be returning to Meadow Lake. As I packed the sergeant informed me that I could take the Meadow Lake police car to use at Loon Lake. "I'll use my private car as long as it's away." This was indeed a concession, and I was glad I would not have to use a saddle horse to come back to Meadow Lake for advice, which I was sure I would need.

Before I left Meadow Lake my replacement arrived. He was a "northern" man. He said that after three years in the Northwest Territories, Meadow Lake was a metropolis compared to the posts where he had been stationed during his stay in the Arctic regions. Meadow Lake might look like a metropolis to me when I returned, after what I had learned about Loon Lake from the sergeant's description. As I packed I made sure I took along the sergeant's "gift", my *Peace Officers Manual*.

On Sunday morning I left Meadow Lake in bright sunshine with my kit stacked in the back seat of old 1092. I travelled, first on graded mud roads, and then on trails which took me through pastures and the barnyards of older homesteads. To get through these I had to open and close dozens of barbed wire gates. I decided then that only a genuine emergency would send me back for the sergeant's advice.

Constable Gillis waited anxiously for me with his car parked outside the office door. He had all the "turn over" documents ready for me to sign. I had only to check the stamps, the transport requisition forms, and the money on hand for the Receiver General of Canada. I didn't bother checking items on charge to the detachment such as tables, prisoners' blankets, chairs and so on, because Gillis was coming back. Then with a quick goodbye, Gillis drove off in a cloud of dust.

The detachment building was a one-storey affair about twenty-four feet square, with the office occupying one half. The other half contained the cell, and a bedroom large enough for two single beds. For some minutes I sat at the desk pondering my latest transfer, and had decided to go to the local hotel for lunch, when an irate Gillis burst through the detachment door. He had returned to tell me that two homesteaders had made a complaint, alleging the theft of two heifers valued at thirty-five dollars each, and that the pertinent information was under the blotter on the desk. He was in the office scarcely long enough to profanely describe why he had to come back fifteen miles to tell me about the complaint – no telephone service in the area. I looked under the blotter, and on a sheet of paper I found the complaint.

After lunch I walked all through Loon Lake in ten minutes. Its two streets crossed each other at right angles. One street led south to St. Walburg, the nearest town, some thirty-five miles away. The same street continued north of the village half a mile to where the graded road became a very rough trail leading to that "God-forsaken place", Goodsoil, thirty-five miles to the north. Loon Lake had a general store, a Red Cross hospital, a doctor's house, a garage, a church, a drug store and some houses. There were also a hotel and a Chinese restaurant, the RCMP detachment, and a shack used jointly by a provincial relief officer and the Natural Resources officer.

During the time I walked around the village I had the theft of cattle case on my mind. I wondered if the C.O. would have sent me to Loon Lake if he knew such a case was waiting to be investigated. Gillis would not have mentioned it for fear of being told to cancel his leave to attend to it. I was sure that Sergeant Coombes was unaware of it when he told the C.O. that "Kelly can handle it". I spent the rest of the afternoon studying my *Peace Officers Manual* and the Criminal Code insofar as they referred to offences dealing with cattle.

The more I read the more I doubted my ability to deal with such a serious case. For theft of cattle, the Criminal Code stated a man could be sent to jail for fourteen years. Probably no one had ever received fourteen years for stealing cattle, but it did indicate the seriousness of the offence. The code also stated that if the theft involved property valued at less than twenty-five dollars, the most a person could receive as punishment was six months in jail.

I would have returned to Meadow Lake immediately to get the sergeant's advice if it had not been for the thought of opening and closing the dozens of barbed wire gates, going and coming. That evening I wondered what the C.O. in Regina, the one who gave us the Saturday morning examinations in the Criminal Code, would have thought of my being responsible for such an important investigation, considering that I had made such a mess of trying to answer his questions. As I sat pondering my next move, I decided that whatever the outcome, I would give it my best effort and if that wasn't good enough, it couldn't be helped. This was the beginning of a philosophy that I would retain for the rest of my police career.

I had been out of the training division only four months, and my little police experience had been broken up by two previous transfers. I decided to get as much information as possible about the alleged theft, and then make a visit to Meadow Lake, in spite of the barbed wire gates. The homesteaders had spoken to Archie

Gemmell, the relief officer, about the theft of the heifers and he had brought the complaint to the police. The next morning I met Mr. Gemmell and asked if he had any means of getting in touch with the two complaining homesteaders. He offered to go and get them in his half-ton truck. When they arrived I soon obtained their story. They each owned one of the two heifers missing from the pasture belonging to one of them. When they had found that the heifers were missing they had done some investigating.

Thinking that the heifers might have broken through the fence, they checked it and found that some fence posts, with barbed wire attached, had been lifted from their holes, then presumably lowered to the ground so that the cattle could walk out of the pasture. About thirty feet from the fence was a seldom-used trail which led to the village of Makwa. Between the fence and the trail were cattle tracks and trampled grass, and on the trail itself were faint tire tracks.

It seemed clear that the heifers had been taken from the pasture and hauled away in a vehicle. The homesteaders seemed to have done the necessary police work up to that point. The question now was, who was the person or persons responsible?

The homesteaders had ideas in this connection. It was rumoured, they said, that the postmaster at Makwa had a reputation for handling "hot" cattle among others that he bought and sold, and that he had a small truck which he used in this business. Further, it was known that he kept cattle in a pasture in the bush, immediately east of the cleared land on his homestead. Obviously the postmaster was a logical suspect, and if indeed he had stolen the cattle, their owners seemed to have done all the police work necessary, except for finding some direct evidence to link the postmaster with the stolen heifers. It didn't take a Sherlock Holmes to figure out the next step – find the pasture to see if the heifers were there.

During our conversation I learned that the owners of the heifers placed a value on them of thirty-five dollars each. I didn't think, however, that I had enough information on which I could obtain a search warrant. I could visit the pasture without the postmaster knowing anything about it, but I would need the homesteaders to go with me to identify the stolen heifers, if indeed they were there.

As we drove to Makwa, on the same road as I had travelled from Meadow Lake, I learned that the postmaster was a political power in the district. He was known as a leading Liberal, with friends in the provincial Liberal government. His appointment as postmaster was pure patronage, which had enabled him to operate the post office on his farm, a mile or so from Makwa village. He also had a voice in the patronage handed out to others in the area.

As the two complainants and I passed the homestead and post office, we could see to the east a large area of cleared land beyond which was light bush which, presumably, was in the pasture. We continued north for about half a mile, then turned east for another half mile until we came to an extension of the bush we had seen beyond the postmaster's cleared land. This would give us cover when we walked to what we thought was his pasture. After walking some distance through this bush we came to a barbed-wire fence which could only be for the purpose of pasturing cattle on the other side. We were about to climb over it when we saw a man come from the post office. After crossing about a quarter of a mile of cleared land, he walked to the pasture gate. He opened it and entered the pasture. After we had waited about fifteen minutes, we saw him leave the pasture and return to the post office, his home.

As soon as we crossed the fence we could see cattle tracks. In a few minutes we came upon a number of cattle, two of which my companions recognized as theirs.

1935, Meadow Lake, Sask. Visiting constable on police horse Kit before Meadow Lake detachment office.

TWELVE

I realized later I could have seized the two heifers when we found them, but at the time I did what I thought best. The two complainants and I returned to Loon Lake. I had each one swear out an information to obtain a search warrant to search the postmaster's farm for the heifers. I knew from my *Peace Officers Manual* that I could arrest anyone found in possession of stolen property, so we returned to Makwa to search the postmaster's pasture. I drove in the police car, the homesteaders in a borrowed truck.

I informed the postmaster that we had warrants to search his pasture and he said he had no objection. We drove over a well-travelled track on his cleared land and through a barbed-wire gate into the pasture. Within a few minutes the homesteaders identified their cattle, and then loaded them into the truck. The postmaster denied knowing the heifers were in the pasture or how they got there. But he was the man we had seen go into the pasture earlier that day. I placed him under arrest.

I took him immediately before the Justice of the Peace in Loon Lake who had issued the search warrants, and had the two owners each lay a charge against him for the theft of a heifer valued at thirty-five dollars, contrary to section 369 of the Criminal Code of Canada.

By now his son had arrived and wanted his father out on bail. There was no objection and I made out the bail forms for the J.P., the first time I had made out such forms. The J.P. and I set a date for his next appearance in court. I knew adjournments should not be for more than eight days, but how to count eight days baffled me. Did we count that day as one day or did we start counting on the next day? Did the day he next appeared count as one of the days? To make sure, the J.P. adjourned the case for seven days.

The homesteaders thought that all they had to do was take their heifers home. I knew that the heifers were now in the possession of the court, but the J.P. allowed the homesteaders to take them home to take care of them until the case was disposed of.

It had been a busy first day at the detachment. Before this I had only made out and served summonses to defendants and witnesses. On this day I had made out, for the first time, an Information to Obtain a search warrant, a search warrant, two charges of theft, and bail forms. I had also seized two heifers, arrested a suspect, and set-tled on the amount of bail requested.

In retrospect it all seemed so simple. Actually, the homesteaders had done most of the investigation. I had just come in at the kill. Later I realized that I had not given the prisoner the official warning, nor had I arrested him by placing my hand on his shoulder when I told him he was under arrest. When I told him he was under arrest, he said, "I guess I'll have to change my clothes." I had made a note in my notebook of his earlier statement that he knew nothing of the stolen heifers being in his pasture.

Next would come the problem of prosecution. Where would it take place? Who would prosecute? How did I get in touch with a po-lice magistrate if one was necessary? Did I have enough evidence or should I be looking for more? As I mulled over these questions I knew that I would have to go to Meadow Lake to discuss them with the sergeant, regardless of how many barbed wire gates I would have to open and close. I had been away only one whole day when I returned to Meadow Lake on Tuesday morning. The sergeant was surprised to see me enter the office.

"Didn't you like it over there?" he asked.

After I had told him the whole story, he said that in spite of the fact that we had seen the postmaster enter the pasture, and that he had admitted it was his pasture, I was advised to get a Natural Resources Officer to prove it in court. In regard to the pasture fence he wanted to know if there was another gate, other than the one we had seen the postmaster enter. This I didn't know so he suggested that on my way back to Loon Lake I walk around the perimeter of the pasture to check on it. If there was such a gate it would allow the postmaster to say that others had access to his pasture. It was a point such as this that my inexperience had caused me to overlook. Then he raised another point.

"What evidence have you got that he stole the heifers?"

I knew I was in trouble. We had no evidence that the post master had gone to the homesteader's pasture and had stolen the heifers, but on my advice the homesteaders had charged him with that offence. I had visions of advising the laying of the wrong charges, and arresting a man when he hadn't committed the crime he had been charged with. Later I learned there was nothing wrong in laying one charge as a "holding" charge and then changing it before a trial. But the sergeant let me "stew" for a while before he said, "Don't worry. The next time you are in court you can withdraw these charges. But in the meantime have the homesteaders lay charges of possession of stolen heifers against the postmaster."

The sergeant also cleared up the other points that had bothered me. With a check of the pasture fence, and a Natural Resources officer to give evidence, he thought there was sufficient evidence to proceed with the prosecution. In my report to the sub/division office, he said, I should set out the evidence I had, along with the steps I had taken in the matter of arrest and bail, and then ask for the police magistrate for the area to visit Loon Lake to sit on the case. The sergeant pointed out that the postmaster could elect to be tried by a judge alone in the District Court, or before a judge and jury in the Court of King's Bench. But the police magistrate could deal fully with the case if the postmaster elected to be tried by him. If he didn't elect to be tried before the magistrate, then the magistrate would deal with it as a preliminary hearing. All this was not very clear to me, but it was enough that in my report I was to ask for the attendance of the police magistrate. All this because each heifer was valued at more than twenty-five dollars. Otherwise two J.P.'s could have presided and disposed of the case.

"Then who will do the prosecuting?" I asked.

"You and I," he replied cheerfully. "I will prosecute the first case and you can prosecute the other, with me at your elbow." He must have noticed a concerned look on my face because he continued, "There's no danger you will mess it up. Anyway, he might plead guilty to both charges, or if he's convicted on the first charge he might still plead guilty on your charge." I certainly hoped he would.

I never thought I would be anxious to get back to Loon Lake, but I declined Mrs. Coombes' invitation to stay for lunch. She wrapped up a loaf cake for me and I left immediately. On my way back I stopped at the postmaster's pasture and walked around the mile of barbed-wire fence. I found there was no gate other than the one the postmaster had entered the previous day. I had learned from the sergeant that the homesteaders could lay the new charges when the accused next appeared in court, thus saving them a special journey to Loon Lake to do so. On the accused's next appearance the theft charges were withdrawn and the "possession" charges laid.

By this time I knew when the police magistrate would arrive in Loon Lake, so that date was set for trial. Now the accused was represented by counsel, Mr. "Rookie" Blackburn of St. Walburg.

Sergeant Coombes arrived the night before the trial and I showed him the "brief" I had prepared. He found it in order. I told him that I thought he should prosecute both cases, but in his usual jocular fashion, he said, "You are old enough and ugly enough to prosecute your own case. By the way, how old are you?" He knew my age. I had just passed my twenty-third birthday.

The trial took place on a very hot day in July. A festive air prevailed and the small detachment office was crowded, a few onlookers even sitting on the bed in the cell. Vacationers from the lake mingled with homesteaders who had come to Loon Lake for the entertainment. I opened the windows, not only to allow some air into the office, but so that the people crowding around them outside could also hear what was going on.

The Police Magistrate, in shirt sleeves, sat behind my desk. It was pushed into a corner to make room for onlookers. The postmaster and his lawyer, Mr. Blackburn, also coatless, sat near the desk. The sergeant and I, dressed in breeches and boots, brown serge jackets, collars and ties, stood perspiring alongside some filing cabinets, waiting for the trial to begin. The sergeant nudged me and I opened the court with, "I declare this court open in the name of the King." The magistrate told the accused that he could be tried by him, or by a judge without a jury, or by a judge and jury. But if he wanted to be tried by one of the others, he would proceed with a preliminary hearing. Mr. Blackburn said the accused would like to be tried by the police magistrate. He entered a plea of not guilty on both charges.

Magistrate Stan Mighton was well known to the lawyer and to the police. The accused's decision to be tried by him arose from the fact that Mighton had the reputation of being lenient when it came to punishment. Lawyer Blackburn believed that if his client was found guilty he could expect a more lenient penalty than one imposed by a judge in a higher court. The magistrate decided to hear the charges separately, even though the evidence would be exactly the same in each case.

In the first case, one homesteader gave evidence about examining his pasture, the fence, the tracks on the trail nearby, identifying his heifer in the accused's pasture, and the value of the heifer. I gave evidence about the small part I had played in the investigation, about seeing the accused visit his pasture the morning we saw the stolen heifers in his pasture. I also said that I had walked around the pasture fence and found only one gate, the trail from which led directly to the postmaster's house. The Natural Resources officer showed from his records that the pasture was owned by the postmaster.

The postmaster gave evidence, but all he had to say was that he did not know the heifers were in his pasture, and they must have been put there by someone else until such time as they could be removed. On cross-examination he agreed that if it was another person who stole the heifers, he would have to go through the postmaster's barnyard to get into the pasture through the gate we had seen him use. "Unless," he said, "someone had taken down the fence to put the heifers in the pasture." To take them out they would have to do the same thing. Had he seen anyone cross his land and enter the pasture? "No," he said. Why did he go to the pasture the morning he was seen by Constable Kelly? "To check my cattle," he answered. Did he see the stolen heifers there? "No," he replied. The police and the homesteaders saw them there a few minutes after he left the pasture, so why didn't he see them? He didn't know. He could only say he didn't see them.

The magistrate said he would hear the second case before giving his decision on the first. The sergeant told him the evidence would be the same on the second charge and suggested that the evidence of the first charge be accepted. The magistrate was prepared to do so, but Mr. Blackburn, for some reason, thought the second trial should proceed. I was sorry about this, and then I heard the sergeant say, "Constable Kelly will prosecute this one, Your Worship."

As prosecutor and witness in the case, I followed the practice of giving evidence first, although it was out of sequence.

As expected, the evidence was exactly the same as in the first case for both the prosecution and defence. I had no problem, knowing that the sergeant would prevent my going wrong. The magistrate said he would give his decision in both cases after lunch. I stood to attention and adjourned the court.

For some unknown reason, Mr. Mighton, Mr. Blackburn, the sergeant and I went to the Chinese restaurant and not the local hotel. We were sitting in a small booth when the sergeant left to say a few words to an acquaintance at the cash register. As we waited for service Mr. Blackburn asked the magistrate, who was known as a bit of a humorist, what decision he had arrived at.

"Well," said Mr. Mighton, in a slow drawl, and a half grin on his face, "I'm going to find him not guilty on the first charge, and guilty on the second." Neither Mr. Blackburn nor I could believe what we had heard. "But the evidence is the same on both charges. He's either not guilty or guilty on both," Blackburn retorted.

"I am aware of that," said Mighton, "and *I* think he's guilty on both charges. But think of how the sergeant is going to feel when he learns that I don't think he proved his case beyond a reasonable doubt, whereas this green constable, obviously prosecuting his first serious case, did so." He looked at me as he spoke, then continued, "anyway, it won't make any difference to the punishment. I'm going to send your client to jail for six months, Mr. Blackburn. If I convicted him on both counts, the punishment would be a further six months, but to run concurrently with the first. Do you have any objection, Rookie?" As the magistrate spoke I could only think of the accused's evidence, supposedly on his own behalf. In my mind it was this, as much as the evidence of myself and the homesteaders, that showed his guilt.

I couldn't believe a court case could be disposed of in this way. I agreed with Mr. Blackburn. Whatever the verdict, it should be the same on both charges. Before the sergeant returned Mr. Blackburn commented, "I would rather you found him not guilty on both counts, but if that's the way you're going, there's nothing I can say."

When the court reopened after lunch, the magistrate asked Mr. Blackburn if he had anything to say. As though the conversation in the restaurant had not taken place, Blackburn said there was ample grounds to give his client the benefit of the doubt. Anyone could have put the heifers in the pasture after they had been stolen. His client, a man with a good reputation, was hardly the man to steal cattle from homesteaders. Both charges should be dismissed, he concluded. Knowing what the magistrate was going to do, I listened to Mr. Blackburn, realizing how easy it would have been for the magistrate to dismiss the charges as Mr. Blackburn had suggested.

Sergeant Coombes spoke for both charges. He did not know what the magistrate was going to do, as I did. He pointed out that there was only one gate to the pasture, on a trail leading from the postmaster's cleared land. Anyone going there would have to pass through the postmaster's barnyard. He was seen to visit the pasture, clearly to check over the animals there. He must have seen two strange heifers, but made no effort to inform anyone of this. He might have bought them from the person who had stolen them, but he had not claimed so in evidence. There was no doubt about his guilt and he should be found guilty on both counts.

Mr. Mighton did exactly as he said he would. Not guilty on the first charge and guilty on the second. There was a collective gasp from the people present. They knew as well as we did that it was guilty or not guilty on both charges. But no one was more surprised than the sergeant, and he showed it by the expression on his face.

"Would you like to speak to sentence, Mr. Blackburn?" the magistrate asked. He did, and made a strong plea for a suspended sentence, repeating his earlier words about his client's good reputation in the community. When his turn came the sergeant pointed out the seriousness of stealing cattle from homesteaders whose lives were difficult enough without having to protect themselves from cattle thieves. He asked for a "salutary" sentence. As I now expected, the postmaster was sentenced to six months in the common jail at Prince Albert. I immediately closed the court, knowing that I had a prisoner to escort to jail, or at least as far as North Battleford.

The sergeant was quite upset and wanted to discuss the verdict with the magistrate, who excused himself, saying that he had to be back in North Battleford that evening and should leave immediately, which he did. The prisoner and his counsel discussed a possible appeal, but they decided they would rather handle the matter through some form of clemency, calling upon the federal Liberal M.P. in North Battleford and the Liberal Attorney General in Regina for assistance.

I couldn't bring myself to tell the sergeant about the conversation between Mighton and Blackburn in the cafe until several months afterwards. When I did so, he said, "That bastard! I knew he was playing a trick of some kind." I did not stay long enough at Loon Lake to know whether the postmaster received any clemency or not.

I completed my reports so that I could take them to North Battleford when I escorted the prisoner there. In the conclusion of case report, when it came to the disposition of the first case, I had to enter "Not Guilty". In explanation I could only say that the magistrate had given the accused the benefit of the doubt, even though the evidence in both cases was exactly the same. I could hardly report what I had heard in the cafe. Although somewhat shocked at first, in thinking over the matter I could only conclude that justice had been done. People in the district had told me before the trial that the postmaster, with his political "pull", would never go to jail. Many recalled the political interference with the old Saskatchewan Provincial police in the 1920s, which had resulted in scandal and the taking over the provincial policing by the RCMP.

As criminal cases go, this one was not unusual except to me, seeing it was the first serious criminal case I had dealt with. I had learned a great deal about what I should know about the law. It included the jurisdiction of J.P.s, magistrates and judges. My thanks to the sergeant and my *Peace Officers Manual*. This case did much to bolster my confidence in dealing with other serious matters.

THIRTEEN

S oon after the cattle case was over it was time for Gillis to return. Very early one morning during this period I received a visit from an elderly homesteader. With a European accent, he said he wanted to make a complaint about the theft of hay. As I prepared to take down the details he said he didn't want to make a complaint. I thought this was strange, but guessed he had something on his mind when he asked about "the other constable".

I asked if he meant Gillis, and he said he did. I told him that Gillis had been on leave but would be returning any day as his leave period had expired. I asked that if he didn't want to make a complaint, just what did he want of the police. He clearly showed his reluctance to speak to me about it. He then said he had visited the detachment on previous occasions and that he knew the other constable quite well. He was obviously stalling as he tried to make up his mind whether he would talk to me or not.

"You look rather young to be in charge of a detachment," he said. "I wonder if you have had any experience in the matter I came to talk about?"

"You'll never know unless you tell me about it," I responded.

"Do you know how a person can get a reward for reporting a still?"

Actually I new very little about it. All I had done to date was ac-company Sergeant Coombes on a couple of unsuccessful searches of two homesteads north of Meadow Lake. About the only thing I knew was that a reward could be given and that, after an Excise seizure, the submission of forms was a formidable exercise for someone unacquainted with them, as I was. But I wasn't going to admit to my visitor the limit of my knowledge.

So I indicated that I was well versed in the procedure. I thought our conversation had gone on long enough without me knowing who I was talking to, so I asked him his name. He refused to give it.

"I will have to know your name if you expect a reward for reporting a still." Then I added quickly, "That is if the case is concluded successfully," having in mind the unsuccessful searches at Meadow Lake.

"The case will be successfully concluded if you will do your part," he said.

I began to see why he was so evasive. He had expected a more mature man than I was, and he was wondering if I had sufficient experience to deal with the matter he wanted to tell the police about. Then he wondered how he could be sure that, if he gave me his name, I would report it and not that of some other person. He didn't say so, but I suspected that he was implying that the name I would send in would be fictitious, and that I would keep the reward for myself when it arrived.

I was trying not to show my visitor that I was getting annoyed at the game he was playing, but then I thought I could play it for as long as he was prepared to do so. I told him that he would have to trust me. He would know if an illicit still had been seized, and if he didn't get the reward, he could always write to RCMP headquarters asking why he didn't receive it.

Then I said, "If you have given information before, you must have trusted the constable then. Would you give me the name of the person you informed on then?" To my surprise, without hesitation he gave me the name. I drew the file from the cabinet and could see the name of the informant in that case, presumably that of the person sitting opposite me. Then it occurred to me that this person might not be the previous informant at all. He might be the convicted person, who, in the absence of Constable Gillis, was trying to find out who had given the police information that had led to his conviction. After the manner in which he was approaching an ordinary complaint, I was quite willing to believe that he might be pulling off this sort of thing. Then I decided the game had gone on long enough.

"Unless you are prepared to positively identify yourself," I said, "I'm bringing this interview to a close."

Just then the office door opened and in walked the relief officer for the district, Archie Gemmell. He looked at my visitor and said, "Hello, Mr. -----, are you coming in to see me later?" The name Gemmell had called my visitor was that of the informant on the file I had before me. I wondered later how our "game" might have ended if Gemmell had not come into the office. Gemmell, seeing I was busy, excused himself and left.

I would not have been surprised if my visitor had been one of the "crackpots" who gave the police information that was nothing more than a figment of their imagination. We had two such quite respectable people in Meadow Lake who came in regularly with information which was completely without foundation. Sergeant Coombes dealt with them as he would any other person, but when they left the office he threw the notes he had taken into the wastebasket. He had learned from experience. Later on I had similar experiences, and they tended to make me sceptical of the "facts" I had been given.

Having his name come out so unexpectedly, with no further mention of any reward my visitor then gave me the information he had about a neighbour who was about to operate an illicit still. His neighbour, he said was going to run off a batch of homebrew that very morning, in order to have a supply ready for a dance that weekend. He operated his still on provincially owned land adjoining his homestead, "on the back end". He was so definite about everything, I wondered if he had been cooperating with his neighbour and now had quarrelled with him.

He then gave me some more details. There was a faint trail from his neighbour's barnyard to the provincial land, and the still site was about 250 yards farther along, in fairly heavy bush. With this information I went to the local J.P. and obtained a search warrant to search the still operator's homestead. I didn't need one to search on provincial land. I went to the homestead by police car because the informant had said the trail was good enough for car travel. But the trail was so full of dried-out potholes that I was sure that if I had used the police team I would have made better time.

As I bumped along the trail, I thought that, as this was my first investigation under the Excise Act, I would be happy to find the homesteader in possession of a distilling coil, or some illicit spirits, even, if not a whole still. Punishment for these offences was the same as if I had found a complete still, a minimum fine of $100 or three months in jail in default of payment of fine. To find an illicit still operating was more than I could hope for.

A neatly dressed young woman came to meet me as I drove into the homestead's yard. I asked for her husband. She said he had gone to visit a neighbour and she didn't know when he would return. I told her I had a warrant to search for a still or anything else that indicated illicit distilling on the homestead. I didn't know if she was lying about her husband's whereabouts, but I suspected that he was at the still site. If she was telling the truth, and I went to the still site, it could give her time to dispose of the distilling coil if it was hidden in the barn. If I stopped to search the barn, that would give her time to go to the still site to warn her husband.

I decided to go to the still site. I could see a faint path leading to the back of the homestead, and I followed it the length of the homestead, about half a mile. I could see it continue into the rather heavy bush which I presumed was provincial land. As I walked to this point I had some doubt as to whether this was the path to the still site. It seemed that it hadn't been used much. I wondered if there was another path that I had missed. Then I thought of the informant whose view of my suspected inexperience would be confirmed.

I noticed some tire tracks leading off the homestead. These were surely made by the Bennett buggy I had seen in the yard, and the team of horses I had seen in the barn. This indicated that the moonshiner had probably hauled materials and equipment to a still site. Back in the bush all was quiet. I knew the slightest noise would carry, so I was particularly careful to make none. I had gone about 100 yards off the homestead property when I saw smoke and steam rising into the high trees. As I got closer I could see a man moving about what I then believed to be a still. He was so intent on what he was doing that it wasn't until I was within twenty yards of him, and politely said "good morning", that he noticed me.

When he saw my uniform, he threw up his hands and sat down on a log nearby, holding his bowed head in his hands. The still was in full operation, something I was never to see again, in spite of many successful Excise Act searches yet to come. Boiling on an old kitchen stove was a boiler full of fermented mash. The boiler lid was sealed with dough to prevent any steam from escaping. A hole in the centre of the lid allowed the insertion of a copper pipe, about half an inch in diameter, and this was also sealed with dough. This pipe was part of the coil, in a barrel of cold water. The end of the coil went out through the bottom of the barrel in order to carry the condensed steam, now potable alcohol, into a shallow dish.

Nearby were a large number of various-sized containers, from medicine bottles to gallon jugs, some of which contained the alcohol already manufactured. Near the stove was stacked about half a cord of stove wood. A few feet behind it were two barrels, one full and the other half-full of mash ready for boiling. As he got to his feet the homesteader's first words were, "Who told you about me?" Then he waved his hand as if to say, "Don't answer. I think I know."

I took two small bottles of alcohol and set them aside. Then using the homesteader's axe, I smashed all the bottles and the barrels of mash. The homesteader helped me douse the fire and dismantle the still. I kept the coil and smashed the stove, the barrel and the boiler. The coil was sufficient for my purpose. So with the coil, two bottles of alcohol, and the homesteader carrying his axe, which I allowed him to keep, we returned to the house. On the way he wanted to know what the penalty would be. I told him if this was his first offence, which he assured me it was, then he could expect the minimum fine of $100 or three months in jail. He was silent for a while. Then he blurted out, "Then it's going to be jail."

As we travelled toward the house I again noticed the tire tracks. If I could prove that he had used the team and the Bennett buggy to haul materials to and from the still, I could seize them "in the name of the King". I asked if he had used his team for this purpose, but he denied it, and I did not pursue the matter. I was rather glad. I thought going to jail was enough punishment without my taking away the means by which he could "prove up" on his homestead.

His wife was waiting for us in the exact spot where she had been standing when I left her about an hour before. I realized then that I hadn't told the homesteader he was under arrest, but he accepted the fact that he was. His wife wanted to know if she should prepare lunch. He nodded, and I was invited to eat with them. They discussed the possibility of getting the $100 from some relations down south. They thought of selling the cow, but he finally ended up by saying that jail was the only option. His wife would be alone, but there was nothing for her to do but feed the chickens and milk the cow. The horses could be put out to pasture. She could always go into Loon Lake with a neighbour for her relief order. My prisoner and I started off for Loon Lake, taking the exhibits.

As we reached the next homestead he asked if I would mind stopping. He wanted to see if his neighbour would help out his wife if she needed assistance in any way. As we drove into the yard I was not surprised to see my visitor to the police detachment that morning come out of the house. No sign of recognition passed between us, and he readily agreed to give whatever assistance the wife required. I could only wonder how he felt at seeing his neighbour being carted off to jail as a result of his informing on him. Was he so hard up that he had done it for the sake of twenty-five dollars? He had done the same thing before, so perhaps the money was the incentive. In any case, without such sources of information, the product of illicit distilling would find its way into the hands of other homesteaders, who would spend money for homebrew that would be better spent for food and clothing.

The federal government encouraged the giving of information in these cases by offering twenty-five per cent of any fine meted out. This helped the RCMP to enforce the Excise Act, but sitting in that barnyard, watching the homesteader request help from the informant, made it difficult for me to remember that he was performing a service for the community, all of whom were on government relief. As we travelled on to Loon Lake the prisoner and I talked of many things. At one point he burst out laughing and said, "it'll be a dull dance on Saturday night." I answered that all the trade would now go to his opposition. He answered. "There isn't any." It was good to know.

The homesteader had committed an indictable offence, triable at the discretion of the Crown by way of summary conviction. This allowed me to take his fingerprints. Ordinarily a summary conviction case would be disposed of by one Justice of the Peace, but in Excise cases it required two J.Ps. The homesteader pleaded guilty and was sentenced to the minimum fine of $100 or three months in jail. I escorted him the 135 miles to North Battleford, where I left him to be escorted by someone else to the Prince Albert common jail. Before I left the next morning the staff sergeant told me I would have company on the return trip. A Constable Jack King was taking the place of Constable Jack Gillis, who was not returning to Loon Lake. For some reason he was not even returning to Saskatchewan.

King had more service than I had, and I was most appreciative of his assistance in filling out the several forms required by the National Revenue department in Ottawa. These forms were unnecessarily complicated for someone like me, just learning his trade. I had known enough to send in an Advance Notice of Seizure direct to Ottawa as soon as I returned to Loon Lake from the homestead. Even with King's help, it took most of the morning to complete the forms.

I could not imagine then that in twenty years I would be the Chief Preventive Officer of the RCMP, responsible for the Force's activities in enforcing the Customs and Excise Acts all over Canada. Nor could I have guessed that in that capacity I would be pleading with National Revenue officials to simplify their complicated seizure forms.

I spent my last day at Loon Lake turning the detachment over to Jack King. My seven weeks at Loon Lake had been a busy time as a result of the cattle case and some routine investigations. If it had not been for the cattle case I would have spent a rather dull time there.

As I returned to Meadow Lake in Police Car, Code No. 1092, I opened and closed innumerable barbed-wire gates. But I didn't seem to mind doing this. It seemed a natural thing to do. When I arrived at the outskirts of Meadow Lake, it didn't seem to be the metropolis my replacement there had thought it to be after his several years "in the north". But it was certainly an improvement over Loon Lake. It had telephones, wooden sidewalks and even a few street lights. I felt I had come home.

FOURTEEN

Before returning to Meadow Lake it had occurred to me that I might not be staying there if my replacement had been satisfactory. As a single man with little experience, I could be used as a relief constable when required on any one of the thirteen detachments in the sub/division. But on my first night back an incident happened that enhanced my chances of staying at Meadow Lake.

Although liquor was prohibited in a detachment, my replacement, I'll call him Jim, had arranged to have a bottle brought to him from North Battleford. Jim started to drink after supper and as the evening wore on the time between drinks got shorter. By the time we went to bed Jim was drunk.

During the evening he had told me about his northern service. Babysitting for Eskimos was not his cup of tea, he had said. By bedtime he had made it quite clear that dealing with anything other than "big crime" was a waste of time. I could take a drink or leave it. That night I decided to leave it. We had only been in bed a short time when the sergeant rushed into the office, saying that he had received a call from Dr. Rafuse who had been requested to go to the Indian reserve to attend to some injuries resulting from a drunken brawl. The sergeant wanted Jim and me to accompany the doctor to help "clean things up".

The sergeant soon became aware of Jim's condition. He ordered him back to bed, and said he would accompany me to the reserve.

There were a number of head injuries and the doctor did the repairs by stitching the heads that I had shaved. With a couple of Indians under arrest, we returned to the detachment and put them in the cell to await a court appearance the next morning, charged with drunkenness and assault.

The sergeant never said a word about Jim, but I knew he was thinking about Jim's failure to be in fit condition for duty. The next morning he asked me if I had been drinking the night before. I was glad to be able to say I had not. Then he told me to groom the horses. He was going to talk to Jim. When I returned to the office Jim was in a cheerful mood. He said the sergeant was sending him back to North Battleford after talking to the C.O. on the phone. He had been afraid that he would be staying at Meadow Lake, he said.

Apparently, the sergeant had told Jim that he was going to overlook his misbehaviour, which could have resulted in his appearance in Orderly Room, charged with being drunk, being drunk when required for duty, and importing liquor into police quarters. I was not sure that Jim appreciated what the sergeant had done for him.

This was one side of RCMP discipline that I was to see frequently. Unless an NCO was forced by circumstances to prefer a charge against a subordinate, the subordinate went unpunished. I realized that because the sergeant had dealt so leniently with Jim, he had put himself in an awkward position as far as I was concerned. He could hardly treat me any differently if I broke rules and regulations some time. This, and a number of similar incidents elsewhere, led me to believe that when a man ended up facing charges in Orderly Room, the chances were that it was not the first time he had committed a breach of the regulations.

Jim's misbehaviour ensured his transfer from Meadow Lake and I was glad. I began to enjoy the few amenities Meadow Lake provided. I sang in the church choir and took part in plays. But few newspapers reached Meadow Lake, there was no library, and it was at a time when it was not thought that having a radio was necessary. There was ample police work to keep us busy, and innumerable escort trips to North Battleford. A highlight of my work that fall was when the sergeant told me to accompany two Natural Resources officers on a several days patrol into the woods east and south of Meadow Lake. I took the police team and democrat, along with saddles and bridles, and feed for the horses. The officers took bedding and a supply of food.

For several years the Resources officers had been receiving complaints about the number of deer being shot before the hunting season began. The offenders would dress the deer and hang them in trees, high enough so that coyotes or dogs could not reach them. Then when the season opened the illegal hunters would act as guides, mostly to American hunters. If these people failed to get their allotment of two deer, they purchased one or two deer shot out of season to take home. Many American hunters drove back to the U.S. proudly displaying, on the front fenders of their cars, one or two deer that had been illegally killed and illegally purchased.

We hoped that by patrolling the woods for a few days before the season opened we might come across the hunters and, if not, our presence might prevent some from hunting. We drove the democrat into the woods as far as possible and then patrolled the bush with saddle horses. We stayed out three nights and two full days. We did not see any hunters but there were plenty of signs that they had been there before us. At various points we found six deer hanging from the trees, dressed but with the hides still on. There was no point in waiting for the hunters. As long as we were in the woods they would not put in an appearance. So we cut down the deer and gave them to the Meadow Lake hospital.

As winter came on, it became necessary to use the police team more. Driving a team and sleigh was not a novelty to me. I had been accustomed to it for several years in New Brunswick before I joined the RCMP. But I had never driven a team like Kit and Bess. To them a sleigh drive was an extension of their exercise periods. It seemed that the sleigh and driver were no more to them than a tail was to a kite. To them a long winter patrol was a happy time away from their drab stable. Quite often such patrols were made, not because they couldn't be made by police car, but because the horses needed a workout.

On one occasion we received instructions to interview a trapper who lived on Green Lake, about fifty miles northeast of Meadow Lake. Actually the trapper lived in the Big River detachment area, but because the horses needed the exercise the sergeant decided that I should make the inquiry.

On a beautifully clear crisp winter morning, with no wind and the thermometer reading about twenty degrees below zero Fahrenheit, I travelled to Green Lake village. I drove through pine woods and sand hills, following the bank of the meandering Beaver River. The sleigh bells rang out and the harness traces snapped in the cold air.

The horses wanted me to give them their heads. They might have thought we were just out for an exercise run and would soon be returning to the stables, not starting out on a 100-mile patrol. I had difficulty in keeping them down to a reasonable trot, but how pleasant to have a team that one had to hold back. I was warmly dressed in heavy woollen underwear, three pairs of woollen stockings, moccasins, heavy cloth breeches and brown patrol jacket, a hip-length buffalo coat and a muskrat fur hat, and bundled in a large buffalo robe. We travelled through real "Rose Marie" country. Not unlike Nelson Eddy, of whom very little if anything had been heard at that time, I did a lot of singing to keep myself company. I remember thinking that I was even being paid for what I was doing.

There was no habitation at all between Meadow Lake and Green Lake village. I arrived there in about three hours, but if Kit and Bess had had their way we would have made it in two. As usual when in Green Lake I paid a visit to the Hudson's Bay factor. Over a cup of coffee, when I told him where I was going, he warned me that a recent snowstorm had obliterated the trail made down the lake by the trapper I was going to see, and his pair of wolf-like dogs. He said I should stay away from the shoreline as the recent snow had built up there in deep drifts. He knew the middle of the lake was safe for travel because he had been fishing there the day before and had found the ice over a foot thick.

What I had to fear most, he continued, were the trapper's two "damned dogs". They appeared to him to be too vicious to run loose. Every time the trapper came to the village the factor was afraid the dogs would attack the Indian children playing there, and he had warned the trapper about it. I was used to visiting trappers' cabins and seeing the yapping dogs I usually found there, so I didn't take much notice of what he was telling me about them. As I left he invited me to lunch on my return.

Soon I was driving down the lake through about a foot of fluffy snow. It gave the horses no trouble, even though it piled up against the sleigh's dashboard. The horses had more trouble with the light crust that had formed before the last snow. My only concern was that after coming fifty miles I might not find the trapper at home.

As I travelled down the lake I recalled that Commissioner Irvine of the North-West Mounted Police had, some fifty years before, in the summer of 1885, made a patrol to this same lake. He was searching for the renegade Indian Chief Big Bear after the Riel Rebellion had ended. Big Bear and his followers had ransacked the Hudson's Bay store in which I had just had a cup of coffee with the factor. On June 14, Irvine and his police party, on horses, had patrolled from the south end of Green Lake through the heavy bush. He didn't find Big Bear, who was arrested some weeks later by a lone constable on patrol many miles to the southeast.

I appreciated the difference between the way Irvine had to travel and my situation. I sat comfortably in a warm sleigh, whereas he had to battle mosquitoes and blackflies for days on end, and protect his horses from them as well.

As I approached the trapper's cabin, which was about fifty yards from the shoreline, I was pleased to see smoke coming from his stovepipe chimney. As I turned off the lake I could see the trapper coming toward me with a shovel, in case the horses had difficulty with the deep snow. As I drove toward the cabin I heard his dogs barking and was surprised not to see them. The trapper said he had heard my bells from a way back, and had shut his dogs up in a shed, because they too had heard the bells. They got excited when visitors came. I stopped the team before his cabin, but it could be seen that the horses were already upset by the continuous barking.

I hurriedly concluded my business with the trapper, who asked if I would stay for a cup of coffee. I told him I was concerned about the horses and the barking dogs. Then he told me how valuable the dogs were to him. He used them to draw a toboggan when he went to the store, then as pack dogs when he went out on his trapline. He wondered what he would do without them. I didn't waste any time getting away, and let the horses travel faster than I should have, just to get away from the dogs. After a while I slowed them down, thinking we were far enough away not to be troubled by the dogs any more. As I did so I heard a faint barking and, looking back, I could see the two dogs racing toward us along the track I had made. The horses, too, had heard the barking, and wanted to travel faster. I was afraid that if they went any faster they were likely to stumble as a result of breaking through the shallow ice crust, then get off the trail and possibly overturn the sleigh. The dogs gained on us, and the nearer they got the more excited the horses became. In my attempt to keep the horses on the track we had made on the way down, I had slowed them up enough to allow the dogs to get to within fifty yards of the sleigh.

My problem was to watch the now snarling dogs and at the same time keep the horses on the trail. At one point, while looking back at the dogs, I inadvertently pulled the horses a considerable distance off the trail. Guiding them back allowed the dogs to catch up to the sleigh. I hadn't noticed that the buffalo robe was hanging over the side of the sleigh until one of the dogs tried to grab it. I pulled it back just in time. The horses by now were very excited and wanted to get away from the snarling and barking dogs as fast as they could.

Instead of continuing to trot they wanted to gallop. My holding them back made them plunge ahead. I now realized that I was on the edge of a catastrophe. At any moment the sleigh might overturn, leaving me and the horses at the mercy of the dogs. They seemed ready to tear us apart; I had two mad dogs to deal with.

Up till then I had been sitting in the sleigh, fearing that if I stood up I would be more easily thrown out. But now I decided that it was the dogs' lives or mine, and that I should shoot them. I had thought earlier I might have to do this, but I recalled the trappers' story about how valuable the dogs were to him. As I stood up to shoot them, the robe fell off the sleigh and the dogs stopped long enough to tear it apart. I hoped this would be enough of a distraction for them to stop following us, but they soon started after us again.

Soon the dogs had not only caught up with us, but one of them was racing alongside the near horse. It attempted to jump on the horse's back but, fortunately, due to poor footing, it fell back. Both dogs were frothing at the mouth and their snarls were even more vicious. I had drawn my Colt .455 and was trying to steady myself while aiming at the dog which had fallen immediately behind the sleigh. I realized that, standing in a sleigh bobbing up and down, and being jerked by a galloping team of horses, any chance of hitting a dog was indeed slim. But perhaps even the noise of the revolver would stop them. As they followed I had only their heads to aim at. I realized, too, that I had only five bullets in my revolver. Under the circumstances I might expend them all without killing a dog.

I had another fear. I couldn't see between the horses for the steam rising from their bodies, and that prevented me from keeping the horses on the trail. There were mounds of froth at all points where the harness touched them. I felt that they were so overheated they might stop dead in their tracks, dogs or no dogs. As I tried to keep the team on the trail, I turned to the dogs and aimed at the nearest snaring, frothing dog, about eight feet away. I couldn't keep his head in my sights but I fired anyway. The crack of the revolver in the very cold air frightened my already highly agitated team. The sleigh lurched ahead, throwing me down on the seat. As I fell I looked behind and could see both dogs still running behind the sleigh. As I thought that I had failed to hit the dog I had aimed at, it fell motionless in the snow.

I decided to shoot the second dog, but it fell on the dead dog and began tearing it apart. I had expected the live dog to take up the chase, but it kept tearing at its mate. I could hardly believe that the chase had ended. The horses continued at the same speed for some distance before they realized that things had changed. I could now bring them down to a half-walk, half-trot, and eventually to a plodding walk. Before this they had thrown off enough steam to prevent frost from building up on their bodies, but now, cooling down, lace-like patterns of frost were forming over their faces and sides.

The incident had covered more than three miles and had ended about two miles from Green Lake village. As I sat in the sleigh, all heated up, I missed the buffalo robe. My muskrat hat had been on the floor of the sleigh since the chase began and, heated as I was, I was glad to put it on with the flaps down over my ears. I was glad to get my team into the Hudson's Bay Company stables, blanketed, but too tired to eat the hay I put before them. I knew the forty-five-mile journey back to Meadow Lake would be a less lively drive than that I had experienced on the way to Green Lake that morning.

I went over to the Hudson's Bay store where I told the factor what had happened. He wasn't really surprised, he said. He knew of an incident at a northern post where similar dogs had attacked and killed a child right in the village. He always thought of it when the trapper and his dogs came to Green Lake. Anyway, he said, he was glad one had been shot, and now he would insist that the trapper shoot the other one.

I had a leisurely lunch with the factor and his wife, as I had no intention of returning to Meadow Lake until I was satisfied that the horses had rested sufficiently. I was on my way to the stables to give the horses some water when I saw the trapper, carrying his snow-shoes, come into the yard. I expected him to be very annoyed at me for shooting his dog. Instead he assumed all the blame. He shouldn't have let the dogs out of the shed so soon after I left, he said. When he saw they were not going to turn back he grabbed his snowshoes and followed along the trail. He passed the place where the dogs had torn up the buffalo robe, and when he heard a shot he guessed what had happened. As he approached the dead dog, the other dog ran away across the lake and into the trees. He had seen how the sleigh had swerved on and off the trail, and wondered how I had been able to keep it upright.

With the factor as witness, I took a written statement from him, outlining what he had told me, along with his statement that he would be responsible for any damage and that he was going to kill the live dog. As he said this the factor said, "I will help you do it."

It was several hours before I thought the team had cooled off and rested sufficiently to start on the return journey. There were none of the high spirits of the morning, but occasionally they would break into a slow trot for just a short distance and then return to a walk. I let them take their own time. I was snug enough under a robe borrowed from the Factor, but there were times when I wondered if we would ever reach Meadow Lake. However, I didn't care how long it took. We were alive and we'd get home sometime. The horses deserved all the consideration I could give them. I credited them with saving my life. A lesser team would have left me at the mercy of the two mad dogs.

It took nine hours to travel the forty-five miles to Meadow Lake. When I arrived after midnight the sergeant was waiting up for me, knowing that something must have gone wrong. I told him what had happened and he looked the horses over very carefully to make sure there were no injuries. He could find none, only a pair of tired horses. The only thing missing was the buffalo robe. Up until now I had thought it was police property, but the sergeant said it was his own.

The next morning I gave both horses a good grooming and took them for a long walk without saddling either. Instead of wanting to get ahead of me as they usually did, they were willing to travel at my speed. It took about a week of good care before I was satisfied that they were their old selves. I had put in a report on the incident "in case the trapper changed his mind and wanted the Force to pay for his dog," said the sergeant. I embodied the trapper's statement in the report and never heard another word from headquarters.

On a hot July day about four years later, I was crossing the Regina barrack square on my way to the crime laboratory with some exhibits. The Green Lake incident was far from my mind. A team pulling the garbage wagon came out from between two houses. The horses were fat, and from the way they walked I concluded they were lazy. There was something familiar about them, and then I realized the horses were Kit and Bess. I knew they had been transferred from Meadow Lake to Depot Division and I thought they would be used in recruit equitation, seeing that they were far better horses for it than the ones I was trained on. Instead they had been employed on the garbage wagon, collecting garbage each day and delivering it to the incinerator.

This was far from the lively team I had known at Meadow Lake, the team which I credited with saving my life that cold winter day on Green Lake several years before. I felt badly that such a fine team should end up so ignominiously. But as I thought about it I concluded that this was a good way to end their years. They might have been sold separately to people who would use them for much harder work. Their present work was nothing more than exercise. They were well looked after, as their condition showed. Indeed this was the best form of retirement for them.

I stopped them and talked to the driver. I told him I had used them as a detachment team and what a fine team they were. I didn't bother telling him about the Green Lake incident. I stood and watched them go to the next house, thinking of that morning on

Green Lake just a few years before. Now, apparently contented, they plodded along like two ordinary horses, a far cry from the high-spirited horses I used to know at Meadow Lake. I would never forget Kit and Bess, as they used to be. But to see them now, they were hardly the horses that Constable Lilley had told me would jump like kangaroos.

FIFTEEN

Police work in Meadow Lake dropped off in the winter. General weather conditions limited travel for most people who had complaints to make to the police. But we had plenty of work arising from the Indian reserve close by, from the Indians at Green Lake, and minor offences in and around the area close to Meadow Lake. I frequently patrolled the 220-mile return trip to North Battleford, escorting prisoners to jail and occasionally a mental patient to hospital. There were always enough inquiries to make "in the country" to keep the horses well exercised.

The height of my and the sergeant's social life was curling. We played on natural ice in a shell of a building that kept out the cold winds, although the temperature indoors was as cold as that outdoors. Like most curlers in small Saskatchewan towns and villages, we curled quite happily when indoor temperatures stood at thirty degrees below zero Fahrenheit. Toward spring, as the weather became milder, we often curled after midnight or in the very early morning hours when the ice had "firmed up".

We not only took part in the scheduled games, mostly in the evenings and on weekends, but in "pick-up" games during weekday afternoons if our work permitted it. We usually dressed with a mixture of civilian clothes and uniform, which was against regulations, breeches and Indian beaded moccasins below, sweaters and fur hat above.

We never curled in the afternoons without giving some thought to incoming calls to the detachment and, more importantly, from the C.O. at North Battleford. We asked the sole operator of the telephone system to take the caller's number, then telephone the rink so that we could return the call from there. One afternoon, after a heavy snowstorm the night before, there was little travel around Meadow Lake. The sergeant and I felt quite safe in joining a "pick-up" curling team. Certainly, it was not weather for the C.O. from North Battleford to make a sneaky inspection visit to Meadow Lake, as he usually did, since that was the only way he could see how we normally operated. We were occasionally warned of his coming by an anonymous telephone call telling us "the old man is on his way".

On this particular afternoon we were halfway through a game when a young girl dashed into the rink yelling, "Sergeant Coombes! Sergeant Coombes!" She told him that Charlie Aaron, a fur buyer from North Battleford, had just arrived at her mother's hotel. He had mentioned that he had been pulled through a snowdrift at Cochin, about twenty miles north of North Battleford on Number 4 highway, and the RCMP inspector's car was among the others waiting to be pulled through. This was enough for Mrs. Evans, the hotel owner and the widow of a NWMP ex-member. She knew why inspectors came north and wanted us to be advised of his coming.

As the sergeant and I dashed from the rink he told me to go directly to the stable and groom the horses, something I had been doing most of the morning. But then I had been dressed in fatigues, not in the most inappropriate dress of a white roll-neck sweater and beaded Indian moccasins. Soon after I started to groom I sensed the presence of someone in the stable doorway.

"A fine get-up for grooming horses," Inspector Spriggs said.

He could not help but notice the forbidden Indian moccasins and my roll-neck sweater. He could see, too, that the horses were well groomed. After a few comments about them he went to the detachment office. By the time I decided to go into the office he had left for Mrs. Evan's hotel. The sergeant said he had been "ticked off" for wearing beaded moccasins and for allowing me to do the same. A better example should be shown to young constables, the inspector had said. Nevertheless, he accepted the sergeant's invitation to supper that evening. I knew as soon as I heard the inspector was arriving that the supper invitation I had received would have to be postponed. Constables didn't eat with inspectors unless it was unavoidable. It seemed that being invited to supper was part of the inspection process.

I ate supper at the hotel with the C.O.'s constable-chauffeur. As they came north through the deep snow the C.O. had chuckled when he had said, "Those fellows at Meadow Lake will be surprised when I arrive for an inspection in this weather." How right he was, but not nearly as surprised as we might have been had he arrived and found us curling in the middle of the afternoon, when we should have been in the office. I didn't say a word about being alerted to his arrival. Even constables were known to become chatty with their C.O.s on long boring journeys. Many years later the inspector, after he had retired, told me that he often announced he was going to a certain detachment and then went in another direction, in order to arrive at a detachment unexpectedly.

We had our inspection the next morning during another heavy snowstorm. The C.O. seemed less concerned about the inspection than about being unable to get on to Loon Lake and Goodsoil, and possibly not being able to get back to North Battleford. He might have to wait days, he feared, until the road grader cleared the snow off the highway. As it was he was forced to stay another night in Meadow Lake. The next day several stormbound travellers decided they would travel in convoy to North Battleford, and would be pleased to have the C.O. join them. Even at that we wouldn't have been surprised if they had been forced to return to Meadow Lake. The sergeant and I smiled at each other. We didn't say a word, each knowing how the other felt – that will teach the C.O. to arrive unexpectedly after a heavy snowstorm, and in the middle of a curling game . . .

During the nearly eighteen months I was with Sergeant Coombes at Meadow Lake, which included the seven weeks I spent at Loon Lake, I learned a great deal about police work. I had long forgotten that, in training, the two things I had wanted most when I was transferred were – to get away from Saskatchewan, and never to be on a detachment where there were police horses. Now I was so used to both that I never thought of them. I'm sure I was just as happy as if I had been allowed to choose my posting.

But the summer of 1935 included a not-so-pleasant interlude. I went to Glaslyn detachment for two weeks to replace the regular man in charge. It was about the dullest two weeks of my whole service. Glaslyn was an old settled area only forty miles north of North Battleford, on the highway leading to Meadow Lake. About all I had to do was patrol the highway and check drivers' licenses. A check of the files indicated that this was normal, making me wonder why the RCMP kept a detachment there at all. I decided then that if ever I had a detachment of my own like this one, my service in the Force would be brief, although I learned later that Glaslyn was an exception. It occurred to me that I might be stationed there permanently if the man

I replaced did not return, as Jack Gillis had failed to do the year before at Loon Lake. Fortunately he did, and I gladly returned to Meadow Lake. But not for long.

When fall arrived my happiness at being at Meadow Lake came to an end, "out of the blue" as usual. I was transferred again, this time back to Loon Lake to take charge of the detachment. Constable Jack King had been rushed to hospital with a burst appendix. I was not surprised at the transfer, after my earlier transfers to Loon Lake the year before and more recently to Glaslyn. I anticipated being called upon for relief duty anywhere in the sub/division. I was disappointed, nevertheless. But I was cheered somewhat when I thought that when King regained his health I would return to Meadow Lake. Little did I know that I was never again to be stationed at Meadow Lake.

As in the year before, I was allowed to take the police car "old 1092" with me. This helped me overcome the misery of travelling with Loon Lake's mismatched team of horses. Loon Lake was much the same as when I left it the year before. If anything it was more drab, two muddy streets requiring rubber boots when it rained, no street lights, and no loitering summer visitors to the lake.

But there was one great improvement – a telephone system had been installed. By now I was aware that the last battle in the 1885 Riel Rebellion had been fought just a few mile west of the village, but this historical fact didn't help me to better appreciate my transfer.

I had only been in Loon Lake a few rainy days when I received a telephone call from the C.O. He advised me that a detective sergeant from the North Battleford CIB would arrive in Loon Lake in a day or so. I was to take him to the Beacon Hill district in the Goodsoil detachment area. I wondered what kind of serious crime had made it necessary for a CIB man, and a detective sergeant at that, to make the investigation. I had to decide on how we would travel, by team and democrat or by police car. Beacon Hill was nearly fifty miles northwest of Loon Lake, and beyond Loon Lake village there was not a yard of graded road. I made inquiries and learned that after the recent rains the trail would be impassable by car.

I didn't want to think about travelling over such trails, on what would be at least a 100-mile patrol behind the slow-moving Loon Lake horses, but that was the only way to travel. It seemed that I was at last going to see Goodsoil – the "God-forsaken place".

SIXTEEN

Ever since I had heard about Goodsoil detachment, about a year and a half before, it seemed that I was destined to go there. Each of my three transfers had put me closer to what everyone, except Sergeant Coombes, referred to as that "God-forsaken place". Little did I think that the detective sergeant's visit presaged my being transferred there.

He arrived early in the morning two days later. He was a short, rotund fellow, well under the required height for the RCMP. As a member of the CIB he was in civilian clothes. It was just as well. He wouldn't look right in uniform. He had been a member of the Saskatchewan Provincial Police when it was absorbed by the RCMP in 1928. He had stayed overnight at St. Walburg, 30 miles south, rather than push on to Loon Lake, over the muddy and rutted highway after dark, where the hotel accommodation was at least fifth rate.

He was in a foul mood, because of the difficulties he had had that morning keeping his car out of ditches on the "bloody" road, and because he felt that the C.O. should have given the "job" to Sergeant Coombes. He also gave the impression that such a "job", was beneath the dignity of a detective sergeant who usually investigated such serious crimes as murders, rapes, safeblowings and burglaries.

From the moment he arrived his speech was peppered with colourful profanities. Later on he became even more profane, when he climbed with difficulty into the high democrat and we began to slowly make our way toward a homestead in the Beacon Hill district, about twenty-five miles west of Goodsoil. Half a mile north of Loon Lake village the roughly graded mud highway gave way to a winding trail through a sixty-six-foot road allowance, carved out of the bush a few years earlier by unemployed men from the cities on a "make-work" project. For a few miles we passed the occasional uninhabited tar-papered shack, which indicated that it was a homestead that someone had "filed" on.

The rains of the past few days had left the trail nearly impass-able, with large mudholes. The horses waded through them up to their bellies, and the democrat roller-coasted over hidden hummocks in the mudholes. The short roly-poly sergeant found it difficult to hang onto his seat. This brought on a continuous symphony of profanity. In his Lancashire accent he threatened dire consequences to the C.O. for sending him to such a place. After a couple of hours I learned the reason for the patrol, and this, too, was in the form of a complaint. "That damned fool constable should have had more sense than to get involved with a married woman."

Bit by bit I learned that the woman lived on a homestead, and that her husband worked away from home in Edmonton, Alberta. He had written to the C.O., saying he had heard from neighbours that the Goodsoil constable frequently visited his homestead, too often for all the visits to be connected with police business, and he wanted the matter investigated.

After about eighteen miles, over a trail which had exhausted the police team, we came to the Beaver River. A bridge led us to the foot of a steep hill, where an old settler named Seeley kept a general store. He knew the country well and assured us that we had covered the worst part of the trail. From there on it was hard and rocky. After feeding ourselves and the horses we started up the steep hill. At the top we came to an area known as Flat Valley, a newly settled area with not much cleared land. From here we took the trail northwest to Beacon Hill, instead of going straight north to Goodsoil and then west to Beacon Hill.

The trail was hard and rocky, as Seeley had said, but the horses had brightened after a good rest. At first we passed through an area with poor land, rocky and with stunted trees, that did not appear to be settled on. Then we came to where homesteaders had been set-tled for some time. Their farms showed hard work and great care. After making several inquiries we finally arrived at the complainant's homestead, about four o'clock in the afternoon.

Fortunately, the woman the sergeant wanted to interview was at home. I hesitated to think what the sergeant would have said if she had not been at home, in which case we would have had to stay in the district, sleeping on the floor of a homesteader's cabin. We couldn't have made sure that she would be home on our arrival as the nearest telephones were thirty-odd miles to the west, at Beaver Crossing, Alberta, or fifty miles to the southeast, at Loon Lake. We could not have arranged an appointment in any event as homesteaders were not likely to have telephones.

The interview was a short one, partly due to the sergeant's wish "to get the hell out of here", and the woman's ready admission of her relationship with the constable. The sergeant recorded the facts in a written statement, signed by the woman and witnessed by the sergeant and me. As we were ready to leave she asked if the matter could be kept from her husband. The sergeant was not in the mood to consider her feelings, and he told her that if it hadn't been for a complaint made by her husband, he wouldn't have made a "bloody" journey of 200 miles from North Battleford to Beacon Hill. As it was nearly suppertime, she offered to make us a meal, which the sergeant declined. Soon we were heading for Goodsoil detachment twenty-five miles to the east, where we planned to spend the night, not southeast to Loon Lake.

I had given the horses a feed of hay on our arrival at the homestead and some oats before we left. After a mile or so past the homesteads, we reached a good trail which led through Big Head Indian reserve. At the edge of the trail stood a lone building, Manderson's store, where we stopped for a few chocolate bars and some soda pop. The trail through the reserve was flat and sandy, at first on open plain and then through pine woods.

Even the sergeant was impressed with the scenery, but he wondered who would want to live in such a "goddamned" place. By now it was dark. We could see the reflection of the moon on shimmering Lac des Isles on our left. It reminded me of my patrols to Green Lake, alongside the Beaver River, but now the silence was broken by the occasional scream of a loon and, of course, the creaking democrat.

Our reverie was broken when we came to a cutline road allowance that led us away from the lake. It, like the one near Loon Lake, had been cut out of the bush a few years earlier by unemployed workers. The darkness made travel hazardous. The hilly trail rambled from one side of the cutline to the other, and was full of water-filled mudholes with hidden hummocks. The sergeant was now at his profane best, again finding it difficult to stay on his seat. We couldn't see if the horses were on or off the trail, or when they were about to take us in or out of a mudhole. By this time the horses were showing signs of fatigue, but we didn't know how much farther we had to go. We had travelled about seventy miles, and now we were in the dark, on a trail every bit as bad as the one we had started out on that morning. Even after this we might not find the Goodsoil constable at home.

The constable might be anywhere in the 4,000 square miles of his detachment area, and might not return for several days. But I didn't mention this to the detective sergeant. I had visions of breaking into the detachment so that we could spend the night there.

By now I even felt some sympathy for the sergeant. His short legs made it difficult for him to brace himself against the dashboard to help keep his seat. He had called several times on the Lord to save him from making another such journey. At last we came to a better trail, and at the same time saw a dim light in a window off to the side of the road. Surely, we thought, this must be Goodsoil. But we still had several miles to go. The horses seemed to brighten, and moved as though they knew the journey was coming to an end. We passed several homesteads and the silhouette of a large church against the night sky. When we came to a place with two or three buildings alongside the road, and a brightly lit two-story house with a flagpole, we knew we had arrived at Goodsoil RCMP detachment.

Mr. Johnson, who owned the detachment building and lived nearby, was in the detachment. He took over my team, saying he was used to police horses; he stabled the Goodsoil police team.

The constable was not surprised at our arrival. Later I learned that he had visited Seeley's store soon after we had left there at noon, and had found out where we were headed. Out of the sergeant's hearing he asked why we had gone to Beacon Hill. When I mentioned the name of the woman we had interviewed, he simply shrugged his shoulders. He made up two single beds in the unfinished, uninsulated and unheated attic. The sergeant and I were in no mood to be fussy. We washed in the constable's washroom, a bowl on a stand in the corner of his office, then went to bed. We were hungry but that late at night we didn't want to disturb the storekeeper with whom the constable ate his meals.

By the time we awoke the next morning the constable had lit a fire in his potbellied wood heater, and had boiling water ready for us to shave. He was dressed in uniform with buttons and leatherwork highly polished. My mud-spattered uniform and high boots were more in keeping with the country atmosphere of Goodsoil than was his immaculate uniform. We had breakfast with the constable at the general store which was also the post office. The sergeant wanted to interview the constable alone. As I left the detachment to look around, I wondered what would happen to the constable if the sergeant ordered him to give a statement and he refused. Would he be guilty of insubordination?

I then gave Goodsoil the "once over". It didn't take long. I had met one storekeeper at breakfast, so I paid a visit to the other, a bachelor, who lived in the back of the store. He was very friendly and pressed me several times to tell him why the sergeant and I had come to Goodsoil. I was sure that Goodsoil, being something of an outpost, was a place where two policemen visiting the local detachment piqued the curiosity of its few inhabitants.

Next, I went to the blacksmith's log building where I found him making horseshoes, enough to last all summer, he said. The RCMP horses were the only ones to be regularly shod all round. Most homesteaders could not afford to have shoes on their horses, although some occasionally had them shod in front. I then visited Mr. Johnson, who lived behind the detachment in a low log house that he had built when he first homesteaded, some forty years earlier. His conversation flowed. He was of Scandinavian descent and had come north from Minnesota to start ranching. When the country began to be homesteaded he had to give up some of his range, so he turned to a mixture of farming and ranching. Later he gave up ranching altogether. He was the one who had suggested the name Goodsoil when the government decided to have a post office built there. He had built the detachment building to rent to the RCMP. He supplied the firewood and stabled the police team. As the only Justice of the Peace, he sat on all cases the constable placed before him, but he often settled disputes between homesteaders without resorting to court. When I offered to pay him for stabling my team overnight, he refused, saying, "I'm doing all right off the government."

On returning to the detachment I witnessed the statement the constable had given the sergeant. In it he admitted making frequent visits to the homestead of the woman we had interviewed the day before, and acknowledged they had nothing to do with police work. I hastily got the team ready, and in no time we were travelling south on the thirty-mile journey to Loon Lake, eating lunch at Seeley's at the Beaver River. After crossing the river we encountered similar difficulties to those of the day before, but in the reverse direction.

As the horses rested in a large mudhole, the detective sergeant mentioned that he was sure a charge would be laid against the constable "for cohabiting with a woman other than his wife". This was accompanied by more profanity as the laying of such a charge meant another trip over these same "bloody awful" trails, in this "land that God gave Cain". I had always thought this quote referred to Labrador, but the sergeant was in no mood for a contradiction as he continued to vent his anger on the "bloody fool constable", the C.O., Sergeant Coombes, the horses, the trail and that "God-forsaken place", meaning Goodsoil.

As we left Seeley's it had begun to rain, and it continued until well after we reached Loon Lake very late that evening. As we arrived, soaked to the skin, and with no mention of supper, the sergeant jumped out of the democrat, without a word of goodbye. He got into his car and sped away. I chuckled to think of his state of mind after travelling the further thirty miles to St. Walburg in the rain, over a mud highway. I stabled the police team and went into the hotel to see if I could get something to eat at that late hour.

The journey to Beacon Hill had done little to improve my opinion of the police team. During the next few days I collected statistics to show how expensive it was to keep a police team that was used so infrequently. I listed the relatively few miles they had travelled in the last year, the number of days they had remained in the stable, and the total cost of keeping them. The cost per mile of travel amounted to several dollars. For comparison purposes I listed the number of miles my predecessor had travelled by his private car at seven cents a mile. On the basis of these figures I recommended that the team be sold, pointing out that if a team was required for a patrol, one could be hired in the village at a moderate cost.

1935, Beacon Hill, Sask. The log home of an elderly homesteader.

SEVENTEEN

About a week after my return to Loon Lake from the Beacon Hill patrol, the C.O. telephoned me from North Battleford. He had set a date to hold Orderly Room proceedings at Pierceland, a village a few miles west of Beacon Hill, to dispose of the charge that had been laid against the Goodsoil constable. He would arrive by car at Loon Lake early in the morning of the day before the hearing, accompanied by the detective sergeant and a stenographer. By then Sergeant Coombes would have arrived from Meadow Lake with his team. Then that team, Kit and Bess, and the Loon Lake team would transport the five of us to Pierceland, where the Goodsoil constable and his team would meet us. As I put up the receiver I chuckled to think of what the detective sergeant might have said when he heard he was returning to the Goodsoil detachment area.

The "judicial" party arrived as planned. The C.O. and his female stenographer rode with the best team – Kit and Bess – and Sergeant Coombes. The detective sergeant rode with me. There was less grumbling from him this time. I thought he might have decided that grumbling did not make the ride any easier. My team was much slower than the other, and by the time we were crossing the bridge at the Beaver River, the C.O's party had had lunch at Seeley's store and was halfway up the hill on the way to Pierceland.

The detective sergeant and I reached Pierceland well after suppertime. I had just put my team in the livery barn when the Goodsoil constable and his team arrived. His team was unbelievably mis-matched, a fat roly-poly black and a lean nervous, mouse-coloured buckskin that walked about a foot ahead of its partner. At least my horses walked together.

The "hotel" in which we spent the night was a small two-bed-room log bungalow, run by "Ma" Hassler, a brassy frontier woman. The C.O. slept in one bedroom and the stenographer in the other. The rest of us slept on the living room floor, much to the detective sergeant's annoyance, made worse by Sergeant Coombes tongue-in-cheek comments about how pleased he was with such good ac-commodation. "Ma" Hassler slept at a neighbour's house, but she was back in the kitchen before we got up, to make sure we had a good breakfast.

The Orderly Room proceeding took place in a surprisingly large office, vacated for the day to accommodate us, in a building owned by the provincial Natural Resources department. Orderly Room pro-ceedings are quasi-judicial, in that they have the support of federal legislation by way of the Royal Canadian Mounted Police Act. One difference between a regular court and RCMP Orderly Room proce-dure is that even after a plea of guilty, the evidence of both prosecu-tion and defence is recorded. This allowed the Commissioner at headquarters in Ottawa either to confirm the punishment, or to re-duce it, but not to increase it. And under certain circumstances, as only he could decide, dismiss the offending member.

Sergeant Coombes acted as prosecutor. The constable, not rep-resented by anyone, pleaded guilty to the charge of "cohabitating with a woman other than his wife", contrary to RCMP regulations. The detective sergeant gave evidence and entered the statements given by the constable and the woman. The constable did not object to any of it. Then he was allowed to give evidence under oath and be cross-examined on it, or simply give a statement not under oath, on which he could not be cross-examined. He chose to do neither. Sergeant Coombes, although acting as the prosecutor, gave evidence as to the constable's service and his good character. After reviewing the evidence the C.O. gave reasons for the sentence that he was go-ing to pronounce – thirty days in the Regina guardroom. He told the convicted constable that he had forty-eight hours to put in an appeal to the Commissioner if he desired.

Thus ended the formal proceedings, after which the C.O. told the constable that he would recommend his dismissal from the Force. As I stood "at ease" in one corner of the office listening to what had gone on, I realized it was just as easy to lose one's job in the RCMP as it was difficult to join the organization. In this case, the career of a constable with over five years service had been terminated for what amounted to lack of judgment. The lesson was not lost on me.

Our three teams left Pierceland in convoy after lunch, probably the last time three RCMP detachment teams were in one place together. With three teams the seating arrangement changed. The detective sergeant took charge of the "prisoner" and went with him in the Goodsoil democrat. The stenographer went with Sergeant Coombes, and the C.O. rode with me. This surprised me as I thought it only fitting that the C.O. should ride behind Kit and Bess – the best team by far. I learned later why he didn't. On the way to Pierceland he and Sergeant Coombes had a bit of a "tiff". Anyway, I thought, the C.O. would now have the experience of riding behind the team I had recommended to be sold.

The C.O. was a good travelling companion. The countryside around Pierceland reminded him in some ways of the Yukon where, as a constable, he had served for some years. He told me of his experiences there, but he didn't say a word about his reputation of being a real rough and tumble fellow if necessary. I concluded he would have little sympathy for anyone who complained about the "isolation" of a place like Goodsoil. As we neared Goodsoil he asked me where my kit was, knowing that I had moved to Loon Lake from Meadow Lake on a temporary basis. With a feeling of impending doom, I replied, "At Loon Lake, sir."

"All of it?" he queried.

"Yes sir," I answered meekly.

Then I learned that on our arrival at Goodsoil I was to "take over" the detachment from the convicted constable, lock it up, and continue on to Loon Lake. There I would wait for someone to replace me before returning to Goodsoil. Swallowing hard, I asked in what must have seemed a plaintive voice, "Permanently, Sir?"

"Of course," he answered crisply, as though it was the most natural thing in the world that I should be transferred to the "God-forsaken" Goodsoil detachment.

At Goodsoil I signed the necessary documents, counted the "cash equivalents" and locked up the detachment. I informed Mr. Johnson, the landlord, a farmer whose farm home was about 100 yards away, of the arrangements. After a meal at the store we all left for Loon Lake. We arrived very late, in the dark. The C.O. and his party, which now included the convicted constable, left immediately by car on the 135-mile drive to North Battleford. It seemed that no one wanted to stay in Loon Lake overnight, except Sergeant Coombes, who was used to sleeping on the other single bed in my bedroom.

After Coombes left the next morning with his team, I could only think of my transfer to Goodsoil – the seventh in less than a year and a half. Like the others this one had come "out of the blue". My earlier foreboding, from the time I had first met the convicted constable in the Regina guardroom, had now come to pass. Then I realized I was in charge of two detachments – Loon Lake and Goodsoil.

At Loon Lake I awaited the return of Constable King who was recuperating after his appendix operation. While waiting for him I received an acknowledgement of my reports recommending the sale of the police team. My instructions were to post enclosed notices, advertising the sale of the police team by way of sealed bids, which the bidder would send directly to the Divisional C.O. in Regina. I was surprised that my recommendation for the sale of the team had been accepted, and cheerfully posted notices throughout the district. Even so, the transfer to Goodsoil was on my mind. I had often heard the expression about someone "being in the right place at the right time". In my case it seemed that I had been in the wrong place at the wrong time.

Eventually Constable Ernie Nesbitt came to replace me, instead of Constable King. He was there long after I was transferred from Goodsoil. It had been several weeks since I had "taken over" Goodsoil detachment, and my return there was over a trail made much worse by the recent rains. The Goodsoil team had remained in Loon Lake, waiting for me to take them back north. The wait did nothing for the fat black horse. He still walked about a foot behind the mouse-coloured buckskin. This would be my fifth journey over that weary trail in about six weeks, and the fall rains had made the trail more difficult to travel over. The mudholes were larger and deeper.

In some mudholes, with water up to their bellies, the slow, fat black horse didn't seem to care if he got out or not, whereas the buckskin couldn't get out fast enough. If there had been only a few such holes it wouldn't have mattered, but there were dozens of them. Getting the horses to work together became a steady chore. In a mudhole, with one or two wheels of the democrat on hidden hummocks, I had to make sure I hung on securely as the buckskin tried to pull the democrat and his black partner through it. When I had a chance to think of my new posting, I could only wonder about the "fickle finger of fate" which had given me such bleak knowledge of the Goodsoil country in the Regina guardroom eighteen months before, and then had consistently pointed the way toward it ever since.

On my arrival at Goodsoil I lit a fire in the pot-bellied heater to warm up the detachment, which had been empty for some weeks. As

I unrolled my bedroll to make my bed, I thought that only a few weeks back, at Loon Lake, I was expecting to return to Meadow Lake to continue my police career under the tutelage of the sergeant. Now I was thirty miles farther north in the bush, with no telephone, not even one mile of graded road in the roughly 4,000 square miles I had to police, and with a toilet out back among the trees.

But I had achieved something that was the aim of most constables leaving the training division – a permanent detachment. This could hardly be expected until they had served a much longer post-training period than I had done – one and a half years. As I mulled over my situation, it occurred to me that if my predecessor had not misbehaved I would probably have stayed in Loon Lake permanently. At that time, if I had been given the choice, I would have chosen to stay there, but a time came when I knew that would have been a very serious mistake.

I was getting ready for bed when Mr. Johnson, my landlord, J.P. and general factotum, came to the office to bid me welcome. Not having had the opportunity of discussing local conditions with my predecessor, I appreciated his visit. Having been a J.P. for many years he had a good general knowledge of local conditions as they applied to police work, and even some of the more specific problems facing the Goodsoil constable. Many of the homesteaders were immigrants of German origin, who had emigrated from German settlements in southern Russia some years before. They had settled in southern Saskatchewan until forced by drought to come to new homestead country. There were a few families whose mother tongue was English. All the settlers, whatever their language, were generally law abiding, but some of the younger element, he said, "lived so far in the bush they believed they did not have to obey the laws."

One problem in the community was the "squabble" between the priest of the local Roman Catholic church, himself a German immigrant, and a German faction in his church that disagreed with him on many things. The situation was so bad that it surprised no one when the leader of the opposing faction stood up in his pew during a service and criticized the priest. The RCMP came into the picture when the priest requested the constable to lay charges against this man for disturbing a religious service. Up to now the police had refused.

The priest, said Mr. Johnson, had tried for years to get a Roman Catholic constable stationed at Goodsoil. My name being an Irish one, he wondered if I were such a constable. I assured him that my background was strictly Methodist. Not that it would have any effect on how I dealt with the priest.

The leader of the anti-priest faction, also a German immigrant, had not been in Canada long enough to obtain citizenship. He was aggressive, ambitious, and very prominent in the Liberal Party, then in power provincially. He was also a school trustee. Earlier he had insisted on trying to get a German-speaking teacher so that the children could be taught in German. He was a bachelor who lived with his parents and three brothers, all extremely hardworking. Mr. Johnson concluded by saying that, although he was not taking sides with the priest, Bill Bendt was a troublemaker.

In the other faction was another troublemaker, a retired university professor, who lived with his daughter and her husband on their homestead. He was the priest's right-hand man when the priest communicated with any government department or with politicians. He let it be known to all who would listen that he knew people in high political circles. I later found this to be true, particularly when my police work was the subject of his letter writing. As I listened to Mr. Johnson, I realized that my predecessor had not mentioned any of his troubles when he spoke to me in Regina about Goodsoil. But it was clear that I had been dropped into a community where religion and politics played important parts in the lives of the settlers.

I thought that this kind of activity might be the result of living in unorganized territory, where everything had to be done by a distant provincial government, and where the area was so far from the influence of older and more well-settled communities. I appreciated Mr. Johnson's "briefing", and told him that being forewarned was a great help.

Just a few minutes after Mr. Johnson had left, by way of a side door, there came an authoritative knock on the front door. I opened the inner front door, expecting then to open a storm door to see who was there. My visitor had already opened it, and as I opened the inner door he almost fell into the room. Without saying a word he pushed past me into the office. He was the man Mr. Johnson and I had just been talking about, a sharp-featured, middle-aged man with a clerical collar, Father Schultz. I suspected that he had been waiting outside until Mr. Johnson left.

In a strong German accent he explained his strange behaviour. He had pushed passed me so unceremoniously, he said, so that no one would see him entering the detachment. One would think we were on a busy street in a suburban setting instead of in an isolated house alongside a northern trail.

"Are you a Catholic?" he asked abruptly.

"No," I replied, knowing my answer was a disappointment.

Then he launched into a long attack on "Bill Bendt and his gang" for interrupting his church services. He had asked my predecessors to lay charges against these men, but nothing had been done. He had even complained to the provincial Attorney General about the police inaction. I had begun to wonder if there was any record of the matter on file. Mention of the Attorney General indicated that there might be. I checked the priest's name in the filing cards, and then drew a thick file from the cabinet, headed "Rev. Father ------, Complaint of: Goodsoil, Sask."

The file contained a report of an earlier visit by the priest in which the constable suggested that the police take no action. If a charge was to be laid it should be done by the priest himself or one of his congregation. The Attorney General in answering the priest's first letter of complaint agreed with this view. Copies of more letters of complaint were on file. They were well written and I could see the hand of the ex-university professor in them. The Attorney General always gave the priest the same answer, in effect, if he wanted charges laid, he must lay them himself.

As I read the file the priest came up behind me and looked over my shoulder. I pointedly closed it. I told him that although he had not asked me to prefer charges against Bill Bendt, the Attorney General's view must stand. Then he made a stiff bow, turned, and with an abrupt "goodnight" left the office.

Bill Bendt might be "a dangerous man", but the priest was certainly a strange one. I was to remain in Goodsoil for nearly three years, but I never talked to the priest again. As I lay in bed soon after the priest left, I wondered how he knew I had arrived. No doubt one of his scouts had been on the job.

1936, Goodsoil, Sask. Waiting for the trails to dry up.

Goodsoil, Sask. Unpainted and uninsulated.

1936. Goodsoil police team on Lac des Isles trail between Goodsoil and Pierceland.

EIGHTEEN

In the next few days I learned many things about the area I had to police. It was roughly 4,000 square miles, mostly lakes, rivers and forest. The southern boundary, six miles south of the detachment office, was the Beaver River, a tributary of the Churchill River that ran into Hudson's Bay. There was no set boundary to the north.

Originally, the newly settled area, six miles wide on the southern edge of my area, had been solid forest. Now the homesteaders, all on government relief, after some years of hard work had cleared a few acres of land. One mile north of my office, the Waterhen River ran from west to east, nearly parallel to and a tributary of the Beaver River. North of the Waterhen there was no habitation; unbroken forest reached to the treeline in the Northwest Territories. The western boundary of my area was the Fourth Meridian, which divided Saskatchewan from Alberta. To the east about thirty miles was my eastern boundary, which was the western boundary of Meadow Lake detachment.

The settled areas of my detachment were comprised roughly of two ethnic groups, the eastern half was mainly German and the western half was mainly English. The Big Head Indian reserve lay in between. From the many closed files I read, I saw that patrols had been made by horse and democrat, horse and sleigh, saddle horse, dog team, canoe, with and without an outboard motor, snowshoes and even by foot. I added one more mode of travel, a float plane.

Soon after my arrival I received a delegation of four men, two English and two German. They wanted to know if I could do something to prevent drinking at the local dance hall built on the lot next to the detachment. Rowdy young men frequently interrupted dances which were often abandoned halfway through the evening. Drunken young men fought on the dance floor, and the disturbances caused people to stay away. My visitors wondered if I would "police" the dances, including the one coming up on the following Saturday night.

I asked them how long this had been going on. They didn't answer in words but by shrugs and hand gestures, both being an implied criticism of my predecessor. I then asked how the young people obtained the liquor. It was locally manufactured, they said, but they couldn't tell me who manufactured it. I was sure they had some idea of who it was, but they weren't prepared to voice their suspicions to the police. As a result, I thought that they were partly to blame for the conditions they wanted me to correct, and I told them so. They said the liquor was brought to dances in the buggies carrying the young people. It was hidden in the grass between the RCMP detachment and the dance hall, at the foot of the fence where they tied their horses.

I told my visitors I might stop a few fights if I attended the dance, but if I were visible it would allow the drinkers to watch me and be free to go to their liquor supply with impunity. I could search around the fence for liquor and destroy what I found, but this would not get to the root of the matter. I would see what I could do, I said, not knowing then that I couldn't do much of anything, other than "police" the dance as they had suggested, and possibly destroy the liquor hidden in the grass. They left without any assurance from me that I would take any particular action.

I was somewhat disturbed about conditions that existed "under my nose", which probably included hiding the "homebrew" on police property. I could stay for the dance and search for the hidden homebrew and destroy it, but that would allow the owners of it to go free. I might even arrest one person in possession of some of it, but that would alert the others. I thought about how much better I could deal with the situation if I were stationed where I could call on a neighbouring detachment for assistance. After much thought I decided to leave Goodsoil on Saturday evening, leaving no lights on in the detachment.

Meanwhile, I told the storekeeper where I ate my meals that on Saturday night I was going to visit a friend of a friend of mine, a homesteader three miles south of Goodsoil, and would be away until quite late. The storekeeper, very sarcastically, said I could use my time better if stayed to police the dance. I knew that what I had told him would be spread among those who came to his store during the remainder of the week.

As planned, I left Goodsoil early Saturday evening, driving the police team so that the few residents could see me leave. I visited the homesteader, had supper with him, and told him of my plan. I asked if after dark he would drive me to within walking distance of Goodsoil and take my team back to his place for the night. He agreed and dropped me off half a mile from the dance hall. I was in plain clothes and walked in the dark to the detachment office.

The dance was in full swing. I could see the horses and buggies tied to the fence at the sides and back of the hall. In the fence, immediately behind the hall, there was a gap that led to Mr. Johnson's house and the back of the detachment building. If I arrested anyone that was the route I would have to take to avoid passing in front of the dance hall.

In the dark, I unlocked my side and front doors and made sure the cell door was open. Then I put a pad and pencil on my desk to enable me to keep a record in case I made more than one liquor seizure. I walked through the gap in the back fence to where the horses and buggies were tied. Hiding behind a buggy, I waited for a solitary person to come out and partake of his hidden liquor.

I knew I could effectively deal with only one man at a time. If I tried to arrest two men at once, they might not only start a fight and destroy the liquor, and possibly escape, but the commotion would alert others, who would then stay away from their hidden liquor. So I let pairs approach their "caches", take a drink and leave. When the first lone person came out I followed him to his cache. As he put the bottle to his lips I snatched it from him, threw him over my hip, and dragged him to the detachment. In the dark I put him in the cell, asked his name, wrote it on a sheet from the pad, and placed it with his liquor bottle on the floor in one corner of the office.

I arrested three men in this fashion before the alarm was raised. The last one had come out of the hall alone, but was soon followed by another, who, seeing what I was doing, tried to help his friend get away. I hung on to my prisoner as well as his bottle of liquor while the second man ran to the hall to give the alarm. This allowed me time to get the third man away, through the gap in the fence, and into the detachment cell. I made sure the three were safely locked in before I lit my gasoline lamp, locked the detachment door, and with a flashlight went to search for more liquor in the grass around the fence. I found about a dozen more bottles at various places and smashed each one on the nearest fence post. Then I returned to the detachment to find a number of people wanting to know who I had arrested. I let them into the detachment where they could see three prisoners in the cell.

By now I could feel a large lump over one eye. The next morning I had a beautiful black and blue bruise around the eye, the result of the fight with the man who tried to free my third prisoner. I cleared the office of the "friends", and fingerprinted each prisoner. I made out the Information and Complaint forms, charging them with being in possession of illicit liquor contrary to the Excise Act. I swore to the charges before Mr. Johnson that night, and released the accused on their own recognizance to appear in court the following Monday morning. Later that night I learned the identity of the man who had tried to help his friend get away from me, and who was responsible for my black eye. I charged him with assaulting a peace officer.

On Sunday morning I made out another charge against my assailant for obstructing a peace officer in the execution of his duty, and also a warrant for his arrest. I needed another Justice of the Peace to sit with Mr. Johnson on the Excise charges, so I walked the three miles to where my team had stayed overnight and drove on to a settlement known as Northern Beauty. Another Justice of the Peace lived there and, at my request, he agreed to come to Goodsoil the following morning to sit with Mr. Johnson on the "homebrew" cases. He would have to make a sixteen-mile round trip with no hope of collecting costs. In spite of such inconveniences I never knew of a J.P. who refused to sit on a case when requested.

The three accused pleaded guilty and were sentenced to the minimum fine of $100 or three months in default of payment of the fine. One paid the fine and costs, which enabled the visiting J.P. to pay for a meal before leaving for home. I now had two prisoners to take to jail. After the conclusion of these cases Mr. Johnson pointed out one of the men who had accompanied the accused to court. He was the one for whom I had a warrant to arrest. I arrested him and reopened the court. He pleaded guilty before Mr. Johnson, sitting alone, and was given three months in jail. Mr. Johnson said it was only fair that he should spend as much time in jail as the others.

Charging these men under the Excise Act, rather than under the Saskatchewan Liquor Act for being in possession of liquor, meant that they would be punished more severely. The punishment for assaulting a policeman was probably more severe than the accused would get in a court in a well-settled community. I had pointed out to the J.P., in the latter case, that a lone policeman in an isolated area such as Goodsoil needed the support of the court in maintaining good public order, and I asked for a salutary sentence.

I hired a light truck to take the three prisoners to North Battleford, but at Loon Lake I found that "old 1092" had not been returned to Meadow Lake. I borrowed it and went on to North Battleford where I left my prisoners to be taken on to Prince Albert common jail by another escort. I returned to Goodsoil the next day. Fortunately, at that time of the year the mudholes had frozen, making it possible to drive vehicles over them. However, the trail remained very rough and there was always the danger of breaking a spring. These cases showed me that even though I was stationed in isolated Goodsoil detachment, I could always expect a trip to the outside. But strangely enough, for the nearly three years I was at Goodsoil, whenever I made a trip south, mostly escorting prisoners, I was always anxious to get back because there was no one "keeping the shop".

The arrests at the dance hall had a very salutary effect. The dances from then on, while not always models of propriety, were conducted in a more decorous manner. My friend who had driven me back to Goodsoil on that Saturday night kept me informed about local gossip. The new policeman, it was said, "meant business". When I went in to lunch on Sunday, having missed breakfast to go to Northern Beauty to get the second J.P., the storekeeper was quite sheepish. He, like everyone else, had heard about the arrests. Henceforth, he said, he would look after his store and leave police business to policemen.

I had grumbled when at Meadow Lake about the 220-mile return trip when escorting prisoners as far as North Battleford by car. From Goodsoil the return journey was 340 miles, seventy miles of which was over the roughest possible trail, often by teams and democrat, but I even got used to that.

Mr. Johnson, on his first evening visit, had warned me of the letters that would be sent to the Attorney General about the manner in which I carried out my duties. If they were not about things I had done, they would be about things I should have done, he said. Such letters were not returned to me for an explanation but were sent to Sergeant Coombes who, in his capacity as a patrol sergeant, visited Goodsoil about once a month. Then I had to give him a full statement on whatever circumstances were involved. He would take statements from the complainant and whatever witnesses he had to interview. On most vistits he had a complaint to investigate.

The first complaint arose out of the arrests at the dance hall. Someone wrote to the Attorney General and complained that I was not carrying out my duties in uniform. I explained that I deliberately

wore civilian clothes so that I could carry out my duties more effectively. I heard nothing more about the matter, but I was sure the
sergeant would report that, from what he had heard at Goodsoil,
most homesteaders were pleased about the manner in which the
trouble at the dance hall had been cleaned up.

The subjects of the complaints against me were varied, but one
continued to be made all the time I was at Goodsoil. It had to do with
homesteaders wanting to lay charges of theft against persons to
whom they had sold something, such as a cow, or a horse, or a
wagon and so on, but had not received payment. Usually the seller
had given the buyer time to pay, and when this period expired, with
no payment made, the first thing the sellers thought of was going to
the police. The only reason they wanted to lay charges was to get
back the property they had legally sold.

My answer to such requests was that the matter was a civil one,
not criminal, and one in which I could not become involved. I could
only suggest to each complainant that he should see a lawyer, with
the view of starting a civil action to collect the price of the item sold.
Even if the complainant had enough money to pay a lawyer, the
nearest one was seventy miles to the south. I never knew one complainant who decided to follow my advice. I sympathized with these
people. I'm sure that under similar circumstances I would have been
as frustrated as they were.

It was on one of the sergeant's visits that he told me about his
plans to take his pension. When he had completed twenty-five years
service, he planned to start up a mink ranch on Vancouver Island
with another sergeant who had the same number of years of service.
They had come out from England on the same ship to join the Force.
In the RCMP one could take a pension at twenty years service, but
there was an incentive to serve twenty-five years, as the additional
five years counted double toward pension. As a result of this talk
with the sergeant I began to think of my future in the Force. If I could
reach the rank of sergeant with twenty-five years, I would be young
enough to retire and then follow another line of work. And that was
my goal for some years. I could not have imagined then that I would
serve nearly thirty-seven years in the RCMP.

1936, between Pierceland and Mudie Lake, Sask. Crossing Beaver River by ferry with my "new" 1929 Ford Coupé.

1936, Pierceland, Sask. Outside of Reverend Frank Myer's "Manse".

1936, Pierceland, Sask. Another view of the United Church "Manse".

*1936, Mudie Lake, Sask. Trail built on muskeg
through cutline for proposed road.*

NINETEEN

A few months after my arrival at Goodsoil, I visited a homestead on some police business and found that the homesteader had a 1929 Model A Ford Roadster on blocks in a log garage he had specially built for it. He had bought it when he first arrived and had never driven it. He said he would like to sell it and set the price at $100. I looked it over, saw it had a fairly high axle which would allow it to pass over rough ground, and I bought it. The only thing I didn't like about it was the canvas top which could be raised or lowered.

I knew that I could use the car in the summertime under ideal conditions, but from late fall to early spring, the snow-covered, frozen ground would allow me to use it extensively. I rented a log garage from the owner of the store where I ate my meals, and arranged for him to dig a hole in the back of the garage, large enough to put in a stove made from a forty-five-gallon gasoline drum. This would enable me to thaw out the car on very cold mornings, before I went on patrol.

With no heater in the car, I knew that in wintertime I would have to dress the same way as if I were travelling by open sleigh, but the car would be much faster, and even with only a canvas cover, much more comfortable. To make sure the engine didn't freeze up during a patrol, I filled the radiator with pure antifreeze.

There wasn't one gasoline pump in the Goodsoil detachment area. The one or two trucks in the district brought their gasoline in by the drum. My supply came from the high-test gasoline that the storekeeper brought in for use in gasoline lamps used by myself and some settlers. The price in 1935 at Goodsoil, seventy miles from a railhead, was fifty cents a gallon.

There was always a risk in using the car in both summer and winter. I had little mechanical ability and a breakdown of any kind would mean, with no one to repair the car, that I might be stranded far from any habitation. It might even mean a walk of many miles at thirty below zero Fahrenheit. Travelling by car over rough trails was hard on tires, so I carried several spare tires and tubes. The breaking of springs, although less frequent than tire trouble, caused greater difficulties. They always seemed to break far from any assistance, hence the need for a spare new spring and a number of spring "leaves". But, in all the time I drove the car, I never had a breakdown which left me stranded.

I soon learned that I had to be prepared to deal with these and other problems such as being stuck in mudholes or being faced with a heavy snowdrift. In addition to spare tires and the springs, I filled the rumble seat of the roadster with the equipment I needed – a shovel, an axe, a block and tackle, a set of four chains, a hammer, several kinds of pliers, a logging chain and plenty of hay wire, and the jack which came with the car.

When I needed blocks to hold up the car, and a prise pole when I repaired a spring, I cut them from trees nearby. The latter was as important as any tool I had, when I found myself in a deep mudhole and had to build a base of blocks in order to get the car out of it. I found myself in such difficulties on many occasions, and never once did anyone come along whom I might ask for help.

After an hour or two working myself out of a mudhole, I often thought that travel by team, even the poor team I had left in the stable, was preferable. But that was the only time I thought so, and I kept using the car.

After a few months I was not only an expert at repairing a spring in the bush far from any habitation, but at installing a completely new spring. Fortunately, I never had any engine trouble, for which I gave credit to the high-test gasoline, but the thought was always with me when I made long patrols, and especially in much-below-zero weather.

On very cold mornings when I had a patrol to make, I would fill the oil drum stove in the garage with the only fuel available – dry Jack pine, throw some kerosene on it, light it and leave it. In about an hour the once-frozen car started easily. Often the body of the car was so hot I could hardly touch it. I had no thermometer so I couldn't tell the exact temperature. One cold and beautiful morning in February 1936, I patrolled the thirty miles to Pierceland.

The sun shone brightly and there wasn't a cloud in the sky. Neither was there any wind, and the smoke from the chimneys at Goodsoil went straight up in the air without a wrinkle. I enjoyed travelling through the pine woods along Lac des Isles, through Big Head Indian reserve and farther on as the trail passed through Beacon Hill. It was a pleasant drive.

On reaching Pierceland I was surprised not to be met by the usual pack of howling dogs. The only sound I could hear was the blacksmith's hammer on his anvil. I drove to his shop and slid open the door to be met with:

"Why are you travelling on such a morning?"

"Why shouldn't I?" I countered.

"Just look at the thermometer," he said, nodding his head to a small dirty window. I went to it and saw the thermometer outside did not register any temperature.

"It's broken," I said.

"Then go outside and check it out," he said as he began to hammer away again. Outside, with difficulty, I clambered over a pile of broken machinery before reaching it. Taking off my heavy mitten, I blew on the thermometer. I held it in my warm hand for several minutes before the mercury began to rise as high as the lowest registration point – sixty-five degrees below zero Fahrenheit. The actual temperature must have been at least five degrees lower, making it at least seventy degrees below zero.

I hastened to do my business in Pierceland and returned home without any trouble, in weather equally as cold and windless as in the morning. I had no desire to stay in Pierceland overnight. There the only way of starting the car in the morning would be to empty the antifreeze from the car and run pails and pails of hot water through the block. No one in those days thought of taking the battery indoors at night to keep it warm, to help the starting process in the morning.

That day was the lowest temperature in which I had patrolled. It was also the coldest temperature I had experienced. But the patrol during which I suffered the most from the cold, I made in the "moderate" temperature of twenty-five degrees below zero. It was with Armand Carter and his six-dog sleigh team, from Cold Lake, Alberta. We travelled about twenty-five miles north to Wapati Lake in Saskatchewan, by way of Primrose Lake. This is now the area used as a bombing range by the RCAF. From the beginning we encountered a strong, raw northeasterly wind which threatened snow. This was before we had first heard the term "wind chill factor". Even so, we knew it made dog team travel more difficult, and we were much colder when cold winds blew.

Both Carter and I were chilled to the bone, in spite of our having to run behind the dogs mile after mile. On the way north we stopped several times to make tea, which was unusual as my travelling partner had the reputation of being better than an Indian in the bush. I found the Indians I had come to see, living in tents at the north end of Wapati Lake. I quickly concluded my business with them. On the return journey the same crosswind prevailed. We hastened to reach the Ranger's cabin on Primrose Lake where we planned to spend the night, and where we had left ample frozen fish to feed the dogs.

After travelling in the dark for some time we came to a mink ranch on Primrose Lake, still about five miles from the Ranger's cabin. The mink rancher who had heard us coming was on the verandah of his cabin to greet us as we pulled up. Through the open door we heard a radio blaring. A loud voice was saying,"Hello, hockey fans in Canada and Newfoundland . . ."

It was Foster Hewitt broadcasting a game from Maple Leaf Gardens in Toronto. This told us the time – six o'clock. The hockey broadcast began at eight o'clock Toronto time. Not only did we have a good meal, but we also had the unexpected pleasure of listening to a hockey broadcast. By the time it was over it was too late to start for the Ranger's cabin so we stayed overnight, sleeping on the floor. Before going to bed we obtained some dog feed from our host and went out to feed the dogs. All was still. The stars shone brightly and the wind had gone down. Our overnight stay with the rancher was a pleasant interlude after an utterly miserable day – the coldest I ever experienced.

I never had a thermometer at the detachment to tell me how cold it was, but this didn't stop me from knowing roughly what the weather was like in winter. The detachment was in an uninsulated frame building. The inner walls were made of heavy cardboard-like material fastened to the outside studding.

That was all there was between the inside of the building and the outside. In the wintertime it did not do much more than keep out the wind, hence my dependence on the pot-bellied heater that I used for heating the building and water to bathe and shave. In the winter, before going to bed I filled the heater full of dry Jack pine and closed off the dampers, hoping it would last until morning. It never did. My temperature gauge was the pail of fresh water I obtained from Mr. Johnson's outdoor pump. I placed it on the heater before I went to bed. In the morning if the water had just a skimming of ice, I knew it was cold. If most of the water was frozen, except for enough to heat for shaving, then I knew it was very cold. But when the water was completely frozen, I knew it was very damned cold, especially on the mornings when the north wall was covered with frost.

I made many patrols with Natural Resources officers, summer and winter. I had as much authority to enforce the laws in which they were interested as they did, such as the Fishing regulations, the Fur Act and the Game Act. Trappers gave us no problems. They were always careful to obtain whatever licenses were required. We always turned a blind eye to whatever big game they shot over the limit for food. But they knew that shooting game for dog feed was taboo. There were plenty of fish in the lakes. On one occasion Carter and I were staying overnight in a trapper's cabin. He whispered to me that the trapper had shot a caribou. I asked how he knew. "I can smell it," he said. The next morning he accused the trapper, Louis Lundgren, with doing so. Louis admitted it. He hadn't mentioned it because he thought the shooting of caribou was prohibited. Neither Carter nor I knew if it was and had never bothered to find out. They were so seldom seen that far south. On another occasion, under the same circumstances, Carter turned to me and said, "I can smell a bear."

Sure enough, the next morning the trapper led us to a skinned bear hanging from the branch of a tree about 100 yards away. I had seen a skinned bear once before and had been impressed, as I was this time, with how human-like were a bear's forearms.

In the more settled areas most of the homesteaders were on relief, and only a few obtained licenses which allowed them to trap for fur, fish or shoot game. In dealing with this problem I was to learn a good lesson. At first, rather than prosecute for a first offence (not necessarily the first, but the first they had been caught committing), I gave a warning. This I decided was using "police discretion". At the same time I prosecuted those where there was evidence that they had broken the law for some time. As a result they complained to the Attorney General that I was showing favouritism to those I didn't prosecute. This resulted in another investigation by Sergeant Coombes, and a long statement from me.

As a result I became very careful in the use of "police discretion", which resulted in further complaints to the Attorney General about my being too zealous, and another investigation by the sergeant. The only alternative it seemed was to prosecute all or none. The latter I could not do, and soon the complaints stopped. I knew that the Attorney General could hardly instruct the police not to enforce the law, even if the Department of Natural Resources officers were told not to do so, when the politicians had their way with the Minster of Natural Resources. This meant more work for me. The officers increased their requests for me to accompany them on patrol, so that I and not they could charge anyone found committing an offence. I didn't mind assisting them. They often assisted me.

Another lesson I soon learned was not to accept a complainant's story at face value, even though many seemed sincere about the facts they gave me in the initial interview. If a man came to me and said someone had stolen a cow, I would want to know how he knew that it had been stolen and had not simply strayed away from his homestead. He may or may not have had the facts to support his allegation. But often complaints were somewhat more complicated, as evidenced by the following. A woman travelled many miles one morning to lay a charge of assault against her husband. He had assaulted her, she said, by hitting her with a piece of "2 x 4". She had two black eyes, her face was cut and bruised, and she had severe bruises on her arms.

The facts seemed clear. I made out the necessary charge and had the woman appear before Mr. Johnson, the J.P., to swear to it. I thought she should lay a more serious charge than common assault, such as an assault occasioning bodily harm, but she insisted the common assault charge was sufficient. I obtained a summons for the defendant and the next morning I patrolled to her homestead to serve the summons. The wife was absent, she had gone to Loon Lake to see the doctor at the Red Cross hospital, something both her husband and I had suggested she might profitably do.

The husband told me his side of the story. They had quarrelled in the kitchen and, as he left to go outdoors, he had called his wife a dirty name. She had followed him into the yard and on the way she picked up a piece of "2 x 4", which he showed me, and began to beat him about the head and shoulders. He tried to take the piece of wood away from her, and in the struggle she fell to the ground with him on top of her. The piece of wood was between them. Unfortunately it was across the woman's face. His story, plus the bruises on his back and shoulders, seemed convincing enough to provide a reasonable doubt in the mind of the J.P. who would preside on the case.

There was nothing I could do. The summons had been issued and he would have to appear on the date stated in it. On that day husband and wife appeared before Mr. Johnson in my office, which was being used as the courtroom. She asked that the charge be withdrawn. Mr. Johnson could have charged costs, but as usual he didn't. They probably hadn't enough money to pay them anyway.

This was the first of a number of cases that I investigated in which members of a family were at loggerheads. Sometimes they laid charges and disposed of them in court, which usually created bad blood between family members. More often than not they withdrew the charges that had been laid in the heat of the moment. It reached the stage where I always tried to get families to patch up their differences rather than deal with them in court. Courts seldom resolved family differences satisfactorily.

During my first spring at Goodsoil I received instructions to locate a gold watch owned by a trapper who had drowned in Primrose Lake a year or two before. The file showed that the drowning was accidental, but there was no mention of a gold watch in the list of the deceased's belongings. The man's family now wanted inquiries to be made to see what had happened to the watch, because they would like to have it returned to them.

The report showed that George Revell, the Natural Resources officer now working in the Goodsoil detachment area, had accompanied my predecessor during the investigation. He had assisted at the trapper's burial on a sandy knoll on the west shore of Primrose Lake. The next time I saw Revell I asked about the drowning and the gold watch. He remembered the facts very well, but he had never seen a gold watch. He had made the casket and had put the body in it. He was sure that there was no watch on the body. There was nothing more that I could do and I reported it accordingly.

Some weeks later I received further instructions, along with an official document authorizing me to disinter the body of the drowned trapper to search for the missing watch. With Revell I went to Primrose Lake, making the last stage of the journey by canoe. I felt somewhat apprehensive about disinterring a body that had been buried for nearly two years. But the task was not too unpleasant because the dry sandy knoll had helped to preserve the body. I searched the clothing but found no gold watch.

After closing the grave we rested and looked over to the eastern shore, about a couple of miles away. We could see smoke rising from a cabin there, and I asked Revell the name of the person living in it. He told me the name of the trapper living there, then said that the man whose grave we had just opened had lived with him for few months before he drowned. We crossed the lake to ask the trapper if he knew anything about the watch.

When he saw us coming the trapper came down to the dock to welcome us. When I told him why we were there, without saying a word, he went back to his cabin and returned a few minutes later a swinging a large gold watch by a heavy gold chain.

"Is this what you are looking for?" he asked, then he told us his story.

The deceased had been ill for several years before he drowned, and a number of times he left his own cabin, a few miles farther up the lake, to stay with the man we were talking to. During the deceased's last stay of several months he had given him the watch and chain to help pay for what he had done in the way of assistance and care. But, said the trapper, if the family wanted the watch and chain they were welcome to it. As I listened I recalled that Revell had told me that the drowned man had been sickly for a number of years.

He had also told me that at the time of the drowning nothing showed that the drowning was other than accidental, but there was a suspicion that the accused had committed suicide. That might have been the case. With suicide in mind, the deceased might have given his last valuable possession to his benefactor. There was no reason to believe that the story the trapper had told me was anything but the truth. I told him to keep the watch and chain until he heard from me again.

I reported the facts and said that I believed that the trapper under the circumstances had a legal claim to the watch and chain, but that he was prepared to give them up. Some weeks later I received word that the family wanted the trapper to keep the watch and chain, and they wanted him to know how much they appreciated the care he had given their relative. I visited the cabin later that summer when I flew in a Canadian Airways float plane to take the quinquennial census. The trapper prepared a meal for the pilot and me, and as we sat down I noticed the gold watch hanging by its chain on the wall, ticking away.

My patrols to Primrose Lake made pleasant breaks from other work, which usually involved prosecutions, prisoners, and often long patrols taking them to jail. As these Primrose Lake patrols kept me within my detachment boundaries, although far away from the detachment office, and with no means of communication, I had no particular desire to return to the detachment. This was quite different from the feeling I had when, for example, I escorted prisoners beyond my own area. Then I always wanted to get home as quickly as possible. At first I wondered if I was "bushed". Later, I realized that I looked upon any place in the 4,000-square-mile detachment area as home.

Winter, 1936-37, Primrose Lake, Sask. Outside ranger's cabin with Ranger Armand Carter.

1935-36, Goodsoil. Winter dress including buffalo coat, breeches, fur cap and moccasins.

1937, Primrose Lake, Sask. During winter patrol.

Winter, 1936-37. Wapati Lake inhabitants and visitors.

1937, Cold Lake, Alberta. The dog team I used for winter travel in the Primrose Lake area. The dogs are at home in the village of Cold Lake, Alberta, where the Saskatchewan Natural Resources officers lived for convenience in moving about their territory.

Winter, 1935-36, Primrose Lake. Saskatchewan Natural Resources officer's cabin.

1936, Pierceland. Rev. Frank Myers behind my car at his "Manse".

Winter, 1935-36. On patrol in the Primrose Lake area.

TWENTY

B ill Bendt, who led the anti-priest faction in the Catholic church, had never given me any trouble. As far as I was concerned he was a model citizen. The first time I met him was in Mr. Johnson's court where he had come to listen to the proceedings. As soon as he had five years residence in Canada he became a citizen. I thought the process of granting him citizenship had been rather fast. His Liberal friends had been at work, I thought. I was sure of it when a few weeks later he was appointed a Justice of the Peace.

In an early report I had requested that, in view of the large number of German-speaking settlers in the Goodsoil area, consideration should be given to appointing a German-speaking J.P. I presumed his appointment resulted from my report.

Soon after Bendt's appointment I had occasion to charge a sixteen-year-old youth with shooting a moose out of season. Normally this would be routine, but he happened to be the brother-in-law of the Natural Resources officer, who had now built a small house across the road from the detachment. The boy's mother was the postmistress at Flat Valley, with whom I was frequently in contact. The prosecution didn't make for smooth relations. Nevertheless, the charge was laid before Mr Johnson, and the youth appeared before him on an appointed date. Bendt was among the spectators.

After the court opened, but before the charge was read, the youth said he would like Mr. Bendt to sit on the case. Mr. Johnson had no objection and waived his jurisdiction in writing on the face of the charge. Mr. Bendt took over and read the charge to the youth who pleaded guilty. I pointed out to the court that the provincial Game Act provided for a minimum fine of fifty dollars, and in default of payment, a mandatory thirty days in jail. Bendt sentenced the youth to the fifty dollar fine but, in default, to only eight days in jail.

I pointed out the improper sentence but he did not change his mind. The fine was not paid, leaving me with a prisoner I would normally take to Moosomin juvenile jail over 400 miles away in southeastern Saskatchewan. This would mean an 800-mile return journey for me, so that my prisoner could serve eight days in jail, less the travelling time of three or more days.

I had never heard of a prisoner not being taken to jail after a court had ordered a constable to take him to one. But it seemed ridiculous for me to travel nearly a thousand miles, using nearly a week of my time, to take a prisoner to jail when he would have served nearly half of his sentence by the time we reached the jail. He would be released just two or three days later, perhaps even before I got back to the detachment. Not having a telephone by which I could have received some advice, I decided to keep the prisoner at the detachment where I put him to work on my woodpile, splitting stove wood.

In my report I explained the reasons for keeping the prisoner at Goodsoil, where he probably suffered more than if he had gone to jail. My woodpile was near the road. Everyone who passed by saw him working and knew the reason. Some young people hooted as they passed, others stopped and jeered at him. All this was under the eye of his sister who lived in the house across the road, and kept looking at her brother working out his fine.

I mentioned in my report Bendt's disregard for the penalty set out in the Game Act, even after having it brought to his attention. Mr. Bendt was running true to his reputation, which was that when he was involved in anything, things were done his way. I submitted another report, asking that it be forwarded to the Attorney General, outlining the facts. I suggested that it was only the beginning of how things would be handled if Mr. Bendt continued to sit on cases. I never knew if or what pressures were brought on him, but he never asked to sit on another case, nor did he visit the detachment when other cases were dealt with. But I suspected that his political connections had given him some advice.

Soon after the "moose" case I received some information that Bendt "and his gang", as the priest called them, had formed a sort of Nazi "Bund". I was careful not to give it too much weight, thinking that the information might, indirectly, originate with the priest faction. But further information from an unconnected source supported the first story. Now there were new reports to place on the file I had opened with my report on Bendt's participation in the "moose" case. After I had left Goodsoil, my successor, Constable Lloyd Bingham, gathered enough information to have Bendt and several other German-Canadians interned when World War II began in September 1939.

I first met Bingham, an ex-school teacher from Weyburn, Saskatchewan, on one of my many escort trips to North Battleford. Any time I went there I enjoyed the shower facilities, so different from the crude bathing facilities at Goodsoil. It was during a shower we were taking in adjoining stalls, without having seen him face to face, that I had my first conversation with him. He knew who I was and that I had been stationed at Meadow Lake. He had just been transferred there and wanted to know what kind of man was Sergeant Coombes. He seemed unhappy so I tried to cheer him up.

I told him that soon the sergeant would be boasting that Bingham "was the best damned constable in the Force" as were all constables stationed with the sergeant. It didn't improve his state of mind when I told him about the police team, and as Lilley had told me about a year before, that they could jump like kangaroos. That began a long friendship with Bingham, who later became an Assistant Commissioner in the RCMP. He retired to become Chief of the Edmonton City police, where he died in a tragic accident.

After an escort trip to North Battleford, I returned to Goodsoil at dusk one late November day to find a homesteader waiting for me. Since noon that day he and some neighbours had been searching the bush surrounding his homestead for his four-year-old daughter who had wandered off some time before noon. Men were still searching for her and he wanted me to alert the countryside so that the following morning an organized search could begin with as many men as possible. I arranged to have messengers contact homesteaders, and sent a youth by truck to Loon Lake to have the constable there notify the sub/division headquarters that I wanted a tracking dog immediately. I had no idea where such a dog could be found, but I had heard that there was one in southern Saskatchewan. At daybreak a large number of men had gathered, and soon an organized search began.

Unfortunately, the homestead was on the edge of the settlement. The forest ran north for hundreds of miles, with a break at the Waterhen River about two miles north of the girl's home. The homesteaders in this area had cleared very little land. It was late enough for all the leaves to have fallen and they made a heavy cover on the forest floor. The searchers were required not only to look for the child, but also to kick through the leaves to make sure the child was not hidden by them. The lack of wind and the sunshine streaming down into the trees would have made for a pleasant day, except for the job on which the homesteaders were employed.

We all knew that the child had been dressed only in panties, a lightweight dress, and sneakers with no socks. As night came on without success, we could only think of how she must have suffered the previous night in nearly below-zero Fahrenheit weather. We continued our search until the evening of the fourth day, with additional men each day who had come from miles around. That evening, after the child had been missing about eighty hours, we postponed the search until the following morning.

Now we all believed, as some of us had done for a couple of days, that we were searching not for a live child but for her body. We had thought from the beginning that she might have been attacked by a bear. On that fourth evening, I returned to the office prepared to continue searching the next day. I wondered if the tracking dog was on its way. It could still help us search even if the child was dead. Believing that the child must be dead, I walked to the store for supper. Before entering the store I saw a man on horseback riding madly toward me. I waited for him to arrive. He had a message for me. The child had been found – alive!

She had been found by a Métis who lived on the shore of Lac des Isles. He had been walking home through the forest, after searching all day, when he heard a child crying. He found her sitting beneath a large tree crying bitterly, but apparently unharmed. He had taken her home immediately. I went to the homestead that evening and she seemed in fine fettle; the cold nights had brought out the rosiness in her cheeks. Because she had spent so long outside in cold weather, I hired a light truck, the one which had taken the request for the tracking dog, to take the child and her older sister to the Red Cross hospital at Loon Lake.

She returned home in a couple of days, quite healthy. The nurses at the hospital found that she had existed on grass and berries. She had slept during the day and stayed awake all night because she was afraid of the dark. Her parents could not afford to buy her even a cheap doll but the nurses had given her a teddy bear as big as herself.

I was getting ready for bed that night when an RCMP dog master and his charge presented themselves. He had come as fast as he could after hearing he was wanted. He had started to complain about the last thirty miles of trail when I told him he was lucky that the pot-holes and mudholes were frozen over. When I told him the child had been found, he immediately wanted to inform his detachment that he was returning, and wanted to know where I kept the telephone.

"We have no such frills," I said.

Then he wondered aloud how anyone lived in such a "God-for-saken place". To me it was not nearly as "God-forsaken" as it used to be.

Winter came early in that part of Saskatchewan. If a plough was left in the furrow on October 31, it stayed there until April the next year. When the lakes froze it was time for the commercial fishing "season", a period of three or four days, and sometimes less. A certain amount of fish was arbitrarily designated as the season's catch. The Natural Resources officers decided when the season began, monitored the individual catches, and closed the season when they had totalled the full catch they had earlier decided upon. There was a similar "season" in the summertime.

It was believed that early Icelanders in Ontario devised the first "jiggers". Then their use spread to Manitoba among Icelanders there. The jigger took the place of a sixty-foot pole that the fishermen had used to push the net under the ice from one hole to another. The jigger was a short narrow board to which, on the upper side, a series of sharp metallic teeth had been rivetted. With rope and pulley attached the jigger was inserted under the ice at the first hole, with the teeth next to the bottom of the ice, and the loose end of the net attached to it.

The jigger's teeth, forced by the water pressure, grabbed the undersurface of the ice, and by the rope and pulley system the loose end of the net was propelled to the second hole. The end of the net was taken out and tied to a stake in the ice.

The holes froze solid overnight and the ends of the net had to be chopped out the next morning. The wet net and the fish in it were pulled through the hole. The fish were thrown on the lake surface where they soon froze in the twenty to twenty-five-degree-below-zero weather. Trucks drove onto the ice near the fishing holes, loaded the fish, and hauled it to cities as far away as Winnipeg and Chicago.

At first the jigger had been a boon to fishermen, but it resulted in so much fish being caught that fishing periods became shorter year after year, and the catch smaller. Then came pleas from the fisherman to be allowed to fish with nets of a mesh smaller than five inches, so that more of the small fish could be caught during the season. I do not know what transpired after I left the area, but some of the fishermen were talking about organizing a group to fish farther north, in lakes accessible only by air. Before I left Goodsoil I had met one fisherman who tried it on his own.

I enjoyed the few days among the fishermen. I had nothing to do but accompany the Resources officers as they patrolled from fisherman to fisherman in a Model T Ford truck. It was hardly anything more than four wheels on a chassis with two seats open to the air. My presence in uniform, my companions said, made their job much easier, as there were no arguments when they told fishermen the short season was over.

At the end of one summer "season" the Natural Resources officers and I stayed overnight at a cabin on the northeast corner of Cold Lake. We were about to leave when the senior officer, my old friend George Revell, looking to the west along the north shore of the lake, exclaimed, "Those bastards." We could see along the straight shoreline for several miles, and saw smoke rising from the bush, which we estimated was about three miles away. Revell had suspected that a former employee of his department, a man named Stillman, fished out of season. The smoke came from the mainland, behind an island about a mile off shore. The fishermen must have presumed the island would hide their illegal activities from anyone looking from the south, the only place easily accessible to people. North of the lake, forest stretched to the Northwest Territories.

"I'll bet that that's bloody Stillman," said Revell.

We had no intention of leaving the fishermen to their law breaking, but could we get to them without alerting them? If we used the outboard motor and canoe they would hear us coming and flee. If we used the canoe without the motor, they would see us. The only other way was by walking west for about three miles along the shore, through heavy untravelled bush, and approaching them from the north, a direction from which they would hardly expect game guardians to arrive.

As we walked through the bush, attacked by clouds of flies and mosquitoes, we doubted if anyone had travelled that way before. We were exhausted, after clambering over deadfalls and fighting the flies, when we eventually arrived right behind the rising smoke in the suspected fishing camp. There we found four men, two attending the fire and the smokehouse from which we had seen the smoke rising. Two of them were coming to shore with fish they had just caught. Revell seized all their equipment, canoes, nets, motors, axes, shovels, as well as the fish, smoked, half-smoked and fresh.

We used seized canoes and motors to return to the cabin, and then went on to Pierceland by truck, where Revell laid charges against the fishermen. I was pleased we had caught them early in their illegal operations, because even that early they had caught several hundreds of pounds of fish. A few more days of fishing would have made it difficult for us to handle the amount caught. It was all salmon trout, which, if the fishermen had been allowed to continue without interruption, would have found a ready sale many miles to the south in Alberta.

I prosecuted the cases and, after the four men had pleaded guilty, I asked for a salutary sentence. They were heavily fined by William Gill, a homesteader J.P. He was Scottish, and in his heavy accent called himself "Bull Gull". This was how we always referred to him.

Having earned enough money during the fishing season, each man was able to pay his fine and thus avoided going to jail, much to Revell's disgust. He thought that Stillman, at least, should have received a jail term, since he was a former game guardian. But the fines and the loss of valuable equipment amounted to a substantial penalty, enough for it to act as a deterrent to them and others who might be tempted to do the same thing in future. Revell took the fish and gave it to the hospital at Cold Lake, Alberta. Although he was an employee of the Saskatchewan government, he lived there for convenience sake.

I was not unhappy about the fishermen being fined. It had cost them most of the money they had earned during the fishing season, and the loss of costly equipment appeared to be punishment enough. As they had paid their fines I did not have to escort them to jail, which saved me a very tiresome 400-mile journey.

Not long after that I met Louis Lundgren, who had flown in to an isolated lake to see if fishing there was any better than in Cold Lake. In broken English with a strong Swedish accent, he told me that the cost and the trouble of flying to and from the lake made the idea impracticable. He had warned the pilot of the plane that dropped him at the lake to be sure to return at the appointed time to pick him up.

"If you don't," he had warned, "I'll report you to Constable Kelly of the RCMP." I asked Louis how he could have got the message to me, but he hadn't thought of that. "I'd have got the message to you somehow," he said.

Another interesting person I frequently met when I was in Cold Lake was Flynn Harris. Flynn was in his seventies and married to an Indian. He always wore breeches and boots and a Mounted Police Stetson. When his wife went to take him home each day from the local beer parlour, they walked in single file, the intoxicated Flynn leading the way.

Flynn was born in Nova Scotia and claimed to be the son of a Chief Justice of that province. I had no reason to doubt it. As a young man he had gone west and joined the North-West Mounted Police. He told many stories of his life in the Force and later as an Indian agent, and repeated them again and again to anyone who would listen. One story concerned his police service in the north. He had had serious difficulties with a local priest and had been ordered out under escort.

One night on the way south, he and his escort camped beside a judicial party going north to conduct an Eskimo murder trial. By morning Flynn had convinced the judge that he could not properly conduct the trial without Flynn's great knowledge of Eskimo ways. The judge ordered Flynn's escort to wire the Commissioner in Regina to have him authorize Flynn's return to the north. The answer came back very quickly. "Constable Harris will proceed to Regina as originally ordered." Flynn remembered several names of the policemen in the judicial party. One name was "Spriggs", and I wondered if it could be my present commanding officer, Inspector Frank Spriggs. On his next visit to Goodsoil detachment I asked if he had heard the name Flynn Harris. I told him the story Flynn had told me and asked if it was true. It was true, he said.

Spriggs told me other stories of Flynn's unusual behaviour while a member of the Force. One concerned the time when Flynn joined a Salvation Army gathering one Saturday night on a Regina street corner. The intoxicated Flynn, who was in uniform, insisted on leading the band. Soon, by request, a policeman led him away and he returned to Barracks – under escort. Needless to say, his service in the Force was relatively short.

1936, Cold Lake. This picture was taken facing south. Stillman and his partners were found fishing illegally in the narrow strip of lake between the island and the north shore of the lake. The Martineau River is in the top half of the picture.

1935-36, Primrose Lake. Natural Resources officer inspecting commercial ice fisherman.

TWENTY-ONE

I don't know if mental illness was more prevalent on the prairies in the 1930s than in other areas of Canada, but there was plenty of it. RCMP members at all prairie detachments experienced the sad drama of someone being committed to one of the two mental hospitals in the province, at Weyburn and North Battleford. The first mental case I had anything to do with, the one in Regina in which I accompanied a senior constable, was disposed of in a few hours because of good roads, telephones and available doctors. How different it was at Goodsoil detachment where we had none of these things.

A mentally ill patient could be committed to one of Saskatchewan's two mental hospitals in one of three ways. He could commit himself; two doctors could certify that a person was in need of mental treatment; or a charge could be laid by an interested party, usually a member of the family, under the Mental Diseases Act. In the latter method, a patient appeared before a Justice of the Peace, and based on the evidence of the witnesses, one of whom had to be a doctor, the patient could be committed to a mental hospital. In such cases the family usually found it convenient to have the police involved as they, after committal, took the patient to the hospital.

I escorted a number of patients to the North Battleford hospital when I was stationed at Meadow Lake and at Loon Lake. I recall one Meadow Lake case because it was unusual, and also my first such case there. One day a very tall, heavily built man came into the detachment. Sergeant Coombes greeted him like an old friend. He spoke to the sergeant in a whisper and left.

The sergeant told me to get ready to take our visitor to the mental hospital at North Battleford right away. He seemed so normal that I asked if he could go alone by bus and have himself committed. The sergeant then told me the story. About three years before, our visitor had been committed to the mental hospital for the first time after his wife had complained to the police about his behaviour. It showed he was obviously mentally ill. When Sergeant Coombes and his second man went to pick him up to take him before a J.P., he was so violent that it took four men to put him in a straightjacket. From the build of our visitor I could imagine the fight he must have put up.

On each of three similar journeys while I was at Meadow Lake I found him to be a pleasant travelling companion. About six months later he would return home, after being told to return to the hospital whenever he felt he needed treatment. Sergeant Coombes, with the memory of the trouble occasioned by his first committal, always agreed readily with the man's request.

In another case, in the Maidstone area where I was to be stationed later, one morning a farmer, who had had no previous damage done to his crops by hail or drought, saw a very small cloud on the horizon far to the west. He told his son that it was a hail cloud and that he feared for his wheat crop. The son thought his father unduly apprehensive and told him so. But by noon the cloud had gotten bigger and closer. By midafternoon, when it was right over the farm the hail from it destroyed the farmer's crop. The last words his father had spoken as the hail fell on his crop were, "God, if I were a God, I'd be a God and not a God-damned fool."

After a few days the son called the doctor. Several days later he advised the son to have his father committed to the mental hospital. I came into the picture when the son came to me wanting to prefer a charge against his father under the Mental Diseases Act. The son accompanied me when we took his father to hospital, and in six months the elderly man was well enough to return home.

During my last period at North Battleford detachment I was detailed to handle police problems at the local mental hospital. In spite of the watchfulness of the attendants, there were occasional suicides. Each case required a Coroner's inquest and sometimes a postmortem. Seldom was a lawyer appointed to represent the Crown, so it became my duty to present the evidence and examine witnesses. When patients wandered away I took part in organized searches. In one case in midsummer, a patient wandered from the mental hospital. When he was found that evening, he was naked and so badly sunburnt that he died a few days later. Another inquest.

My official duty was not all that took me to the hospital. My fiancée taught the children of the doctors and attendants who lived on the grounds. We often played golf on the nine-hole course which had grass greens. At my club we only had oiled sand "greens". We always had the same patient as our caddy. Otto had been recommended to us by one of the doctors. He also caddied for my fiancée when she played alone. Some of the fairways were along the well-wooded north bank of the North Saskatchewan River, and I didn't like her being alone with Otto, who after all was a mental patient.

I decided to find out why Otto was in the hospital. The only thing we knew was that he wasn't violent, and that he appeared quite normal. One afternoon, as we went around the course, I asked him why he was in the hospital. Without giving me a direct answer, he said, "Those damned Mounted Police," not knowing that I was a member of the Force. I questioned him further and he said the police had no reason to put him in the hospital. After some prodding he said something about a cheque he had written.

I thought he might have written a cheque on someone else's account. But he would have none of that. "No," he insisted, "on my own account." Even if he had written a cheque without sufficient funds he wouldn't normally have ended up in a mental hospital. Did he have sufficient funds to cover the cheque, I asked. "Of course," he answered, "otherwise I would not have written the cheque." From the tone of his voice he obviously thought me a little stupid. I was stumped for a while and then, after another hole or two, I asked what was the amount for which he had written the cheque. He didn't hesitate, "One million, three hundred . . ." I knew there must be more to the story than just his having written a cheque, but I was satisfied that Otto could safely caddy for my fiancée, even when she played alone. That was long before anyone had asked, "What's a million?"

On one occasion Constable Benny Greene had escorted a prisoner from North Battleford to Prince Albert jail. It frequently happened that such an escort would return with a patient for the mental hospital. The day Greene was due to return I received a telegram from him, from a railroad station en route, saying it was imperative that I meet him at the station that evening, "in civilian clothes".

Greene stepped off the train followed by a very pregnant woman. She in turn was followed by a matron. Greene immediately introduced me as "Dr. Kelly", then whispered to me that the woman objected strongly to being taken to a mental hospital. Greene had promised to have a doctor meet her at the train. She initially refused to move off the platform, but I was able to coax her into the waiting room. She refused to go any further. She would wait there for the train back to Prince Albert the next day, she insisted.

In the meantime she told me all about her pregnancy, including some of the difficulties she had had up to that time. She was eight months pregnant she said, and she looked it. There was little I could do but try to convince her, on the basis of my "medical experience" and her "condition", to at least spend the night in the hospital. But she would have none of that. In the meantime Greene had called for help from the hospital. It came in the form of a nurse and two attendants who stood just outside the waiting room. After about two hours she became tired and agreed to spend the night at the hospital. In my capacity as "Dr. Kelly" I drove her and the matron there.

On my visits to the hospital during the next week or so I enquired about "my patient". After about a month she gave birth to a bouncing baby girl. I never knew the name the mother gave the child, but the nurses called her "Kelly" after her mother's "doctor". Kelly and her mother left the hospital soon afterwards.

Not all mental cases ended so happily. The two most poignant cases in my experience occurred when I was stationed at Goodsoil detachment. One evening in mid-April, just as the trails were "breaking up", I received a visit from a haggard-looking, poorly dressed homesteader. He had walked about eight miles over trails covered with deep potholes filled with melted snow water, and in deep mud where there were no potholes. Due to his exhausted condition it was some time before he was able to tell me the purpose of his visit. His wife, he said, was seven months pregnant and seriously mentally ill. Until now he had been able to take care of her and their two young children, two and four years of age, but he was no longer able to do so. He had to watch her constantly to ensure that she did not wander into the heavy bush around his cabin. He had spent many hours searching for her on the various occasions when she had escaped his vigilance, and each time she objected violently to being taken back home.

I asked who was looking after his wife while he came to tell me about her. No one, he said. He had tied her to the bed, spread-eagled, with her arms and legs tied to the four corners. He didn't know if she could free herself, but if she did it meant another long search in the bush, perhaps into the night.

He wanted to know if I could arrange to take her to Dr. Grandy at the Red Cross hospital in Loon Lake, some thirty-odd miles south, as he had no means of taking her there. Until now his only thought was to put her in the Loon Lake hospital. We agreed that Dr. Grandy might decide that his wife should go to the mental hospital at North

Battleford. I said I would take him and his wife to Loon Lake the next morning, and before he left for home I arranged for him to have a meal at the store where I ate mine. As he left he looked so beaten down that I wondered if he would reach his homestead without collapsing. He seemed to be in need of a doctor's care himself.

This case was similar to others I had dealt with, relatives of mentally ill persons seeking medical attention only when it was unavoidable, and often too late. It seemed that assistance was always sought when the condition of the trails made travel difficult. Such was the case with my recent visitor. I knew I would encounter difficulties in reaching Loon Lake. In other parts of my area, where the trails were much better, I had been waiting until they improved to make necessary patrols. But the trail southeast to Northern Beauty, the area in which the homesteader lived, was worse than I could have imagined. Water from melting snow had overflowed the whole trail, hiding the deep potholes and the hummocks. They were impossible to avoid. With some wheels of the democrat on hummocks and others in the potholes, I found it nearly impossible to hang on to the seat as I roller-coasted along. Sometimes I wondered if my team could pull me out of the precarious positions in which I found myself.

When I arrived at the homestead I thought my horses were unfit to go any farther, but I realized when I went into the cabin that I had to try. The one-room, twenty-four-foot-square log cabin was in a pitiable state. A table full of dirty dishes sat in one corner, covered with sawdust that presumably had fallen from the homesteader's makeshift ceiling insulation. In a second corner stood a washstand, and in the third corner a double bed on which the sick woman lay, spread-eagled and tied as her husband had described to me the day before. Two young children, scantily clad, undernourished and barefoot, stood wide-eyed beside the bed. Near the fourth corner was the doorway.

Soon after I arrived a woman neighbour came to help dress the sick woman. Even I had to help restrain her. We tried to encourage her by telling her she was going to see Dr. Grandy, who had attended her some years before. Normally, when I escorted a woman patient or prisoner, a matron came with us. In this case the husband came instead, leaving the neighbour to look after the children. In any event it would have been impossible to take a fourth person along. The journey would have been difficult enough for normal people, but with one a pregnant woman, it would obviously be extremely uncomfortable. We had some difficulty in persuading the woman that she should get into the democrat. For the first six miles we travelled on a sandy ridge, and then a few miles more, south to the Beaver

River, where we stopped for a rest and lunch at Seeley's store. Mrs. Seeley had just arrived from Loon Lake the night before. When she saw the patient's condition she tried to convince the husband that we should return home. She was satisfied that the woman could not possibly stand travelling over the next eighteen miles, the worst she had ever travelled over, she said.

But the husband wanted us to go on. He realized that no matter what problems we experienced on the trail, they would be less difficult than those his wife had created at the homestead. As we left Mrs. Seeley gave us a bag of sandwiches. "It might be a long time before supper," she said.

After crossing the river bridge our troubles began. Although the trail was not as bad as from the police detachment to the homestead, it had many shallow potholes and deep mudholes. The water-laden mudholes were sometimes so large they were longer than the democrat and horses combined, and deep enough for the water to be level with the horses' bellies. Fortunately, there were no hummocks. I wondered, time after time, if my nearly exhausted team could pull us out of them. But they did. The journey was difficult enough for the husband and me, and I wondered how much longer the pregnant woman could put up with it. Both her husband and I tried to make sure she didn't fall as the horses jerkily carried us through the mudholes and over the potholes. I was afraid we might have a baby on our hands at any moment.

As I rested the horses in one mudhole, the woman began a tirade in her native German. Her husband calmed her down, and after we started again I asked him what it was all about. His wife had been blaming me for her pregnant condition and didn't want to ride with me any farther. He told her I owned the team and without me they couldn't get to Loon Lake. By then it was dusk, and I knew we could not reach Loon Lake before darkness set in. When we finally reached a road allowance, several miles from Loon Lake, we had to follow a deep, heavily rutted trail as it meandered from side to side.

For these last few miles in the dark I had to depend on the horses to keep us on (or in) the trail. Most of the time they did, but often the wheels were on the edges of the ruts and would fall off them with a bump. Fortunately, there were no mudholes. But with the combination of deep twisting ruts and the darkness, this stretch of trail was the most difficult of the whole journey. After eleven hours we pulled up to the Red Cross hospital in Loon Lake with our patient fast asleep.

We got the patient into the hospital. Soon the doctor came from his home nearby. After listening to the husband for a few minutes he said the woman should be taken to the mental hospital as soon as possible. The woman, now wide awake, was sitting in a chair. The doctor thought she should sleep and gave her a pill. She hid the pill under her tongue. The doctor forced her to swallow it, but she would not move from the chair to go to bed. She seemed to be dozing off, and once I thought she would fall. I leaped from where I sat to protect her. She met me with a fist to the jaw. After all, I thought later, she was only getting back at the person she thought was responsible for her pregnancy.

The woman spent the night in the hospital, and the next morning we had her committed to the mental hospital. I hired a matron and a car, and the four of us drove the 135 miles to North Battleford. The matron, the husband and I returned immediately to Loon Lake, in the early morning hours. The husband wanted to leave for his home immediately, due to concern for his two children. But we were so tired we slept for a few hours at Loon Lake detachment, he in the cell and I in the constable's spare bed.

On the way back north the journey was just as difficult for the horses. But without the patient, the husband and I didn't mind being thrown about as we went in and out of deep mudholes. We crossed the bridge at the Beaver River and called into Seeley's for a cup of coffee. Mrs. Seeley was anxious to know how we had made out. She was surprised that we had made the journey without incident.

We continued on north until we reached the point where I would have to drive six miles east to take the husband back home. But knowing the kind of trail from his homestead to the police detachment, he decided to walk home. That left me six miles to go, north on the main trail to the detachment I had left sixty hours before.

As I put in my report on the case, I realized that not having medical facilities as readily available as they were in older and better established communities was a penalty homesteaders had to pay for their attempt to find a new way of life. This comment also applied to the following case which occurred during my stay at Goodsoil detachment.

Late one cold November night, I received a visit from a big hulk of a man, who looked even bigger in his winter outer garments. He was very cold so I sat him down beside my pot-bellied heater. When at last he spoke, in a German accent, his soft voice belied his size. He told me that he had walked from his homestead at Flat Valley, about seven miles south of Goodsoil and one mile west, on a seldom-used trail. He had just returned from British Columbia, where for about nine months he had been a patient in a mental hospital. After his release he had lived in Vancouver for about a month. While there he had written to his family in Germany, asking for enough money to pay his way back to Germany by train and ship, there being no air flights in those days. His family was well off and he expected the money any day.

He had gotten over his mental sickness, he said, but would feel better if, when I was in the vicinity of his homestead, I would pay him a visit to see that things were all right. I gladly agreed and after a cup of coffee he began his long cold walk home. He told me his name but I will call him Hans Schmidt.

My work didn't take me near his cabin very often, but a week later, when only a mile from his place, I paid him a visit and found he was not at home. I could see that the only work he had done to prove up on his homestead, was to build his log cabin near the trail that ran through his property. I could tell from the faint heat in his cooking stove that he had been at home that morning. I left him a note saying I had called. The next week I did not call on him, but inquiries at the Flat Valley post office showed that he had turned up on mail day, the day before, to see if he had received a letter from Germany.

The German-speaking postmistress told me that Hans had spoken to her of the letter he was expecting and what he hoped was in it. But there was no letter. I visited Hans again about ten days later, and again he was away but there was some heat in his stove. I left him a note. I visited him only once more. Again he was away; there was heat in the stove and I left a note. But I continued to call at the post office, and each time I learned he had not received the long-awaited letter.

Then on one very cold day in February I heard a rider galloping up the road on horseback. He stopped at the detachment, tied his horse to the gatepost, and ran up the wooden walk. When I met the young man at the door he told me that Hans had been found dead in his cabin. He had shot himself while lying on his bunk. Hurriedly, I hitched my horses to the sleigh and drove to Hans' homestead. Several neighbours were there, awaiting my arrival. A blanket covered the body. When I removed it I saw that Hans had shot himself in the head and that he lay in a foetal position, completely frozen. His rifle was on the floor nearby.

He must have been dead for several days. A neighbour who lived half a mile away seemed to be the last one to have seen Hans alive. At that time he appeared to be in good spirits. They had talked about the letter, and Hans believed that it would arrive soon.

The nearest coroner was Dr. Grandy at Loon Lake. I wrote him a letter telling him of the circumstances. I sent it to him by the young man who had brought me the news of Hans' death. I had asked the coroner if he wished to visit the body or conduct an inquest. The messenger brought back his answer. Everything showed a clear case of suicide. He didn't think his presence was required, and I had his authority to have the body buried. At that time of the year it was a very difficult thing to do. Nevertheless, the neighbours thawed the body to straighten it, and dug a grave in the frozen ground.

About a week later I attended the funeral, and on my way home called in at the post office. I did not receive the usual greeting. The postmistress came from the kitchen, and without saying a word turned to the pigeon holes on the wall behind her, took out a letter and handed it to me. It was the letter Hans had been expecting. I opened it and found that it contained the necessary funds for Hans' journey back to Germany.

The postmistress translated the accompanying letter. It mentioned the date when Hans had written the letter in Vancouver, asking for money. As soon as his relatives received it, about two weeks later (all mail went by surface in those days), they made application to the German foreign exchange authorities for permission to send money out of Germany. Hitler was in power and had established strict foreign exchange control regulations. Another two weeks elapsed before permission was granted, after which the family sent the money to Hans at his last-known address – Vancouver. The money probably arrived about six to eight weeks after Hans had first written his request.

Now there was a further delay of some weeks as the letter lay in the Vancouver post office, waiting for Hans to pick it up. Meanwhile, Hans had returned to Flat Valley without telling his family in Germany that he was doing so, and without leaving a forwarding address at the post office. So the uncalled for letter was returned to Germany. The family then presumed that Hans had returned to his homestead, and the letter I held in my hand had been sent there. I estimated that, from the time Hans had written his letter in Vancouver until the time the answer arrived at Flat Valley, more than three months had elapsed.

Ironically, the letter had probably been waiting at the Loon Lake post office, for the once-a-week Flat Valley mail pickup, when Hans shot himself. The postmistress had several times suggested to Hans that he go to the nearest telegraph office, some forty miles south, to send a telegram to his family in Germany. But he had always been sure the letter would be in the next mail.

"I began to think he was imagining it all," the postmistress said.

I nodded my head. I had begun to think so myself.

TWENTY-TWO

A lthough I received rather cursory inspections every month by the patrol N.C.O., Sergeant Coombes, they did not take the place of inspections by the Commanding Officer of the sub/division, about once every four months. RCMP policy required the officer to arrive unexpectedly at a detachment, once every three months, so that he saw it operating in normal conditions. In this way he could find out if the records were kept up-to-date, and the office and the quarters kept clean when no visit from the C.O. was expected.

Officers had varying ideas of what an inspection should be. They all inspected the basic things, such as records, the seized exhibits, and the monies on hand. But some gave scant consideration to the fact that a member had been on a patrol the night before, and that his uniform might not be as clean as it should be. One officer had the reputation of paying little attention to the police work done and much more to the cleanliness of the police car, uniforms and detachment quarters. Other officers were more concerned with the police work and its problems, and paid less attention to the condition of a member's uniform and quarters, as long as they were reasonably well kept.

The inspection policy of the officer turning up unexpectedly created difficulties for my C.O. when he wanted to inspect Goodsoil detachment. After travelling over the thirty miles of unbelievably rough trail from Loon Lake, he had no idea if he would find me at home, and if he didn't, when I would return. Once or twice he inspected the detachment in my absence, having obtained the key to the door from the landlord, Mr. Johnson. But this partial inspection did not meet requirements. Once I returned from a summer patrol to see the inspector's car outside the detachment. As I reached the front door, carrying my bedroll and blankets, I heard him checking the items listed in the ledger with his constable chauffeur. The constable was upstairs checking the blankets on the two spare single beds.

"Woollen blankets – eight," shouted the C.O.

"O.K. sir," shouted the constable. I knew immediately I had a friend in the constable. There were only six blankets on the beds, the other two were in my bedroll. Later I realized that, to do a proper check, the C.O. should have been asking how many blankets the constable found, rather than telling him the number recorded in the ledger.

My possible absence led the C.O. to notify me by letter when he would arrive. At such times I greeted him in full dress – red serge, breeches and boots, Stetson hat and full Sam Browne with brass and leather beautifully shined. He gave me some rifle and revolver drill, as much as the space in the office allowed. It amounted to no more than a "present arms" with the rile, the basic revolver "load" and "unload" drill, a few right and left turns, a mark time and a halt, ending with a salute. When this was over I was allowed to change from red serge to my brown patrol jacket, shirt and tie.

Next he paid attention to the detachment records. These included the exhibit ledger, daily diary, stamp account book, the record of my purchases and use of firewood, cleaning materials, and gasoline used for lighting purposes. He checked my transport requisition book, to see that if any had been used it had been on police business. He ascertained that the remaining requisitions were in sequence. He initialled and dated all the record books.

He spent some time on the complaint book. From this he could see what complaints had been made and whether they had been properly dealt with. He questioned any that seemed to be unusually outstanding. He checked all the exhibits being held for court purposes, and those having been so used, such as liquor, which he had to destroy. He then signed a certificate of destruction on each exhibit form. He poured the liquor exhibits on the ground outside the door. He would then deal with anything that needed to be condemned, such as a worn-out uniform or one which a member had outgrown, brooms, pails, blankets and so on. Anything of this nature had been listed on a condemning board which had been prepared for him before he arrived. He would then examine each item and approve or disapprove as he saw fit, then take the condemning board away with him. In due course Division headquarters would approve the "board" and return a copy to the detachment, which meant that condemned articles would be replaced by being issued from RCMP stores or purchased locally.

When I saw the C.O. destroy liquor I was always reminded of the story I had heard at Meadow Lake, probably apocryphal. It was about a member who had a heart attack when he saw the C.O. destroy a full case of seized Scotch before he had time to replace the precious liquid with tea of the same hue. To finish off the inspection, the inspector and I went to the stable for him to see the condition of the horses and the democrat. The inspection had lasted about two hours. Then the inspector paid a visit to Mr. Johnson, our landlord and a Justice of the Peace, and the two storekeepers. This was done not to invite any complaints about me, but if they chose to make any he was prepared to listen.

Members realized that being on detachment was not conducive to maintaining a barracks-like smartness. They also knew that they were always under public scrutiny, and most took pride in their appearance. But it had been known for some people to complain about a member's sloppy appearance. A smart appearance always included a very short haircut, a far cry from the haircuts one sees on members of the Force today, nearly sixty years later. There was no barber in all my detachment area. Keeping my hair short was a problem, but I prevailed on Mr. Johnson's housekeeper to cut it when I knew the inspector was due.

The regulations in this regard, for many years before the 1930s and after, were as follows:

". . . He shall be properly shaved and the hair of the head cut short"

Most Canadians believe the discipline of the RCMP is very strict, and so it is when compared with that in civilian life. But in actual fact RCMP restrictions on a member's behaviour are those related to his responsibilities as a policeman, among which are the following.

> A member shall not:
> Conduct himself in a manner unbecoming a member of the Force,
> Be neglectful or inattentive to any duty which he is required to perform,
> Be intoxicated, however slightly, on duty.
> Attend a political meeting in uniform, except in the performance of a specific duty,

Or take part in any activity, social or otherwise, that might create the impression that a particular political party is being favoured.

Other rules dealt with the abuse of liquor, and prohibited possession of liquor in RCMP quarters, all of which were intended to ensure that a member's behaviour, at all times, was that expected of a person holding a sensitive public office.

On one inspection my C.O. told me that he had received a letter of complaint about not doing enough concerning the "homebrew" problem in my area. I had been doing my best, through the use of informants and the reward system, to find the sources of the homebrew I suspected was being manufactured locally, which meant within 100 square miles. I explained this to the C.O. and he said he understood, but to keep trying.

A few days later I was eating a late lunch in the storekeeper's dining room. The only sounds were made by his wife cleaning up in the kitchen. The storekeeper passed through the dining room from the store and went into the kitchen.

"What does Gus Heinrich do with all the lye he buys?" I heard his wife ask him as he entered the kitchen.

There was no answer, but I visualized her husband signalling to her to keep quiet and pointing to the dining room, reminding her that I was there. Then they began to talk about something quite unrelated to Gus's lye. I had heard of moonshiners putting lye in their mash to give it a "kick", but probably to improve the fermentation process. Immediately on my return to the office I found Gus's name in my file cards, and saw that he had been convicted some five years earlier of manufacturing illicit spirits, contrary to the Excise Act.

I knew him well by sight. His house was near the main trail, and as I passed his place we often waved to each other. Not a word of his being involved in the making of homebrew had come to my notice. That afternoon I drove to his place and told him I was going to make a search of his place under authority of a Writ of Assistance – a permanent search warrant under the Excise Act. I failed to find anything in his house or outbuildings. But in the bush, about 300 yards away, I found two barrels of fermenting mash and several empty lye cans.

It was always a disappointment not to find a still, or the most important part of it, the condensing coil. Even so, possession of mash would result in the same penalty. When I placed mild-mannered Gus under arrest he closed his house. For the first time I noticed that he had no animals of any kind, not even chickens. He must have been living off the proceeds of his illegal activities. After taking his fingerprints in the office, I placed him in the cell and went to tell the storekeeper's wife that there would be an extra person for supper. She didn't ask who it was and I didn't tell her. There was nothing unusual about me asking for an extra meal for a prisoner.

When she saw Gus with me at the supper table she nearly dropped the dish she was carrying. Perhaps she suspected that her indiscreet enquiry of her husband earlier that day had resulted in Gus's arrest. But she never asked me about it.

The next day Gus pleaded guilty before two J.P.s. Because he was charged with having committed a second offence, he was fined the minimum of $500 or six months in jail. He chose the jail term, saying, "I have the money to pay the fine but where else could I earn $500 in six months, with room and board?"

I was pleased to have stopped this source of homebrew. But it had happened so soon after the C.O.'s visit, and his receiving the complaint, that I felt he might think that I made an effort to catch Gus Heinrich only after he had informed me of the complaint.

The Saskatchewan government's liquor policy during the 1930s encouraged the manufacture of homebrew in out of the way places such as Goodsoil and Pierceland. In its way, the government might have thought that not allowing liquor stores to be opened within 100 miles or so of new homestead areas was a way to prevent homesteaders from spending what little money they had on liquor. People could only purchase liquor in older areas if there was a drugstore there, and then only on doctor's prescription. The eventual opening of liquor stores in some of the larger towns put a serious dent in the earnings of doctors and druggists alike. The original policy, and the later one of opening liquor stores in the smaller centres, however, did little to stop illicit distilling in isolated places such as "north of the Beaver" where there were no small towns and no doctors or druggists.

Liquor, whether legal or illicit, created, then as now, problems for the police. It also created family problems. In those depression days money spent on liquor would better have been spent on food and clothing. On social occasions young drunken hoodlums made nuisances of themselves by disrupting dances and committing various assaults. These brought the police into the picture. Wives complained not so much about their husband's spending money on liquor, although indirectly this was the cause of the complaint, but about the prevalence of homebrew, and the apparent freedom of moonshiners to make it. Either the wives had refused to give me any information that would lead to an offender or were unable to do so.

Indian reserves gave police an added problem. In my days on an

RCMP detachment, an intoxicated Indian was guilty of an offence under the Indian Act. The priest on Big Head Indian reserve, Father Cloutier, often complained to me about drunkenness among his Indians. They had three sources of alcohol: homebrew, liquor sold legally in Alberta to someone who then sold it to Indians, and such things as lemon extract and Methyl Hydrate (rubbing alcohol). The last two were purchased whenever a storekeeper would sell it to them. I often prosecuted Indians for being intoxicated, much less often for being in possession of homebrew. Only once did I get a conviction of a storekeeper for selling lemon extract to Indians. Indians were as careful as white people in keeping the source of their supplies confidential. Even when Indians had money to pay their fines they rarely did so. I came to believe that, for most of them, going to jail was more of a holiday than punishment. They were seldom employed.

It was virtually impossible to find a still making homebrew. Even so, I had found one when I was stationed at Loon Lake, when a neighbour informed on a moonshiner. In most cases I had to be satisfied with finding mash, a bottle or two of spirits, or the most important part of the still – the copper condensing coil. In Goodsoil, as at other detachments, the information received about distilling activities was far more plentiful than the successful conclusion of such cases. More often than not, in reporting such cases, the concluding remarks were – nonresultant search.

I had received a great deal of information about two men in the Pierceland district who were alleged to be making illicit alcohol. They both lived adjacent to provincially owned land, about twelve miles apart. All my information led me to believe that both men operated their stills on that land, and I spent many hours searching for their distilling equipment. I found that for a lone policeman, searching for any indications of illicit distillation, in what amounted to tens of square miles of heavy bush, was like looking for the proverbial needle in a haystack. Even finding the location where a still had been operated meant very little, other than to confirm what my sources of information had told me.

One of the two, Bill B., had been homesteading for a number of years south of Pierceland. He had done nothing to prove up on his homestead except to clear two acres around his tar-papered frame house. Everyone liked Bill B., a friendly fellow. The other man, named Jenks, lived with his wife and two grown-up sons on a homestead about four miles west of Pierceland, on a trail that led into the province of Alberta. Their homestead was miles from any other and next to a large tract of provincial land.

The Jenks family had come from Kentucky a few years before, and when compared with other homesteaders were fairly affluent. They had recently purchased a new high-bodied wagon, a rare thing in new homestead country. This, coupled with their apparent affluence, and their connection with Kentucky, made it easy for me to believe what my informants had been telling me. But that didn't help very much in the collection of evidence against them.

I had been a policeman long enough to realize that one could work hard and long on resolving a problem without any success, and then with relatively little effort be unusually successful. So it was with Bill B. and Jenks. One morning I was on my way to Cold Lake, Alberta, to begin a canoe patrol to the Primrose Lake area with George Revell. I had to pass through the village of Pierceland and found that it was relief day. I saw Bill B. and his wife tying up their horse and buggy near the livery barn. George Revell would have to wonder what had happened to me; this was an opportunity for me to search Bill B's homestead without him being present.

I headed for Bill B's homestead in my 1929 Ford Coupé. As I lowered the barbed wire gate to enter his property, I noticed some children watching from the window of the house, about 100 yards away. A pretty, scantily dressed girl about nine years old answered my knock. Two children stood behind her, frightened, I suppose, by my uniform. Hoping to lessen the area of my search, I thought I might get some help from the girl. Gently I told her I knew her father made homebrew, and that I was going to look for his still.

I asked if he sometimes kept the coil of the still in the surrounding woods. She didn't answer. I thought that this indicated she would not answer any questions, but then I asked if he sometimes kept the coil in the house. She vigorously shook her head. I asked if he hid the coil in a tree. She didn't move. I asked if the tree he kept it in was far away. She shook her head again. I pointed to a distant tree and asked if the tree in which he kept the coil was as far away as that. She shook her head. I pointed to a closer tree and asked the same question. She didn't respond. I used the same technique about the direction in which I might find the tree. After she had failed to respond when I pointed west, following the child's unspoken directions I went into the bush and had soon located the cooling coil, high up in a pine tree.

With the coil in my possession I returned to Pierceland and arrested Bill B., just as he and his wife were about to drive home with the groceries they had purchased with their relief voucher. I knew that Bill B. would go to jail because he had no money to pay a fine. Except for his companionship, it would make no difference to his wife. She would only have to pasture the team and feed the chickens. That afternoon, after getting two J.P's to sit on the case, Bill pleaded guilty to being in possession of a part of a still, contrary to the Excise Act. He was fined the minimum $100 or three months in jail.

As we returned to Goodsoil en route to Prince Albert common jail, over 200 miles away, he occasionally took from his pocket a small soda pop bottle from which he took a sip. I asked him what it was. He said soda water for his stomach. I was willing to believe it. He had a pasty complexion, as though he suffered from some ailment. Soon his frequent sips aroused my suspicion. The next time he went for a sip I took the bottle away from him and smelled it. Sure enough it was homebrew. I told him I could lay another charge against him, even though only a few spoonfuls remained. But he only laughed and said I would be doing him a good turn by keeping him away from alcohol for more than three months. I stopped the car and smashed the bottle on a tree.

I thought I had been delinquent in not searching Bill B's buggy. He might have had a few bottles for sale when he arrived that morning in Pierceland. But then I would have had to seize his horse and buggy and I didn't want to do that. I didn't lay a second charge against him. He would probably have been fined again and given three months in jail in default, but to run concurrently with the jail term in the first charge. I could hardly call his possession of a few drops of alcohol a second offence, especially as he had been convicted of another Excise offence that day.

Later that spring I arrested Jenks and one son under different circumstances, within a quarter of a mile of where I had arrested Bill B. on Pierceland's only street. I learned that the Indian agent would be paying Treaty money in Pierceland on May 24 – Victoria Day. Treaty money paid to Indians, along with a sports day, would be too good an opportunity for the moonshiners to miss. I had plenty of work to keep me busy at Goodsoil, but on the night of the 23rd I decided that my presence was required at Pierceland the next day. So as late as it was, I drove through the pine woods, the Indian reserve, and then along a trail which led me to Pierceland. On the way I passed a farm owned by Amié Nault. He was an elderly man who was the son of one of Louis Riel's advisers. His wife was related to Marie Lagimodière, the first white woman in the west. I knew them well and I had a high regard for them and their two sons.

The trail I was on entered Pierceland's only street at right angles. About a quarter of a mile from the village there was a lesser trail, which ran off obliquely to the right through some bush. It would take me to one end of the street. For no particular reason I took this direction, and immediately I was sorry. It was full of dry potholes. I swore at my stupidity as I navigated around them. At one of them my lights shone on a team tied up to a tree some distance off the trail. I swung my car into the bush on the other side, knowing that anyone who had tied a team so far off the trail, and so far from the village, in the late night hours, was up to no good. With the aid of my flashlight I examined the wagon and its contents.

It was a real bonanza. The wagon contained enough cardboard cartons to cover the bottom of the wagon body. They held bottles of all kinds, from small medicine bottles, to wine bottles, to one-gallon jugs. They were all filled with a white liquid which, from the odours that permeated the air, was undoubtedly illicit alcohol. The nearly new wagon and the fine team must belong to Jenks. I sat under a tree a few feet way, prepared to wait for the owner's return, all night if necessary. As I sat there I mentally placed the team, wagon and alcohol under seizure "in the name of the King".

Before long I heard voices, then I saw two men approach the wagon, and go one to each side to untie the horses. I walked up behind the man on my side and flashed the light in his face. It was the elder Jenks. The other man, his son, came hurriedly around to see what was happening. I told them both they were under arrest, and that everything was under seizure. It was night and I was alone, with a large seizure and two very able-bodied men as prisoners. But I had my Colt .455 and I did not hesitate to tell them of the possible consequences if they tried to escape.

I instructed the younger Jenks to drive the team to the livery barn in the village while the elder Jenks and I walked behind. At the livery barn I told the livery man to unhitch the team, and keep it and the wagon until I ordered him to release them, as they were under seizure. He helped me unload the alcohol, and except for two medium-sized, full bottles, with people now watching me, I smashed the rest on the blacksmith's nearby trash pile.

The next morning, before two J.P.s, Jenks and his son pleaded guilty to charges of being in possession of illicitly manufactured alcohol. I was afraid they would receive the minimum fine of $100 each. So I pointed out the differences between this and other cases they had tried. The Jenks had come to Pierceland with the full intention of selling liquor to Indians, being paid by treaty money that could be better spent for food and clothing. Also important was the fact that the still with which they had manufactured the alcohol remained in their possession. I said if any case called for the maximum sentence for a first offence surely it was this one, a fine of $500 or six months in jail.

The elder Jenks spoke for both himself and his son. He handled himself well. He asked for a light fine, seeing that he had lost a fine team and a nearly new wagon, and after all he, too, was a homesteader. But the two homesteader J.P.s took little notice of his plea and sentenced both to a fine of $500 each or six months in jail. Jenks asked for a week to pay, but did so in a couple of days, from money most likely acquired from his illicit alcohol sales. In effect, his being caught resulted only in taking from him money he had earned from his illegal activities. When his team and wagon were put up for auction by sealed bids, I learned that the successful bidder had been acting on Jenks behalf. So he got them back by paying the government some more of his ill-gotten gains.

I was sorry that Jenks was able to pay the fines. I thought that after the trouble he had given me he deserved a period in jail, but I could do nothing about it. However, I was pleased that the arrest of these two men, and that of Bill B., would put a stop to complaints from the Pierceland area for a while at least. No one would be happier about this state of affairs than Father Cloutier at Big Head Indian reserve.

I stayed behind to "police" the sports day and returned to Goodsoil that night. As I did so, stopping occasionally for a deer to stop staring into my headlights and get off the trail, I thought how lucky I was to have decided to go to Pierceland the night before. I would have had a perfectly clear conscience if I had stayed at Goodsoil to clear up my office work, in which case I wouldn't have known anything about Jenks and his load of alcohol except, perhaps, through later complaints. I was attributing my success to luck when I realized that I was usually lucky when I put some extra effort into my work.

1936. On the railroad bed used as a trail from Pierceland, Sask. to Beaver Crossing, Alberta.

1936, Pierceland. View of the village.

TWENTY-THREE

The Goodsoil detachment area was developed only to the extent of the relatively few acres of cleared land on most homesteads. This area, north of those which had their own municipalities and appropriate by-laws, was known as "unorganized territory". There were no council members or by-laws, and the small amount of official business required had to be done by the provincial government through its local representatives, the Natural Resources officers, the relief officers and sometimes the police.

No consideration had been given to the building of roads before or during my stay at Goodsoil, except that years before, road allowances, sixty-six feet wide, were cut through heavy bush by gangs of unemployed men in the late 1920s and early 1930s. Similar road allowances, through which trails meandered, had been surveyed throughout the area. All this was done preparatory to opening up the area for settlement. Only in a few places had there been any attempt to grade a road, and this was done by homesteaders without the assistance of road-making equipment. Their interests lay more in proving up their homesteads than in road making. If they had had some government road-making equipment it might have been different, but there was no such thing in the whole of the new homestead area. No taxes of any kind were assessed or collected, and this might have created some reluctance on the part of the provincial government to go to the considerable extra expense of building roads. Issuing relief to nearly 100 per cent of the homesteaders was probably thought to be sufficient assistance, at least for the time being.

Most of the detachment area was covered with light to heavy bush. When homesteaders first arrived they were fortunate if they found enough open space on which to build a cabin, or to put in a garden. Some took their tractors to the area, but didn't operate them because they could not afford to purchase gasoline. These people sometimes suggested, not always facetiously, that stills capable of manufacturing alcohol be legalized, in order to use the product as tractor fuel.

With their tractors in sheds these people, like the others, cleared their land with horses, axes and logging chains. It took several years before bush could be cleared and used as farmland. Most home-steaders were living in the cabins they built when they first settled, and nearly all were receiving government relief vouchers every two weeks. Goodsoil itself was not even a village. It had the police de-tachment; two stores, one of logs; a log community hall, a log black-smith shop, and two houses, built after my arrival, for the relief officer and the Natural Resources ranger. Later, a machine shop for the repair of farm equipment was erected by a homesteader with some mechanical ability. This was the community of Goodsoil, so small it was not recorded on any map.

It was with some surprise that we locals learned that a "hotel" was going to be built between the police detachment property and the community hall. We wondered where hotel business would come from. Homesteaders travelled long distances to get to Goodsoil, but they had no intention of staying overnight, or eating meals if they had to pay for them. They brought something to eat with them. The few visitors who came to Goodsoil were usually commercial travellers who did their business quickly with the two stores, so that they could return south over the rough trails in day-light. It did not take a graduate in economics to conclude that the fu-ture of the hotel business in Goodsoil was bleak.

Nevertheless, a two-storey house was erected and soon the "hotelier" announced he was open for business. After a few weeks, without even one paying guest he, too, must have realized that run-ning a hotel in Goodsoil was a lost cause. He suggested that I should eat my meals there, and when I declined he wrote to my C.O. asking him to order me to do so. The C.O. sent me a copy of the hotel owner's letter and the C.O.'s answer. It was that where I ate was my personal business.

I found my new neighbour, with plenty of time on his hands, to be a nosey Parker, and a disruptive influence in our small commu-nity. Even his cousin, who operated the second store, the one where

I did not eat my meals, said he wished the hotelier had built his hotel somewhere else. Apart from not liking his type, I had another reason for not wanting to be associated with him. I was investigating a suspected arson case in which a pool hall in Pierceland, half owned by his brother, had burned down under suspicious circumstances.

I also had another reason. I found that quite often people on their way to see me on business first stopped at the "hotel". Coached by the owner they came to me with their complaints. Many were matters in which the police had no interest, such as complaints about the sale of an article or animal for which they had not received payment. These were purely civil matters, but my neighbour continued to advise them that they could charge the debtor with theft. My advice was that the only thing they could do was start civil proceedings through a lawyer and sue for the amount owed. Unhappy with the advice I gave them, many wrote to the provincial Attorney General complaining about my refusing to accede to their requests. And of course they complained to their neighbours about my not doing my job properly.

The Attorney General confirmed the advice I gave them, but that did not stop others from coming to me with similar requests. I blamed the hotelier for this. Actually, they only wanted to lay a charge to regain possession of the item sold; sometimes a cow, or a horse or a wagon. One of the people to whom a disgruntled homesteader had complained about me, told me that he had said things would be different when Mr. so and so (the hotel keeper) became a J.P.

I was concerned about the hotelier getting such an appointment. Since the moose shooting case, Bill Bendt, the German-speaking J.P., had shown no desire to sit on another case. As a result I had recommended to my C.O. that another German-speaking person be appointed, in view of the large number of German-speaking homesteaders. The hotel keeper, although Canadian born, had a German name and spoke the language. Indirectly I obtained information of his possible appointment. The Attorney General requested a character investigation on him. I could say very little in his favour, and I wanted to recommend that he not be given the appointment. But I was not certain that the character investigation was for this purpose.

As I pondered the matter, an incident happened which probably prevented his appointment as Justice of the Peace, if that was what the character investigation was for. Some time before, the storekeeper where I ate my meals had hinted that people could purchase a drink of hard liquor at the hotel. In view of the hotel keeper's financial circumstances I was not surprised. But I had received no further information that he was selling liquor. One morning he came to the detachment, a most unusual event. After a few minutes of talking about things in general, he jokingly suggested that he had the answer to some of the problems created by the making of "home-brew" in the district.

I thought he was going to give me some information about some one making it. Instead, he suggested that I might turn a "blind eye" to his selling the "odd drink" of legal liquor at his place. He said it in such a way that I could not take it as a serious proposition. But I knew he was testing the water, in order to get my reaction. If I had given a hint of agreeing with him, he would have soon become the local bootlegger, using my acquiescence as his protection.

In a similarly jocular way I told him that I didn't know why he wanted my approval. I had heard, I said, that one could buy a drink at his place already. I would hate, I continued, to have to escort my next-door neighbour to Prince Albert, meaning the common jail. I never heard again that anyone could buy a drink at his place. I used this incident in my report on his character.

His visit could only have been for the purpose of finding out what my attitude would be to his selling liquor in the hotel. His friendliness was completely at odds to the very cool feelings that had prevailed between us. He never paid me another visit. I put his suggestion down to the fact that he was getting desperate for money, since the hotel business was absolutely non-existent.

A policeman soon learns, particularly in a rural area where he is the cynosure of all eyes, that he cannot be all things to all people. In one particular matter he would be considered too zealous, and in the same matter others would consider him too lenient. I was sure that if I had turned a blind eye to the selling of liquor by my neighbour, there would be many who thought it was the right thing to do; others wouldn't care one way or the other, but there were those who would object violently. I had had some experience in the use of "police discretion", and I was sure that it did not extend to allowing anyone to sell liquor illegally.

Liquor, the illicitly manufactured kind, was on my mind one May 24, as I drove the thirty miles to Pierceland to police a sports day. Such an occasion gave moonshiners an opportunity to sell their wares to whites and Indians alike. If I caught some of them, all to the good, but if I couldn't do that, I derived some satisfaction by my presence putting a crimp in their business. I arrived in time to see one of the two general stores burn to the ground. It had apparently caught fire from the still-smouldering remains of the pool hall next door. The store owner, Dan Flegel, told me that his store had been partly consumed by flames before anyone had noticed it. In the absence of running water, we could only try to save some goods before the fire took over entirely.

Flegel had just finished extending the store and filling it with a new supply of goods. He had no insurance on either. I knew that a homesteader named "Frenchy" Gauthier operated the pool hall for its two owners, one living in Ontario, and the other, a brother of my "hotelier" neighbour, in nearby Alberta. Frenchy lived on a homestead about six miles away, and was known to be easygoing and lazy. As Flegel and I watched the store burn, we wondered why he had not yet arrived to open up the poolroom for what should have been a busy and profitable day, Queen Victoria Day.

Flegel asked, "Do you think someone set fire to the store deliberately?"

"Obviously your store caught fire from the pool hall," I said. "There's no electricity in your store or a fire from which it could have started. But setting your store afire by first burning down the pool hall is hardly the way an arsonist would go about it."

As I spoke it occurred to me that the pool hall might have been deliberately burned down, and I invited Flegel to go with me to look over the smouldering ruins. We concluded that the fire there had started in the corner where a large pot-bellied heater stood. This appeared suspicious because the weather had been mild for several days. There was no need for any fire in the heater for comfort. It was enough to make me feel that I should investigate.

I drove the six miles to Frenchy's homestead, expecting to meet him on his way into Pierceland. But he had not left home. He was just leaving for Pierceland to open up the pool hall. I told him that I thought he would have gone to Pierceland much earlier to accommodate the sports day visitors, especially the Indians. He explained that he had left the pool hall quite late the night before and had slept in. He seemed genuinely surprised when I told him the pool hall had burned down. He had lit a fire in the heater, he said, but had adjusted the dampers so that the fire would burn slowly all night, and the place would be warm in the morning. I asked why he needed any heat at all, and he said the mornings were chilly, which was a fact, but hardly chilly enough for a fire in the heater.

There were two things wrong with his story. Because of the warm weather there really was no need for a fire, and if things were normal he would not have slept in, but would have gone to the pool hall to take advantage of the obvious business that awaited him. Before leaving him he gave me the names and addresses of the two owners, and said he had no idea if there was insurance on the hall.

When I left him I was convinced that he had arranged for the heater to overheat and burn down the building, giving no thought to the store next door. When I returned to Goodsoil, without having seized any homebrew, as I had hoped to do, I submitted a report voicing my suspicions about the pool hall fire.

As a result a CIB sergeant from North Battleford visited the co-owners of the hall in Ontario and Alberta. Both denied being involved in the fire, but he did find out that the hall and its contents were insured for $3000. All summer I kept track of Frenchy, thinking that if he had received any money for burning the pool hall he would go "outside" to spend it. A bachelor, he had nothing but work to keep him at home. But he stayed home all summer. Late that fall I was passing the trail that led to his place. I knew that if I did not interview him soon, the difficulty of winter travel would prevent my seeing him before spring. By then my chances of getting him to talk would have faded. So I drove to his homestead, where I found him ploughing in a small meadow-like field surrounded by heavy bush. We sat on a pile of logs absorbing the warm November sunshine pouring down on us. I expected him to still deny that he had burned down the pool hall. But surprisingly he appeared anxious to tell me all about it.

Three weeks before the fire, both owners had been to see him. They had offered him $500 to set it. They decided on the night of May 23 because no one would think anyone would deliberately set fire to the pool hall the night before the best business day of the year. So, late that night Frenchy overloaded the heater, lit the fire, and surrounded it with newspaper soaked with coal oil to make sure the fire spread.

The owners were not forthcoming with the money they had promised him, and when he wrote them about it he received no answers. He believed they had no intention of paying him, even though they had made the proposition for him to burn down the pool hall, because they couldn't be linked with the fire except through him. But that would mean he would be involved too, if he gave them away to the police. What Frenchy didn't know was that his co-conspirators had been interviewed by the detective sergeant. Thus any move to pay Frenchy what they owed him might have led the police to learn of their involvement. It was not that they didn't want to pay him, but they were forced to protect themselves as well as they could.

I had never taken a written confession from anyone before, so I paid close attention to the rules. I cautioned Frenchy in the words used at that time, "You need not say anything, you have nothing to hope from any promise or favour, and nothing to fear from any threat, but anything you do say will be taken down in writing and might be used as evidence gainst you." I knew the caution by heart, even though I had never used it, and I thought it practically told a person how stupid he was to tell the police anything that could result in his being charged with a crime.

But Frenchy was in no mood to think of the words in the caution, he was ready to confess. I took his story down in writing, in great detail. After reading it very cursorily, he signed it and I witnessed it. At my suggestion he wrote two letters, one to each co-owner, asking for his money. I mailed them but I didn't think there was any hope of them replying. But if they didn't, even that fact would be some evidence against them. If Frenchy demanded something he was not entitled to, surely it would call for some kind of answer. He got none.

Frenchy's confession and the evidence of the insurance company was enough to charge the three men with arson, conspiracy to commit arson, and conspiracy to defraud the insurance company. The charges were laid at Battleford where Mr. Walter Clink, K.C., the Agent for the Attorney General, who would handle the case for the Crown, had authorized them. A date was set for a preliminary hearing to be held at St. Walburg, seventy miles south of Goodsoil, and about 100 miles southeast of Pierceland.

Setting the place for the hearing at St. Walburg was undoubtedly to avoid the police magistrate and Mr. Clink having to make a 200-mile return sleigh ride from St. Walburg, where the railway ended, to Pierceland in the dead of winter. But witnesses who had to travel this distance, and myself slightly less, had no means of complaining.

No plea is taken at a preliminary hearing, which is held to see if enough evidence has been adduced to warrant a trial in a higher court. I presented Frenchy's confession, and after being cross-examined by defence counsel, Mr. Rookie Blackburn the magistrate ordered it admitted as evidence. Then a member of the insurance company gave evidence about the amount for which the pool hall was insured by two of the accused, and their claim to be paid after the hall had burned down.

To my surprise, Police Magistrate Mighton called the proceedings to a halt, saying that he had heard enough evidence to support a *prima facie* case against the three accused, and he committed them for trial in a higher court. They were allowed out on bail, and all three walked out of the hall in which the hearing was held, laughing and joking together. By now Frenchy probably knew why they hadn't sent him the $500 they had promised him.

1936, Beacon Hill, Sask. "Frenchy" Gauthier, later arrested for arson, beside my 1928 Ford roadster on the trail to his homestead.

TWENTY-FOUR

I went to Battleford a couple of days before the trial in the Court of King's Bench to help Mr. Clink prepare the case. He had advised me that John G. Diefenbaker of Prince Albert had been retained to defend all three accused. Diefenbaker, a future Prime Minister of Canada, was known as an able defence counsel who made dramatic appeals to juries and charged high fees. No one, it was said, could more skillfully play on a jury's heartstrings. One story described how a jury brought in a verdict of not guilty as a birthday present to him. Other tales were about cases where the Crown had overwhelming evidence against the accused, but juries brought in verdicts of not guilty, all attributable to Diefenbaker's ability to sway them in favour of the defence.

Mr. Clink assured me that most of the stories were true. "He'll leave no stone unturned to make us prove the guilt of his clients, and at the same time he'll give us a good show."

Battleford, a small town across the North Saskatchewan River from North Battleford, was the first capital of the Northwest Territories. It was the judicial centre for the Battleford Judicial district, which ran from south of Battleford to the Northwest Territories. All jury trials were held there. The judge turned up under the influence of liquor, and remained in that condition for several days. The Sheriff tried to help him sober up by supplying pitchers of tomato juice laced with Worcestershire sauce.

Meanwhile the trial continued, and each day an overflowing

crowd filled the courtroom, not because the case was unusual, but because John Diefenbaker was defence counsel. They knew he would put on a "good show". Young, tall, handsome and distin-guished-looking in his shiny black gown, he knew he was the centre of attraction.

Not unexpectedly, the three accused sitting in the small prison-ers box pleaded not guilty to the charges of arson, conspiracy to commit arson, and conspiracy to defraud the insurance company. Dan Flegel, the owner of the burned-out store was the Crown's first witness. He described how the store had caught fire from the burn-ing pool hall, and how, in the absence of water, he was forced to stand helplessly by, as the flames consumed his store and the mer-chandise it contained. He described how he had recently enlarged the store and filled it with a completely new stock of goods. He had gone deeply into debt to do so and he had no insurance.

Diefenbaker's cross-examination was lengthy. His questions seemed to imply that Flegel had burned down his own store. At one point he tried to make out that the pool hall had caught fire from the fire in the general store, the exact opposite of what had taken place. Diefenbaker knew the facts. Since the preliminary hearing a few months before, he had been acquainted with the evidence given at it, including the contents of Frenchy's confession. This didn't matter to Diefenbaker. As defence counsel it was his duty to cast doubt on every element of the Crown's case.

Striding back and forth in front of the judge, but looking most of the time at the jury, his left hand on his hip, under his gown, he pep-pered Flegel with questions, hardly waiting for the answers. Several times Crown Counsel had to ask him to let the witness answer be-fore going on to the next question. He played up to the jury. A shake of his head or the inflection of his rasping voice gave the impression that the jury should pay special attention to the question he was about to ask. Then, still looking at the jury, with a half smile on his face, he would ask a question, the importance of which seemed min-imal. At one point he asked Flegel:

"Did you inform the police about the fire?"

"No," answered Flegel flatly.

For a few moments there was silence as Diefenbaker, looking around the courtroom, walked toward the jury and leaned on the jury box. With a look on his face as if to say to the jury, "Now watch this, I've got him where I want him," he turned around and shouted across the room at the witness:

"You mean you had been financially ruined by a fire? You sus-pected the fire had been deliberately set? But you didn't notify the police?"

There was dead silence in the courtroom as the audience waited for Flegel's answer. Was it as important as Diefenbaker was trying to make it out to be? Flegel hesitated.

"Take your time witness," Diefenbaker said.

He turned to the jury with a satisfied smile. He had the witness in an awkward position. Flegel's answer would be interesting and he needed time to answer such an awkward question. Then Flegel answered, "I didn't have to notify the police. Constable Kelly was standing by my side watching the store burn down." Tension was eased and the public relaxed in their seats. Unabashed, and with the confidence of one who had received an answer in favour of his clients, Diefenbaker went on with the next question. Another Diefenbaker technique – if an answer was not what he wanted, he didn't show it.

"What conversation did you have with Kelly when the store was burning?" he continued.

"I asked Kelly if he thought the fire in the pool hall had been deliberately set."

"And what did Kelly say?"

"He said he couldn't tell."

"What else did you and Kelly talk about?"

By now it seemed that Diefenbaker hadn't any more real questions to ask. He was on a fishing expedition, hoping the witness would say something that would lead to more effective questioning. As I sat next to Mr. Clink at the counsel's table, I remembered Flegel talking to me. I thought I knew what I had said, but I was as interested as Diefenbaker in hearing what I said, that is if Flegel could remember. Flegel seemed to hesitate about repeating what I said, or he was trying to recall it. Then slowly he answered the question, " 'But if the fire was set deliberately,' I asked Kelly, 'who do you think would do such a thing?' "

"And what did Kelly say to that?" snapped Diefenbaker, seemingly irritated by the slowness of the answers.

"Kelly said, 'Dan, if there's any son-of-a-bitch that would do such a thing, it's that bastard Frenchy Gauthier.' "

Excepting Mr. Diefenbaker and me, everyone in the court, including the three accused, burst into laughter. I was embarrassed. My face was the same hue as the red serge I was wearing. Mr. Diefenbaker stood with his head bowed, waiting for the laughter to stop. When it did Mr. Clink said to me in a stage whisper, "You wouldn't use language like that would you?" More laughter. I didn't realize until then how emotional I was while looking at Flegel's burning store.

Diefenbaker raised his head slowly showing his scowling face. He turned to the judge who had been just as amused as anyone, and said, "My Lord, I think that answer should be struck from the record."

The tipsy judge, a tall thin man with a bald head, wearing half spectacles on the tip of his nose, leaned over from his high seat so that he could see over the half lens. He said, "Mr. Diefenbaker, you asked the question and you got the answer."

Then he settled down in his seat, and before Diefenbaker could begin asking another question, the judge leaned forward again. He looked down at Diefenbaker, and said, "And Mr. Diefenbaker, you are stuck with it", putting great emphasis on the word "stuck". To Mr. Diefenbaker's chagrin there was another outburst of laughter.

When it came my turn to give evidence, we all knew that Diefenbaker would try to have the signed confession thrown out. Without it we didn't have much of a case. We could then only try to have Frenchy's confession entered on the basis of my conversation with him. Before beginning to question me on the circumstances under which the confession was obtained, the judge ordered the jury from the court. It would not be fair for them to hear anything related to the confession if afterwards the judge ruled it inadmissable.

I told the simple story of my visit to Gauthier's homestead and how, without my questioning him, he willingly told me the circumstances under which he had set the fire at the behest of the two men who owned the pool hall, and who had promised to pay him $500 for doing so. Then Diefenbaker began to question me.

The practice of defence counsel, then as now, more than nearly sixty years later, was to try to show that the confession had been obtained by promises, threats or any form of undue influence. He questioned me on the warning I gave Frenchy. He wanted to know where I got the wording from and I showed him my notebook. He picked the warning to pieces. But it was the warning in my RCMP constable's manual. He knew exactly what the confession contained, so he didn't question me on its contents, only the manner in which it was obtained.

He accused me of threatening Frenchy that he would lose his homestead if he did not confess. Then he accused me of promising him a light sentence if he confessed to setting the fire. He accused me further of promising Frenchy that if he confessed, and gave evidence against the other two, I would arrange for him not to be prosecuted. I could see that he was just fishing.

He was also not above a little trickery in court. At one point in my evidence I answered a question of no great consequence. He turned on his heel and made a "note" on his pad on a table near the witness box. I looked down at what he had written, and to my surprise it was nothing but squiggles. I was still looking at them when he turned to ask the next question. He went to the desk and very deliberately turned the pad over with as much noise as he could make. Meanwhile he looked at the jury as much as to say, "do you see what this sneaky witness was up to?" I am sure his pretence at making a note of my answer was to impress the jury that I had said something significant in favour of the accused.

Eventually the questioning stopped. I wouldn't have been surprised if he had called on Frenchy to give evidence about all the things he had accused me of doing in order to get Frenchy to confess. But he didn't, and the judge ordered the jury to return. He informed them that he had ruled the confession admissible, and asked Mr. Clink to read it to them. In it Frenchy said, in effect, that he had set the fire according to the instructions of the two owners, after being promised $500 which he had never received. As a result he decided to tell the police about it.

There was no doubt that Diefenbaker knew his clients had committed the crimes with which they were charged. But he had no responsibility to bring out the truth in court. On the other hand, even if he knew a witness for the Crown was telling the truth, he tried to make it appear that the witness was not sure of his story, or even that he was lying. It was all within the rules of the court. Diefenbaker's only responsibility, like that of any defence lawyer, was to free his clients from the charges against them by creating as much doubt as possible concerning the Crown's case.

Some years later I read an interview with Mr. Justice Birkett of the High Court of England. He had been a distinguished defence counsel. He felt no qualms, he said, when he helped free a man charged with murder, whom he knew to have committed the crime. Such is our system of justice.

The judge continued to conduct the court in spite of his tipsy condition, but on Friday morning he was so tipsy that counsel, on both sides, concocted a story in order to have the judge adjourn the trial until the following Monday. Diefenbaker asked for the adjournment, saying he wanted to attend the wedding of Mr. Justice Embury's son in Saskatoon the next morning. But he had urgent business in Prince Albert which, without an adjournment, he would have to deal with on Saturday morning instead of going to the wedding.

The story about his attendance at the wedding was true. It so happened that the tipsy judge was also going to the wedding and he was pleased to have an adjournment. But it took him a full hour to adjourn. He spent that time telling us how good a friend he was of Judge Embury, and how he had known the groom-to-be since he was a small boy, and many more things of no interest to anyone else. As we listened, Mr. Clink and I wondered how much of the evidence he would remember the following week.

The trial resumed on Monday morning with a surprisingly sober judge on the bench. By midafternoon all the evidence was in. No witnesses were called for the defence. When Diefenbaker addressed the jury, he barefacedly asked for a dismissal of the charges because the Crown had not proved the guilt of the accused beyond a reasonable doubt. In spite of the judge's obvious intoxication the previous week, he presented all the pertinent facts to the jury with appropriate comment on each. Neither Counsel objected to anything he said.

The jury deliberated that night and most of the next day, but finally concluded that they could not agree on a verdict. The judge discharged the jury, setting a date for a new trial in the fall. One juryman had refused to agree with the other eleven. He was a brother-in-law of the two accused who owned the pool hall. No doubt the judge had a few words with the sheriff, who was responsible for choosing the jury panel.

That fall I returned to Battleford for the second trial. I met Mr. Diefenbaker in the courthouse library where he was changing into his gown. I said, "Good morning, Mr. Diefenbaker, here we go again."

"Not unless they produce $400 before I put my nose into that courtroom," he retorted sharply. Later I wondered if that amount covered the defence of all three accused, or was that amount expected from each. I never found out. They must have produced it because he defended them again. The second trial, before Chief Justice Martin, did not last as long as the first one. Diefenbaker spent much less time trying to get Frenchy's confession thrown out. He spent much less time on the conversation between Flegel and me while we watched the store burn down. He asked none of the questions which had created so much laughter at the first trial.

Chief Justice Martin, although a no-nonsense judge, had a good sense of humour. I drove him to and from the courthouse. One day after lunch we were a few minutes late, and the lawyers in a second-floor window were watching for his return. He saw them, but this did not stop him from throwing a ball around with some children playing on the courthouse steps. I waited at the door for him to enter. Then he said, "Those lawyers, I'm sure, are wondering why a silly old judge would keep them waiting, just to play ball with those children. When they're as old as I am they'll find out."

The confession was admitted in evidence again, and again the accused did not give evidence. In due course the case went to the jury. They started their deliberations in early afternoon. At 10 p.m. the judge called me from his hotel and said, "I think we should go to the courthouse and if the jury hasn't come to a verdict I'll send them to bed."

As we entered the courthouse, one of the two sheriff's officers guarding the juryroom came to the judge and told him that from the noises in the room it wasn't likely that a verdict would be reached that night. I had visions of another "hung" jury, as in the first trial, and due to the same reason – a juryman partial to the accused, regardless of what evidence was produced against them. The judge playfully tiptoed to the juryroom door and put his ear to the door. We all heard someone inside shout, "You agree with us that all three are guilty, but you won't agree to find them guilty. If they go free because of you, I'll break your goddamned neck."

The judge, feigning fear, backed away and asked the guard to get the sheriff to the courthouse so that the jury deliberations could be adjourned until morning. Then the judge and I went to his chambers on the second floor. We waited for the sheriff's arrival for about half an hour. When he arrived he had a surprise for us. The jury had reached a verdict. I knew it could only be a guilty verdict. The juryman whose voice we had heard was in no mood to give in. All three were found guilty on all charges.

Diefenbaker asked for a suspended sentence for all three because it was a first offence. Or if they were to go to jail, however, he asked for short terms in the common jail. In sentencing them the judge said it would be a travesty of justice for these men to go free while Flegel, the man who had lost everything he owned, would suffer for the rest of his life as a result of their crimes.

He sentenced the pool hall owners to three years in the penitentiary, and Frenchy, who was a mere tool of the other two, and whose confession had brought about the trial, to six months in the common jail.

Many years later, after I retired from the RCMP, I was staying in an Edmonton hotel when I recognized the foreman of the jury in this case. I introduced myself. In our conversation I mentioned the case, and of overhearing the voice threatening a juror. I wondered if he remembered it.

"Very well," he said, "I was the one doing the threatening."

The arson case was a part of my continuing education as a member of the RCMP. I had for the first time seen a high court in action, and the way a distinguished defence counsel went about defending his clients who he must have known had committed the crimes with which they were charged. They were not guilty of such crimes, in his mind, until a jury had found them guilty. He would have been quite happy to see them freed, and leave the court without a stain on their characters.

It was easy to see why Diefenbaker was popular with the public. He had a great sense of drama, and he made his cases highly theatrical. He had superb control of inflection and was a master of the biting question. He framed his questions in such a way, or he asked them with an inflection which suggested that a witness was not telling the truth, or was not sure that what he had said was correct. His leaning on the jury box, walking to and fro with his arms waving, and pointing his long bony right forefinger at a witness as he asked a question, were all part of the impression he wished to convey to those who really mattered in the court – the jury.

He sometimes feigned anger. This was done mainly to suggest to the jury that he was finding it difficult to get the witness to say anything in favour of the accused. At other times it would be done to try to emphasize what he thought the witness should have or should not have done.

He modulated his voice, from a whisper to a shout, with telling effect. He spoke to the jury as if they were old friends. He impressed upon them their importance in criminal trials. They must believe the judge on points of law, he told them, but they, and only they, must decide on the facts. He told them this in such a way that they could easily believe that they were more important than the judge, who was just playing second fiddle. He told them about the need to consider how particular witnesses had given evidence. They could believe them if they wished, but they needn't do so. He mentioned the benefit of the doubt going to the accused, and ended by saying he was confident to leave the decision in the jury's hands, as though there was an alternative. Mr. Clink had told me six months before that Diefenbaker would give us a "good show".

I had plenty of time on my journey back to Goodsoil to think of what had happened. The court had been conducted with due decorum, but no more so than in a J.P's court held in my detachment office. In fact, when I thought of the "hung" jury in the first trial, I wondered if there might not be more justice in my J.P's court. But where was the justice for Flegel in all this? Those who had burned his store had been punished, but there was no recompense for him. He had been deprived of his livelihood. He could sue the convicted men for damages in civil court, but it would cost money he didn't have. Even if he sued and won that was no assurance that he could collect damages. Justice had prevailed, but only as it dealt with the criminals. Flegel, the innocent storekeeper, would have to suffer the consequences of their crimes for the rest of his life. It turned out to be very short, he died within two years of the trial.

TWENTY-FIVE

W hen one policeman is responsible for policing about 4,000 square miles, complaints needing investigation usually arrive long after the event. In such cases the "trail" is often so cold that his chances of concluding any investigation successfully are limited.

In the Goodsoil area police problems were compounded by the absence of good roads and modern means of communication, meaning a telephone. But even if telephones had been available to settlers, it would often have been difficult for a complainant to contact me because of my many absences. For several days or a week at a time I patrolled the northern lakes and bush. But there was one time when I was near the scene of a crime soon after it had taken place.

I was driving my 1928 Ford roadster back to Goodsoil, after a four-day canoe patrol in the Primrose Lake district, in the northwest of my detachment area. I stopped at Jack Manderson's isolated general store along the trail at Beacon Hill. As I entered, the storekeeper's only customer laughed and said, "Speak of the devil . . ." He had just asked the storekeeper if he had seen the "Mountie" around.

The customer, a homesteader living a mile or so away, complained that someone had stolen a month-old heifer calf, and its mother was "bawling her head off" over the pasture fence that separated his homestead from the Big Head Indian reserve. I asked him the first thing that comes to a policeman's mind on such occasions.

Did he have any suspects?

Indeed he had, an Indian and a white man he had seen riding around in a light delivery truck. Manderson identified them as Indian George, who lived in a cabin on the reserve, one mile along the main trail to Goodsoil; and White George, a Mennonite who had returned from a Mennonite settlement in South America only a few weeks before. Manderson thought that White George lived with a homesteader near where he used to homestead, a few miles south of the store.

As anxious as I was to get back to my office at Goodsoil, nearly twenty-five miles to the east, there was nothing for me to do but follow the lead of the bawling cow. She indicated that her missing calf had gone in the direction of the Indian reserve. With the informant I patrolled in my car to Indian George's cabin. He stepped out as we drove up. I did not have sufficient information on which to reasonably base a suspicion that he was involved in the theft. His reputation was enough to make me suspicious, but suspicion was not grounds enough on which to apply for a search warrant before a J.P. In any case, the nearest J.P. lived six miles away. So I asked Indian George if I could search his cabin without a search warrant. As expected, he refused, and let loose a tirade against the police, who, he said, always blamed an Indian when they couldn't blame anyone else.

I didn't need a search warrant to search the woods behind his cabin, but I found no sign of the missing calf. We were about to drive away when the homesteader pointed to a dog coming out of the woods about two hundred yards beyond the cabin. It was a whitish dog with red colouring about the head, which seemed strange. We waited for the dog to come closer and could see that the red colour came from fresh blood. We drove to where the dog had come out of the woods, and followed a narrow path for about fifty yards. There we found a fresh calf hide, a calf's head with the brains removed, and the entrails. The homesteader identified the hide as that of his calf. Obviously the calf had been killed there.

Taking the head and hide with us, we returned to Indian George's cabin. The dog was resting in the shade of a tree nearby. Finding the hide and head and the killing place so close to Indian George's cabin created a reasonably strong suspicion that he was involved in the theft. Indeed, finding them so close to the cabin, with no other habitation within a mile, was tantamount to finding him in actual possession of them. I now *had* to search Indian George's cabin. He came outside to meet us. I told him that I had enough evidence on which to arrest him, and if I arrested him I had the right to search his cabin without a search warrant. I believed I was on reasonably sound legal grounds in telling him this. If I had to arrest him to make a search, I would do so. But I didn't want to arrest him just then, and have to haul him around while searching for White George.

If he forced me to arrest him, I told him, I would seize his clothes so that I could send them to the police laboratory in Regina, to test for traces of animal blood. I knew there was a new laboratory in Regina, but I didn't know if they could test for blood. Sending the clothing there and receiving an answer would take at least three weeks, hardly a method to achieve a speedy conclusion of the case.

Indian George thought over my remarks and reluctantly agreed that I could search his cabin. I didn't have to go beyond the small kitchen to find what I was looking for. On a cupboard shelf was a dish with the brains in it. In a cupboard I found the calf's liver and heart, and in still another cupboard there were pieces of veal cut to roasting size. I seized the meat, liver and heart, and then sat at the table to take a written statement from Indian George. He signed it, and the homesteader and I witnessed his signature. In the statement he implicated White George. They had been driving over the reserve, he said, when they saw a calf break out of someone's pasture. They had put it in the truck and killed it where we had found the head, hide and entrails. He said White George had not taken any of the slaughtered calf.

White George, he said, had gone about six miles north with a party of Indians to pick blueberries. On the way there the homesteader and I left our seizure at Jack Manderson's store. We had gone about three miles from Manderson's when we came to a stream too deep for the car to cross. Leaving it we walked on, not knowing how many miles it was to the berry patch. After about two miles we came to several acres in a meadow-like clearing.

In this idyllic setting the berry pickers had erected a number of pup tents in the shade of some poplar trees. There we found an old Indian woman smoking a pipe near one of the tents. She spoke no English, but in reply to my question she waved her hand in a direction which I took to be the place where the others were picking berries. Before leaving to find them, I entered the tents and unloaded the ammunition I found in the rifles. I put the shells under the rolled-out blankets. The clicks of the rifles must have alerted the old woman to the fact that I was emptying them.

About half a mile away we found six berry pickers. Four women and two men, one of whom was White George. I arrested him as he picked berries from a low blueberry bush. The other man was an Indian but dressed like a businessman. He came over to where I had arrested George, and belligerently informed me that I had no authority to arrest anyone on the reserve, and even if I had I could not do so unless I wore my red tunic. I was wearing breeches and boots and shirtsleeves. I ignored him and ordered George to start walking ahead of me. The Indian came between George and me, insisting that I couldn't arrest White George, and threatening me with dire results if I took him off the reserve. I didn't know how my prisoner would take his friend's support, so in order to have some control I put handcuffs on the prisoner.

When the Indian wouldn't stop interfering I told him that he, too, was under arrest. After some argument he grudgingly walked with us to the tents. When we arrived the old woman told him that I had gone into the tents when I arrived at the field. He went into each tent and came out accusing me of stealing the ammunition. I didn't tell him I hadn't and, eventually, with the Indian still threatening me, the four of us moved along the trail to the car. On the way I questioned the Indian. He did not belong to Big Head reserve. He had come on a visit from a reserve in eastern Saskatchewan. By the time we arrived at the car, he had cooled down considerably. On the way I had been debating with myself about whether or not I should charge him with obstructing a peace officer in the course of his duty, but decided to release him so that he could go back to the berry patch. I told him he was free to go back, much to the chagrin of the homesteader, who shook his head in disapproval. So that the Indian would not think then that he was completely in the clear, I told him I would consider whether or not I would lay a charge against him.

We drove back to Indian George's place where I put him under arrest. Now there were four people in my Ford roadster. Indian George and I were in front, the homesteader and White George in the rumble seat. After picking up the meat and hide at Manderson's, I drove to the homestead of a Beacon Hill J.P., a Mr. Fred Bohme. Then with three people in the driver's section, and two in the rumble seat with the meat, we drove on to Pierceland. There I sent a messenger a mile out of the village to ask another J.P., Bill Gill, to sit on the case. I knew that two J.P.s would have jurisdiction if the value of the calf was under twenty-five dollars. If it was over that they could only proceed by way of a preliminary hearing to see if there was enough evidence to try the accused in a higher court. I talked to the homesteader and he agreed to set the value of the calf at $23.50, thus giving the J.P.s jurisdiction to try the case.

The trial was held in "Ma" Hassler's living room late Saturday evening because we couldn't hold court on Sunday. The accused pleaded guilty and were sentenced to the most severe punishment the J.P.s. could give them – six months in jail. In sentencing them, one of the J.P.'s said it was a serious crime in a community where most people were on government relief. Any theft was serious, but to steal a homesteader's cattle was particularly so. The accused, he said, had not just stolen a calf. They had stolen a future cow which, within a few years would not only be supplying milk for the family, but also more calves to help the complainant build up a herd of cows. This last argument had not occurred to me. But the J.P.s, both home-steaders, appreciated the complainant's loss more than I did. They ordered that he keep the meat and hide.

I rented "Ma" Hassler's two bedrooms, one for the prisoners, the other for myself. I hired a night guard to watch over them at the go-ing rate – three dollars per night. The next morning, Sunday, I left for Goodsoil with the handcuffed prisoners on the crowded seat beside me. As we crossed the Indian reserve we stopped at Indian George's cabin to tell his wife what had happened.

We made good progress through the pine forest along Lac des Isles, then the trail angled off into a wide road allowance cut through the heavy bush. The undulating, uphill trail twisted from one side to the other. We rolled in and out of mudholes full of water from recent heavy rains. I managed to get out of them until we came to a very large one. As I tried to avoid it, one side of the car slid into it. If I had been alone it would have taken me hours to get the car out of the hole, but with the help of two healthy prisoners, even though hand-cuffed, I hoped to do better.

When I asked them to help by pushing the car, Indian George re-fused and White George followed suit. As we sat there swarms of mosquitoes attacked us. The handcuffed prisoners were most af-fected. They eventually decided that helping me to get out of the mudhole was the lesser of two evils. We got the car out of the mud-hole, but not before the prisoners had been splattered with mud and water from the spinning wheels. I thought for a moment or two that I would not let them back into the car, but a cleaning with dry grass made them presentable enough. Indian George was in a foul mood. As we started off, he said, "After I get out of jail, the first time I see you crossing the reserve, I'll blow your effing head off." "We'll see," I said.

I remained at Goodsoil long enough to have a meal, to take the prisoners' fingerprints, and to type out a report which I would mail when I arrived "outside". I had planned on being at Meadow Lake, about seventy miles away, that night, but hadn't reckoned with the almost impassable thirty-mile trail to Loon Lake. Halfway there I broke a rear spring trying to navigate a large pothole. It took two hours to partially repair it, which included cutting down a tree to provide small blocks of wood to place under the spring, to keep the car body clear of the rear wheels. All the time the handcuffed prisoners stood around, muttering and swearing and fighting flies.

We arrived at Loon Lake in late evening. I put the prisoners in the Loon Lake detachment cell, and the car in the local garage to have the broken spring replaced with a new one. There were no new springs in the garage, so I gave the garage owner the one I carried, and asked that he order one for me so that I could pick it up on my way back to Goodsoil. I mailed my report that night. On Monday, after the broken spring had been replaced, we went on to Meadow Lake. I opened and closed the innumerable barbed wire gates without the usual grumbling. At least there were no potholes on this trail.

After putting the prisoners in the cells at Meadow Lake I discussed the case with Sergeant Coombes. He thought everything was fine. On Tuesday morning I caught the once-a-week train to Prince Albert and deposited my prisoners in the common jail that evening. I remained in Prince Albert that night. In the morning I returned to North Battleford by train.

Arriving in the early evening at the detachment, the duty constable informed me that the C.O. wanted to see me the following morning before I returned to Goodsoil. I knew then he had received my report and had been talking to Sergeant Coombes at Meadow Lake.

When I paraded before him I found a disgruntled C.O. He thought that the two J.P.s had no jurisdiction to try a "theft of cattle" case. I pointed out to him that I couldn't find anything in the Criminal Code which differentiated between "cattle" and "property". As the value of the calf was less than twenty-five dollars, two J.P.s had jurisdiction. That was my case. Even if they had jurisdiction, he said, he thought they should not have disposed of it. The case should have been tried by a police magistrate. I couldn't argue with his view. He ended our conversation by saying he had written to Division headquarters about it. By now I had begun to suspect the fine "Italian" hand of the Orderly Room sergeant, who was forever picking holes with the work done by detachment men, and who had undoubtedly brought the matter to the C.O.'s attention.

What the sub/division staff did not seem to realize was that if I had these two accused tried by a police magistrate, I would have had to take them to Goodsoil and keep them in the cell there until a police magistrate decided to travel 200 miles from North Battleford, at least sixty miles by team and democrat to the Pierceland district for the trial, taking him a week or more away from his regular busy schedule. In the meantime, all my work would be suspended while I played nursemaid to two prisoners. I didn't bother to tell them this, they should have known the problems that the C.O.'s suggestion would create. And all this time was in addition to the week or more it would take to escort the prisoners to jail and return to my detachment.

The C.O. asked how I was getting back to my detachment. I said I had left my car at Meadow Lake and hoped that I could be relayed there by various police cars. He buzzed for the Orderly Room sergeant and told him to get a car from North Battleford detachment to take me to Glaslyn, forty miles to the north – then Glaslyn would take me on toward Meadow Lake, until we met the Meadow Lake car coming to meet us. By late that evening I had covered the 110 miles to Meadow Lake, where I stayed overnight.

Before leaving on Friday morning I told the sergeant about my talk with the C.O. "I know," he said, "he called me when he received your report. I think the sub/division officer is wrong." Now I felt better. I didn't mind the C.O. saying the cases should have been tried by a police magistrate, but if the two J.P.s did not have jurisdiction I was in a serious predicament. Anyway, I could only wait for the reply from Regina. I arrived back at Goodsoil detachment at midnight Friday, just twelve hours short of a week since I had received the complaint from the homesteader in Manderson's store in Beacon Hill.

The only word I received about the case was when the sergeant made his next monthly visit. On a copy of the letter the C.O. had sent to Regina, was a "minute" to the sergeant. It read, "Please take up Part XVI of the Criminal Code (Summary Trials of Indictable Offenses) with Constable Kelly on your next visit to Goodsoil." We had already dealt with this at Meadow Lake when I returned from taking the prisoners to jail. The case was on my mind when I went to Meadow Lake to visit the Coombes family over Christmas. I looked up the "calf" file and I saw a copy of a letter from the Deputy Attorney General saying that two J.P.s had jurisdiction to try a theft of cattle case where the value of the animal was less than twenty-five dollars. The C.O. had sent a "minute" to Sergeant Coombes in the form of a footnote. "Please correct this mistake on your next visit to Goodsoil." Sergeant Coombes had visited me several times since, but had never mentioned this to me. He had seen months before that there had been no mistake on my part, only on that of the sub/division office.

I had won a point, but it occurred to me that winning a point over one's superiors was not the best way to help one's career. However, it was not the last time I was to get into hot water about the jurisdiction of J.P.s in theft of "cattle" cases. But in the next instance, it was horses, not a calf.

There was a sequel to the calf case. Very late that fall I opened my door to a knock and found Indian George standing there. He had travelled the seventy miles from Meadow Lake that day, mostly on foot, and wondered if he could stay the night in the cell. He was on his way home from jail. I said he was welcome. He hadn't eaten since morning so I arranged for him to have a meal at the store where I ate my meals. As he went to lie down in the cell he said it felt like home. I asked him how he had got along in jail. "Fine," he said, "and they fed good." There was only one thing he missed, he said, without telling me what it was. I thought I knew. When I asked about White George, he said he had gone south, hoping to find his way back to South America.

It happened that I had a court case in Pierceland the next day, I could take Indian George to the door of his cabin. As we passed over the frozen and snow-smoothed mudhole out of which he and White George had helped to push the car a few months before, I reminded him of his threat to blow my head off when next he saw me cross the reserve. He chuckled. "You know, I was so mad that Sunday morning after pushing that car out of that mudhole, that I was sure I would kill you when I got out of jail," he said. "But I've had a few months to think things over. If I hadn't stolen that calf I wouldn't have been in that mudhole."

As the trail passed within fifty yards of his cabin I was able to let him out of the car on the same spot where I arrested him. I often saw Indian George after that. I would stop and chat. He was always pleasant, and I got the impression that his involvement with the police in the calf case had resulted in his having a different, and better, opinion of the RCMP.

Indian George was not the only person to receive free lodging in the detachment cell. Before the "hotel" had been built, the Anglican Church student and the United Church minister always slept in the cell overnight when in the Goodsoil area. They continued to do so after the "hotel" was operating. Surprisingly, no complaint was forthcoming from the hotelier. He must have thought that they were travelling on a shoestring, which they were, and if they had not stayed at the detachment they would have found free lodging with a settler in the district.

The United Church minister, Frank Myers, travelled in a Bennett buggy, drawn by two horses; Andrew Scott, the Anglican student, travelled by saddle horse. Both had their headquarters in the Pierceland district, about thirty miles west of Goodsoil. Myers had his own cabin on the outskirts of the village of Pierceland. Whereas Scott lived with an elderly couple on a homestead. When both happened to be in Goodsoil at the same time, they tossed a coin to see who would sleep in the cell. The loser slept on the office floor.

The men had completely different personalities. Myers was easy going, slow talking, with an amusing quip always on the tip of his tongue. He seemed to be an ideal type, and could quite properly be called a lovable character. I always referred to him as the Will Rogers of the United Church. Scott, on the other hand, was overly aggressive and seemed unsuited for the ministry. When Scott left the area I inquired as to his whereabouts over the years, but never found any trace of him. I was led to believe that he had returned to his home in England. When Myers left, he did not travel very far. He went to a church at Maymont, Saskatchewan, about fifty miles east of North Battleford on the Saskatoon highway. He stayed there until he retired, more than forty years later. That was probably a record in the United Church. But to those who knew him, the length of his ministry in one place was no surprise.

1936, Beacon Hill, Sask. Andy Scott, the Anglican church student on his travels between homesteads.

Rev. Frank Myers' Bennett buggy
(a car with all the mechanical parts removed).

TWENTY-SIX

B y December 1936 I had been in the RCMP three and a
half years, but had not taken any of the three weeks annual leave. In 1934 I had asked that my leave be allowed
to accumulate, so that in due course I could request the maximum
leave allowed, 42 days, to visit my parents. They had left Canada because of my father's ill-health, and returned to Britain. I planned to
leave Goodsoil on December 1, so that I could sail from Halifax, Nova
Scotia, on December 5, on the *S.S. Montcalm*. To arrive in Halifax on
time I would have to leave Goodsoil and travel seventy miles in my
1928 Ford roadster to catch the 8 a.m. train at St. Walburg.

If I made train connections at North Battleford, Saskatoon,
Winnipeg and Montreal, I would arrive in time to catch the ship at
Halifax. I left Goodsoil in the early morning, allowing about four
hours to reach St. Walburg. Normally this would have been ample
time. The thirty-mile forest-lined trail to Loon Lake was frozen over
and snow had smoothed it out. From there it was graded highway.
But when I awoke that morning it was snowing heavily. With all the
arrangements I had made, I simply had to go.

Fortunately the wind was from the north, and as I had to go due
south, it helped me along until I came within half a mile of St.
Walburg, where the highway turned due west. Here, in the open
places, the north wind had built snowdrifts too deep to drive my car
through. In the clear, much-below-zero air, I could see and hear the
locomotive impatiently puffing away. There was only one thing for

me to do – start shovelling.

When I arrived at this point I had one hour to reach the train. Unsuitably dressed for snow shovelling, I nevertheless shovelled through snowdrift after snowdrift, arriving at the station ten minutes before the train left. It was just time enough for me to arrange with the station agent to store my car in the local garage, where it would be picked up by my replacement at Goodsoil, Constable Lloyd Bingham, some time later.

Hot and sweaty, I sat in the train as it travelled through the storm, which appeared to have increased in intensity, thinking that winter travel across the prairies could easily prevent me from making the necessary train connections. Everything went well until I reached Winnipeg, and there the Montreal train, from Vancouver, that I was to catch was two hours late. I went to the coffee shop for a cup of coffee and sat on a stool at the counter. A few stools away sat a man with a fairly short haircut, wearing a peculiar pair of grey socks, just like the RCMP issue socks I was wearing. Surely the haircut and socks could only mean one thing.

"Are you a member of the RCMP?" I asked.

"Why do you ask?"

I showed him my socks and pointed to my haircut.

"Yes," he said very quietly. Then he mentioned that he was there to ascertain if a man sitting over in the corner boarded the Montreal train I was to take. The "plainclothes" RCMP member went unobserved by the public, but to another member he stood out like a light beacon.

The train arrived in Montreal several hours late. But the Halifax train hadn't left. It wasn't until after the train left Montreal that I learned it had been held up because there were so many passengers for the *S.S. Montcalm* on the train coming from the west. The conductor assured us that the ship would await our arrival. It was the first time since leaving home that I felt reasonably sure I would sail.

Within an hour of arriving in Halifax the *Montcalm* sailed. By the next morning we were well out to sea, which was like a sheet of glass, and so it continued all across the Atlantic. I took part in the usual ship's concert in aid of Seamen's Charities, and sang two popular songs of the day, "Rose Marie" and "One Alone". One evening, in mid-Atlantic, we heard King Edward VIII make his abdication speech. He did not reveal anything about his relations with Mrs. Simpson that Canadians had not heard about for the past several months. But I was soon to find that the speech shocked the British nation to its boots.

I left Liverpool by train, in a heavy rain which continued all the way to London. I crossed the city by taxi to catch a train at Victoria station for Hastings on the south coast. I was met by a porter who said the Hastings train left from platform six, and he would see that my trunk was put on board. After a leisurely lunch I returned to find that the Folkestone train left from platform six, and that the Hastings train left from platform eight. As I peered over the shoulder of the ticket taker, I could see my trunk in the guard's van at the rear of the train, only a few yards way. I told the ticket taker I wanted to take it off, but he wouldn't listen to me. I realized he was doing his job. He couldn't let people through to take baggage off the train, but I did not want my trunk to go to Folkestone.

I could see the train guard, with a whistle in his mouth and a small green flag in his hand, walking back to the guard's van, ready to give the start signal to the train driver. I had no time to lose. I pushed passed the ticket taker, ran to the guard's van and pulled my trunk onto the platform, just seconds before the train started.

By then several porters had surrounded me, and in no time they were joined by a very pompous assistant station manager. No one was interested in my problem. They just wanted to know what I was "pullin' orff". When I saw that if I remained to make myself clear I would miss the Hastings train, I grabbed my trunk and dragged it out through the gate and along the platform to the Hastings train which was about to leave.

I handed my ticket to the man at the gate, dragged my trunk to the guard's van and put it aboard, still followed by the porter and the assistant station master. They were still asking me what I thought I was doing, but the guard was getting ready to signal the train's departure. I went to a train compartment and lowered a window. Someone mentioned the police. I said the police could see me when I arrived in Hastings, and as the train began to move I yelled, "I haven't come over 4,000 miles to lose my trunk in Victoria station." No police met me at Hastings.

It was still raining when I arrived there, and I had nine miles to go by taxi to a village named Staplecross. As the taxi driver tied my trunk on the space next to his seat, I asked him what condition the roads were in between Hastings and Staplecross. At first he didn't understand what I meant, then he pointed to the wet pavement, and with great deliberation he said, "Just like that Guv'nor, just like that." I chuckled to myself as we drove along the wet roads. When I had asked him about road conditions, I was only following a practice I had gotten used to in Saskatchewan. Anyone travelling in the backwoods felt it prudent to inquire about road conditions. My taxi driver, probably, had never travelled on anything but hard-surfaced roads, even in the most out-of-the-way places. Where I had come from the trails, and even some of the graded mud roads, changed from day to day and certainly from season to season. I had been in my parent's home some time before I remembered that I had brought a trunk with me. I went outside and found it at the side of the door in the pouring rain.

A few days later I realized again how far I was from Saskatchewan. I arrived at the Hastings railway station to take a train to London, only to find it moving out of the station. I asked a passing porter when I could get the next train. Taking a large pocket watch out of his uniform vest, he studied it for some seconds, then said, "In eight minutes, Sir." I was surprised and must have shown it as I asked, unbelievingly, "Eight minutes from now?" Giving me a strange look, he nodded and walked away.

How could he know that where I came from, if one missed a train in some places one had to wait twenty-four hours for the next one, in other places several days. In Meadow Lake, on the Prince Albert line, we waited a whole week. Eight minutes? That was carrying things to the extreme.

Several times during my stay I concluded that I preferred the weather in Saskatchewan to rain-soaked England. Sunshine and below-zero weather and snow-covered trails, were much better than continuous rain and hard-surfaced roads. I went into Hastings several times during my stay, and on one occasion went into a large hotel to watch a world championship chess tournament. All the world's best players were there, but it was the world champion, Alekhine, who drew my attention. His concentration was intense. All the time he played he wound all his hair into small spirals. When he felt over his head and could find no more unwound hair, he ruffled down the spirals and started all over again, without appearing to know that he was doing anything strange. Of all the things I saw in Hastings, this is the one thing that I remember best.

For the first time in more than eight years I spent Christmas with my parents, two sisters and a brother. Then I visited my grandmother, aunts and uncles in my native Wales. On the trains, in restaurants, on buses and on the streets, all the conversations were about Kind Edward's abdication. They may not have known about his relations with Mrs. Simpson until a week or so before, but the newspapers soon brought everyone up to date on the "royal romance" as it was referred to. I found it hard to believe that what we in Canada had known for months had been kept secret from these people in the "heart of the Empire". But that's the way it was.

By the time I had been in Britain for two weeks I wanted to get back to Saskatchewan. I was prepared to change the depressing British weather for the sunshine of that province, even though I knew I would be returning to much-below-zero temperatures for at least a couple of months. I had arranged to return to Canada so that I would report at North Battleford on January 11, the day my pass expired. It was not to be. The return voyage was as rough as the outgoing was smooth. The *S.S. Montrose* wallowed in troughs forty or fifty feet deep, then rose to the crest of waves equally high for a minute or two before falling back into a trough. No one dared to go out on deck. It was rumoured that even the captain was seasick. There were few passengers who were not, and certainly many of the crew who served us daily were off duty.

The ship's log in the lounge, on which our daily mileage was charted, showed us that we stayed in the same place in mid-Atlantic for three days, and that was the length of time I was behind when we landed in Halifax. By the last day but one, the storm had subsided enough for the usual ship's concert to be held. As I disembarked, although 2,000 miles from Goodsoil, I felt that I was home. I had left my native Wales only nine years before, but it held no appeal for me now, and would never again, as a place to live. To make me feel more at home, I saw a red-coated member of the RCMP on duty in the embarkation shed.

As soon as I cleared Customs I telephoned my C.O. at North Battleford. I was greeted with, "Where are you calling from, mid-Atlantic? We heard there was a bad storm and wondered about you." I told him that had been the reason for the delay in getting back. Then he said to "hurry home", because he was making an inspection trip to Goodsoil and I could accompany him. I couldn't hurry any more, my time of arrival was in the hands of the railroad people. I spent a night in North Battleford before starting out on the 170-mile journey to Goodsoil. The C.O. had hoped not only to reach there that day, but also to inspect the detachment and return to Loon Lake that night. Good roads and good weather would have made such a trip very pleasant, but unfortunately it had snowed heavily a few days earlier. On the C.O.'s instructions his chauffeur put an extra shovel in the car.

In the cold Saskatchewan sunshine we shovelled ourselves out of several snowdrifts, and twice our car was hauled out of deeper ones by local farmers' teams. At one such place the C.O. wondered if the farmers hauled snow onto the highway in order to create work for themselves.

As we waited for a team to arrive I thought of the taxi driver back in Hastings. If he had been with us on this occasion he would have known exactly what I meant when I queried him about road conditions. The delays meant that we had to stay in St. Walburg overnight, and go the remaining seventy miles to Goodsoil the next morning.

Bingham, my replacement, was anxiously awaiting my arrival. When I didn't turn up on the appointed date, he began to wonder if I was returning at all. He did not appreciate the possibility of staying at Goodsoil any longer than planned. The inspection by the C.O., and the turning over of the detachment to me by Bingham, was done poste-haste.

I had no time to discuss with him matters that had occurred during my absence. "It's all in the files," he said. I had been back in Goodsoil about two hours when I said goodbye to the C.O. and Bingham. As I sat at the table which I used as a desk, with the pot-bellied stove throwing out a great heat, I realized that Bingham had taken his sheets and blankets off the bed, and so I went to make it with my own. I was "home".

It was good to be back at Goodsoil, even though I could only look forward to cold winter patrols and no social life. My only enjoyment would be listening to my Northern Electric battery-operated radio. There were three stations which came in very clearly, CFQC in Saskatoon, CJCA in Edmonton, and KOA in Denver, Colorado, at night. My favourite program came from CFQC, which broadcast a program from the *Royal York* in Toronto each day at noon. It was light orchestral music with a baritone soloist named Stanley Maxted. I often wonder how I would have gotten along without that radio.

I spent most of my spare time studying the statutes, both provincial and federal. I often wondered if my interpretation of the statutes was correct, but I approached them with the training division's criminal law instructor in mind. "Don't look for hidden meanings," he had said. "Just take the ordinary meaning of the words." I was glad to remember this. I hadn't the ability to look for hidden meanings. There were times, however, when, if I had had the luxury of a telephone, I would have called Sergeant Coombes at Meadow Lake for some enlightenment. On one occasion, at least, it would have saved me getting involved with my C.O. again over the jurisdiction of J.P.s in dealing with a theft of horses case (See chapter 27).

There was considerable difference in researching the statutes when the results had to be applied to a criminal case in hand, rather than when it was done for a classroom exercise. On detachment one's wits were sharpened when research was done for the purpose of advising J.P.s on the law, so that they could act within it in dealing with accused persons they were trying.

Studying the statutes was like panning for gold. I found that the definition of "cattle" in the Criminal Code meant not only those animals of the bovine species, but also a horse, ass, mule, swine, sheep or goat. I also discovered that "day" meant between the hours of 6 a.m. and 9 p.m., and "night" the rest of the 24 hours. I began to find out how little I remembered of what I had thought I had learned in training. Then I learned it for the purpose of an examination. Now I had to learn it all over again for a more serious purpose. Not surprisingly, this time it stayed with me.

Because of the preciseness required when dealing with the wording of such things as the laying of charges, and the need to know what kinds of offences had been committed, each discovery was a nugget. Although one used the Criminal Code procedures in prosecutions arising from Federal Statute offences, it was good to know where to look to find the authority to do so. It was important to know where to find definitions of various terms used in different statutes, and even in different parts of the same statute. Similarly, knowing when one spouse could give evidence against the other, and the weight placed on the evidence of an accomplice, was important to a prosecuting policeman far from the advice of more experienced members. Such knowledge was the basis of a policeman's efficiency.

The office statutes supplied to each detachment covered only the wording of the law. Fortunately I was assisted by a *Crankshaw's Annotated Criminal Code*, for which I had paid in 1934, the princely sum of twenty-one dollars. I never left the detachment without it. With it, and my Rogers and Magone *Police Officers Manual*, I felt that I had all the answers, if I could find them, to all the questions that could arise, whether court was held in a homesteader's cabin, on a lake shore, or even in a country store. Crankshaw not only stated the law but also, through rulings of previous cases, interpreted it.

The service that country Justices of the Peace have given to the administration of justice in Canada has gone unheralded. For little or no pecuniary advantage they have been true servants of the communities in which they lived. They were usually men of substance within the communities, but were not expected to have a great knowledge of the law, even though they were well enough qualified to deal with the facts produced as evidence in a trial. The relationship of a prosecuting RCMP constable with J.P.s was akin to that of a judge in a high court to a jury. The judge directs on the law and the jury decides the case on the facts.

No small portion of a detachment member's work arose out of the enforcement of provincial statutes such as the Liquor Act, the

Motor Vehicles Act, the Game Act, the Fur Act, the Fishery regulations (made pursuant to the Federal Fisheries Act), and in Saskatchewan about sixty-five more statutes. This kind of enforcement arose from the contracts that the RCMP had with provincial governments to act as their provincial police forces. Before the RCMP absorbed the provincial police forces, the latter enforced three federal statutes: the Criminal Code, the Railway Act and the Juvenile Delinquents Act. Now the RCMP enforced these statutes along with the provincial statutes, but also enforced all other federal statutes when necessary.

All provincial statute prosecutions were by way of summary conviction procedure. Some of these prosecutions could be time consuming, both in preparation and prosecution as, for example, a charge against a bootlegger of "keeping liquor for sale". These cases always had expensive defence counsel. But one simple case I recall took up more time in research than it really warranted. The Natural Resources officer came to my office with a problem. He had warned some homesteaders several times about cutting slough hay on provincial land without a permit, and without paying the required fee – twenty-five cents a ton. His warnings having had no effect, he wanted to prosecute some of them as an example to others, but couldn't find a charge to lay against them.

After searching a number of statutes, using up most of my spare time over several days, I finally found in the Forest Act what I thought to be the answer. The definition of "tree" in this Act included anything that grew out of the ground, including bushes and grass. With this authority the officer laid charges against each homesteader, that he:

> on a certain date did cut trees to wit: grass, on provincial land without a permit, contrary to section – of the Forest Act of Saskatchewan.

I prosecuted each offender, and each paid a small fine.

TWENTY-SEVEN

There came a time when I became familiar with most of the contents of the Criminal Code, especially when they involved the jurisdiction of Justices of the Peace. But I was particularly surprised to find that under certain circumstances they had much more power than I had thought possible.

Before leaving Goodsoil for my holiday in Britain, I had begun to investigate a complaint about the theft of a team of horses. In my absence Constable Bingham had concluded the investigation, laid a charge, and set the date for a hearing to take place in the detachment office. The value of the team was put at $150, and the authority of two J.P.s allowed them only to send the accused man for trial by a police magistrate or a higher court, if evidence was adduced to make out a *prima facie* case against him. As far as I knew this was the proper procedure where the property involved exceeded the amount of twenty-five dollars.

One evening, before the hearing, I was perusing Part XVI of the Criminal Code which dealt with Summary Trials of Indictable Offenses. To my knowledge it had nothing to do with Part XIV, which dealt with Preliminary Hearings. But, to my great surprise, I found that section 776A of Part XVI (Summary Trials) could be applied at a Preliminary Hearing.

It said, in effect, that two J.P.s, sitting together, in Saskatchewan, were considered to be a "magistrate". As long as the conditions outlined in section 776A were followed, those two J.P.s, after having completed a Preliminary Hearing, could dispose of the case in the same way as if the accused had been convicted on indictment. They could even impose the same punishment as a higher court. I was amazed.

My mind turned immediately to the preliminary hearing soon to be held in my office. The conditions set out in section 776A were as follows:

> The Preliminary hearing had to be presided over by a "magistrate" or some higher authority; the case should begin as a preliminary hearing, and if the magistrate found sufficient evidence to commit the accused to a higher court for trial, he or they could then continue by having the charge reduced to writing (which had already been done for the preliminary hearing), and if the accused wanted to plead guilty to it, the magistrate could sentence the accused as though he had been convicted on indictment.

This meant that in the case I had in mind, two J.P.s could sentence an accused who pleaded guilty to up to fourteen years in the penitentiary. But, if after agreeing to proceed in this way, the accused changed his mind before pleading guilty he was to be committed in the ordinary way for trial in a higher court.

I thought I understood the wording of the section quite clearly, and my Crankshaw's code confirmed it. Still, if I had had a telephone I would have called Sergeant Coombes at Meadow Lake for advice. The best I could do was to discuss the section with the defence counsel, Mr. "Rookie" Blackburn, who I knew was going to represent the accused in the forthcoming case. Just in case he agreed with me, and wanted to proceed as provided by section 776A, I arranged for a second J.P., a Mr. Coupland, a local homesteader, to come to Goodsoil and sit on the Preliminary Hearing with Mr. Johnson.

On the morning of the hearing I discussed section 776A with Mr. Blackburn. He was interested. He said that if the J.P.s decided to commit for trial, he would have his client use section 776A. Justices of the Peace, he said, were not used to giving any more than the six months punishment provided by Part XVI for minor indictable offences, whereas high courts dealt out punishment far more severely.

The case began as a Preliminary Hearing, and when the two J.P.s, after hearing sufficient evidence, indicated that they were about to commit the accused for trial, Mr. Blackburn said that he would like to take advantage of section 776A. I had already informed the J.P.s that this turn of events might occur.

The steps in section 776A were followed precisely, and the accused pleaded guilty. Mr. Blackburn and I addressed the court on punishment. After an adjournment to decide on punishment, the J.Ps sentenced the accused to two years in the penitentiary. Mr. Blackburn blurted out, "You can't do that."

Mr. Johnson spoke for both J.P.s.

"But Mr. Blackburn," he said, "you have just told us that we could do it. Your client was liable to fourteen years in jail and we have given him only two. I don't think you can complain about that."

This was an old homesteader speaking. He would know what it meant to have a team of horses stolen from him. Mr. Blackburn then discussed a possible appeal, but he and his client decided that they would deal with the matter through the local member of parliament and the provincial Attorney General. The convicted man signed a Waiver of Appeal, which meant that I could take him directly to the penitentiary instead of his waiting in the common jail for the thirty-day appeal period to expire. As he left the detachment and said goodbye, Mr. Blackburn remarked, "We gambled and we lost."

As usual I typed out my report on the case so that I could mail it when I escorted the prisoner "outside". As I did so I was reminded of the time when my C.O. had raised "Cain" with me when two Justices of the Peace sentenced two men to six months in jail for stealing a calf worth $23.50. What would he think now of two Justices of the Peace sending a man to the penitentiary for two years for stealing two horses worth $150? I could only wonder. I was careful to point out that the unusual proceedings had taken place at the request of the defense counsel. But I expected to receive some criticism for not objecting to it.

When I arrived at Meadow Lake en route to the penitentiary, I stopped there overnight and discussed the case with Sergeant Coombes. He had never heard of J.P.s sending a convicted man to the penitentiary, and although, after reading it, he thought that section 776A permitted it, he said it would have been prudent to have proceeded by way of a Preliminary Hearing, leaving the trial to a higher court. Even a Police Magistrate, he said, required the accused's permission to hold a trial where the value of an item was more than twenty-five dollars. His view was clear. Technically I was right, but in practice I should have dealt with the case more cautiously. But as I said to the sergeant, section 776A must have been put in the Criminal Code to assist the police in isolated places such as Goodsoil. He didn't think that Goodsoil was that isolated.

I deposited my prisoner at the penitentiary and went on to North

Battleford by train, seeing that there was no train back to Meadow Lake from Prince Albert for a week. On my arrival the duty constable handed me a message from the C.O. He wanted to see me the next morning. I knew that by then he had read my report.

Much to my surprise, I found a very mellow C.O. when I was paraded before him. We discussed the theft of horses case, and when he mentioned the propriety of two J.P.s sending a man to the penitentiary I knew he had been talking to Sergeant Coombes. But, he said, the matter was now in the hands of "Regina", meaning the Officer in charge of the CIB and the Deputy Attorney General who handled RCMP affairs. We would be hearing from them in due course. Then there would be ample time to climb my frame, I thought. But whatever happened, I could always say, quite truthfully, that it was the defence counsel who requested that we proceed in accordance with section 776A.

Surprised as I was by the C.O.'s mild reception, I was even more surprised by what happened next. He invited me to sit down and said, "I think you have been at Goodsoil long enough, Kelly. I have been thinking of relieving you for some time, but had no man to replace you, nor any place to put you. Now I have both. Clear up your work on your return to your detachment, and I'll be writing you about the transfer in a few days."

Immediately I thought I was being transferred because of the case we had been discussing, but I recalled that on the last inspection he had told me that he didn't want anyone spending too long a period in a place like Goodsoil. "Isolated and politics ridden," he had said. I had found it mildly so. But I knew that information about the area was fed to my superiors by settlers known to them. Still, I didn't feel happy about the transfer. I had visions of being transferred to another backwoods detachment. There was one in the sub/division, Isle a La Crosse, about 100 miles north of Meadow Lake. It was more isolated than Goodsoil, and its only transportation was a canoe and outboard motor to travel over the detachment area's countless waterways.

With some diffidence I asked him where he was transferring me, and with considerable relief I heard him say, "They badly need an experienced Criminal Code investigator at North Battleford, one who can relieve on detachments. I think that you'll do nicely." I then thought that perhaps the "horses" case had shown him that I did indeed know something about the Criminal Code and its practical application, and maybe that had hastened my transfer from Goodsoil. As far as I was concerned it was no demotion to be considered "an experienced Criminal Code investigator" on the sub/division's busiest detachment.

I was relayed to Meadow Lake by various police cars, and by the time I arrived it was too late to begin the journey to Goodsoil, so I stayed the night. I told Sergeant Coombes and Constable Bingham of my transfer. The first question Bingham asked was about my replacement. I said I didn't know but I thought he would be the logical one as I had been there after having served at Meadow Lake. Bingham had similar thoughts.

"Do you think he's going to send me to that God-forsaken place, Sarge?" he asked Coombes.

Before the sergeant answered I couldn't help but needle Bingham a little.

"Bing," I said, "you are a cinch for the job. After all, the sergeant himself told me you were the best damn constable in the Force."

Before he could respond the sergeant answered his question, "You could be chosen, Bingham, but why worry about it? Your service at Goodsoil will count toward pension every bit as much as if you were stationed at headquarters in Ottawa."

Bingham knew he would not get much sympathy from either of us, and he was not amused. He muttered something about "that bloody place" as he went into the constable's room. The sergeant then raised the "horses" case. He wanted to know if the C.O. had mentioned it. I said he had been quite mellow and had said in effect that we would wait for Regina's reaction. The sergeant laughed. "He was quite 'hot' when he spoke to me about it; he's waiting for an answer from Regina before he'll explode on you from a great height."

"If he does," I answered, "he won't have far to go to find me. I'll be working out of the office next to his."

I was as happy about the transfer as Bingham was glum. "I know I'll be sent to that damn place," he muttered as we went to supper. He knew what Goodsoil was like. He had relieved me for the six weeks I was away in Britain, but I realized that something else bothered him. He had a girlfriend in North Battleford, whom he later married. At Meadow Lake he could take a day off, especially at weekends, and go to North Battleford over a good highway to see her. At Goodsoil, being alone, he could not get away as often, and it meant an additional 140 miles travel, seventy of them over a trail better suited to a slow-moving team and democrat than a car.

The next morning I left early for Goodsoil, taking down and putting up barbed wire gates for the last time. On previous occasions I had been glad to get back and settle into the work that awaited me. Now, knowing I was leaving permanently, I wanted to leave as quickly as possible. The letter confirming my transfer and, of course, my replacement, could not come quickly enough.

I was already looking forward to living in a small city, where I would not be expected to work fourteen hours and more a day, seven days a week, in a place void of any social activity. Keeping busy had been one way of taking my mind off such deficiencies. Nevertheless, I had gained much by having to serve alone in relative isolation, where I had to depend so much upon my own initiative and judgment.

Meanwhile, I attended to incoming complaints, knowing that if I could not complete any investigations my replacement would do so. During this period I began to get more information on some German-Canadians who were involved in German "Bund" activities with definite Nazi overtones. Bill Bendt, J.P., was alleged to be their leader. Further investigation by Bingham resulted in his internment, along with several others, when World War II began a year or so later.

Eventually I was officially notified of my transfer, and the name of my replacement – Constable Lloyd Bingham. He arrived with Sergeant Coombes one evening, and I immediately turned the detachment over to him. We discussed all outstanding matters. One of the outstanding reports that I had not submitted, which I would leave for him to submit, was the annual report for Statistics Canada (then under another title), on the state of the snowshoe rabbit in the Goodsoil area. I knew nothing about snowshoe rabbits, neither did Bingham. I showed him the previous annual reports, all of which were worded in similar fashion. I had followed the practice of my predecessors by reporting that there has been no change over years past. I am sure Bingham followed the longstanding practice.

That evening a few people with whom I had become friendly put on a "going away" party for me in Mr. Johnson's log cabin and they presented me with a signet ring. It was strictly a teetotal affair to which Coombes and Bingham had been invited. I told Bingham he had nothing to worry about. If I could live through a period of service in Goodsoil I was sure he could.

Next morning, as Coombes was seated behind the wheel of old 1092, ready to leave for Meadow Lake, he said to Bingham, as he had said to me nearly three years before, "If you run into any difficulty, you know where to find me." Then he drove off in a cloud of dust. I remembered when he said "goodbye" to me in similar fashion, and how I had stood watching the dust clouds made by his car until it went over the hill in the trail several miles south of Goodsoil. Now I myself was ready to leave, and I felt a little sorry for Bingham. At least when I took over I had a police team for transportation.

Bingham didn't have one. I had sold the team to the priest's letter writer, the old professor who lived with his daughter on a nearby homestead. But that was Bingham's problem.

As I followed in the wake of the sergeant, manoeuvring in and around potholes and mudholes for the last time, in my trusty Ford Coupé, the successor to the roadster, I recalled when I had first heard the name Goodsoil, in the guardroom in Regina Town station, soon after I had left the training depot. The constable had told me all about the lakes, rivers, forest and homesteaders. He also told me about its rough trails, long patrols by dogs and canoe, by car, by team and democrat, by saddle horse and even on foot. I had experienced them all, as well as a couple of patrols by float plane when I took the quinquennial census among the residents along the shores of northern lakes.

From that night in Regina it seemed that I was destined to be stationed at Goodsoil detachment. Every transfer since then had taken me closer to it. Looking back I realized how much I had learned about policing during my stay there; more than I would have learned at any other RCMP detachment. I had gone to Goodsoil as a green constable. I left as one reasonably experienced and confident.

I had been in North Battleford about a week when the sergeant in charge of the crime readers, those who dealt with reports from detachments, showed me a letter from the Attorney General. It was about my "horses" case. It said that "unfortunately" the procedure followed at the trial was perfectly legal, but it was undesirable for J.P.s to exercise the powers given them by section 776A of the Criminal Code. In a year or so this section was deleted from the code. During my stay at Goodsoil I had not made any law, but it seemed I was responsible for removing a small piece of it.

TWENTY-EIGHT

My transfer to North Battleford, a small city of 5,000 people, was not just a change in location, but a change in lifestyle. I now had no responsibility for the detachment administration, which had taken many hours of paper work.

My duties now involved only active policing. I investigated all sorts of complaints, including such things as assaults, thefts, suicides and accidental deaths. I made "burglary and safeblowing" patrols from midnight until 4 or 5 a.m. two or three nights a week, and often on weekends. There was no such thing as an eight-hour day or a five-day week in those days. Nevertheless, compared to my previous detachment, I had a great deal of time to myself.

My interest in music led me to become a member of the local Anglican church choir, because the man I now took vocal lessons from was its director. There were a cinema and library. I was only 170 miles from Goodsoil, but a million miles in culture, limited though it was.

In the same building as the detachment were the sub/division headquarters and the Criminal Investigation Branch (CIB). Members of the CIB worked in plain clothes and were given the added rank of detective for which they received extra pay. A detective constable received fifty cents a day; a detective corporal, seventy-five cents a day; a detective sergeant, one dollar a day. From a detachment member's point of view, it was not only the extra pay, although it would be willingly accepted, so much as the prestige that made the CIB so attractive.

Detachment members looked upon CIB men with a great deal of envy. They seemed to come and go as they liked, and were never called upon to serve on routine duties such as prisoners' escorts or night patrols. They dealt with the more serious crimes, such as murders, rapes and burglaries, some of which included safe-blowing.

My first investigation at North Battleford resulted from a complaint by a farmer that a twenty-foot logging chain had been stolen from his shed, alongside a major highway, about one mile from his home. I went to the "crime scene", and found the shed door unlocked, which would have allowed anyone passing by on the highway to have taken the chain.

There was a curved clay driveway leading to and from the shed. In the clay were a number of clearly discernible tire tracks which I presumed had been made after a rain about ten days before. I went back to the complainant and checked his car, but the tracks were not made by it. I returned to the shed and drew the tire tread patterns of four different tires in my notebook. As I returned to North Battleford I stopped at the town of old Battleford. Walking along the main street, where the cars were all parked diagonally, I naturally looked at the tires on the front wheels of the parked cars. I noticed the two front tires of one parked car had two different tire tread patterns, and they were the same as two I had drawn in my notebook. Checking further I found that the two rear tires had treads differing from each other and the two on the front tires. But the four of them were the same as those I had drawn in my notebook. This was too much of a coincidence for this car to be other than the one I wanted to locate.

I went into the local tavern nearby, made inquiries, and soon found the owner of the car – a son of the complainant. This was the answer to the tiretreads, but not to the theft of the chain, I reasoned. But without telling him immediately what I wanted, I asked if he had been to his father's shed near the highway recently. No, he said, he had no reason to do so. Surely, he was lying. I then told him so, and that I had proof of it, not being quite sure that I did. He still denied knowing anything about the chain, but when I told him I would have to search his farm, he admitted taking the chain to replace one his father had borrowed from him and never returned. He also told me he was a Justice of the Peace. I accompanied him to his farm and took possession of the chain.

When I told the informant about his son, he wanted to lay a charge against him and promised to do so. But after a few weeks he phoned to say that he wouldn't lay any charge. I agreed with him. I had had enough experience with family matters to realize that laying criminal charges against members of the family usually created more problems than they solved. Case closed. But I thought, although it was a simple case, perhaps not worthy of a Sherlock Holmes, it was one deserving of a more satisfactory conclusion. Because the son was a Justice of the Peace, my report on him included an extra copy for the Attorney General.

The church choir in which I sang had entered the local singing festival. Because of the difficulty our pianist was having with piano accompaniments, the choirmaster asked an elderly woman in the soprano section if her daughter could help. She said her daughter was busy with her own children's choir, practising for the festival, but she would ask her daughter if she could help out. At the next choir practice we had the benefit of a new pianist. After the practice the choirmaster asked me if "I would drive Miss Hickson home." She lived at the Mental Hospital, three miles out of town, where she taught the children of the doctors and attendants in their own school. I readily agreed.

On the way she told me that when the choirmaster first approached her, he had said that he could get her a ride home because a "young mountie" (I was 27 years old) sang in his choir and he would drive her home. She assured me that this was not the reason she decided to play for the choir. She had agreed because of the pressure put on her by her mother. This young lady continued to play for our practices and I continued to take her home. I have driven her home many times since then, during our more than fifty-nine years of marriage.

One morning the corporal told another member and me that we would be going with a CIB "team" that evening to somewhere out of town. Later, the CIB sergeant, the same roly-poly detective sergeant I had driven from Loon Lake to the Goodsoil area some years before, told us that we would be going that night to Maymont, a town forty miles east of North Battleford on the Saskatoon highway.

He had received information that safeblowers, that night, would blow the safe at a store in which large sums of money were kept to pay farmers for grain they delivered to the local elevators. He hoped we could surprise them. "Wear civilian clothes," he said.

Along with the sergeant and two other members of the CIB, we two detachment men drove to the store after dark, in two cars. On the way the sergeant told us that he expected the safeblowers to enter the store through a basement window. We went in through a back door which led into the warehouse, then into the store proper. A CIB man remained outside in a police car, where he couldn't be seen, in case the criminals tried to escape from the store. The other CIB man hid behind bags of flour in the warehouse through which the safeblowers would have to pass on their way to the safe from the basement. His job was to prevent any possible escape through the back door. The safe was in the main part of the store, to the immediate left of the door leading from the warehouse.

The store was rectangular, with a long counter on each side running from front to back. At the back of the store was another counter joining the two side counters. The other detachment man and I placed ourselves halfway down the store, each behind a long counter, to prevent any attempt at an escape through the front door. The sergeant sat in a corner about thirty feet from the safe, along the end wall under the light switch, in the dark.

When the time came he would throw on the switch and place the safeblowers under arrest. The planning appeared sound. The only thing now was for the safeblowers to turn up. The sergeant had also told us he had spent many a night when the safeblowers hadn't turned up, even though he had received "sure" information on a proposed safecracking.

As we sat in the dark, the sergeant decided the wooden box on which he was sitting was too "bloody hard", so, in the dark, he got a bag of sugar from the warehouse. He amused us with his remarks to and from the warehouse, not only about the weight of the sugar but also when he bumped into objects behind the counter as he returned. After a while he complained, "If they don't come bloody soon I'll be heading for home." This sort of thing might have been routine to him, but we two detachment men found it exciting, and pleaded with him in whispers not to give up so early.

After the last of several such pleas, we had just stopped talking when we heard the tinkle of broken glass. The safeblowers had broken a basement window. In the ensuing silence we strained our ears to catch any sound that would tell us the safeblowers were inside the store, on their way to the safe. It took so long for them to get to it we wondered if they had entered at all. Suddenly a flash of light appeared at the safe. I was sure they would see the sergeant, but they went about their business, laying out their paraphernalia on the floor in front of the safe.

We all knew the technique safecrackers used. They boiled down dynamite sticks to obtain a small bottle of nitroglycerine. Using soft soap, they made a channel around the safe door, poured nitro-glycerine into the channel and let it seep around the door. They then put an explosive cap on the end of a few feet of fuse, and secured it in a small pool of nitroglycerine, in the soft soap near the combination mechanism. A few seconds after they lit the fuse the safe door would either be blown off, or sufficiently moved to allow access to the contents of the safe.

The sergeant had no intention of allowing the criminals to go beyond showing what they intended to do. For police purposes, finding them in the store with safeblowing equipment, at night, within a few feet of a safe, was ample evidence on which to base a number of charges. We could hear the safeblowers mumbling between themselves, and I wondered why the sergeant delayed putting on the lights. I had taken out my Colt .455 and held it on the counter in front of me, as did my colleague behind the counter across from me. The sergeant had warned us, if there was any shooting, to be careful that we did not shoot each other. Suddenly the sergeant shouted in the dark, "Put up your hands, you are under arrest!"

There was a sound of scrambling. In about five seconds, which seemed like five minutes, the lights went on, revealing two men standing at the safe with their hands in the air. As we approached them we saw their paraphernalia on the floor. The CIB man came in from the warehouse, and I opened the front door for the man who had been watching outside. He brought in a man who he said had been the "look-out" in the "getaway" car. The store owner turned up, pleased that there was no more damage than a broken basement window. We were soon on our way back to North Battleford with the three prisoners and their equipment.

We teased the sergeant about the arrest of the safeblowers in the dark. "I couldn't find the bloody light switch," he said. "I wanted to switch it on at the same time I told them they were under arrest." When we arrived at the cells, one of the CIB men told the night guard that we were turning over to him, for the first time in RCMP history, two of three safeblowers who had been arrested in the dark. We had our joke at the expense of the sergeant. But he had the last laugh. On the Remembrance Day parade on November 11, he paraded in plain clothes with the RCMP group, showing his many medals, including the DCM, MM and bar for bravery in the fields in World War I. He was full of surprises, this roly-poly sergeant. I was even more surprised when I learned he was a very low-handicap golfer.

I had done nothing in this affair but be present. Nevertheless, it had been a very satisfying experience with a certain amount of reflected glory. And indeed there was some envy on the part of other members of the detachment who might have been chosen to accompany the CIB men instead of my partner and me. To be involved, even in a minor way, with the arrest of three prominent members of the safebreaking fraternity had its own reward.

That year the C.O. kept his promise about my relieving at detachments. I spent three weeks at Cutknife detachment while the member went off to get married, he claimed. When they returned the married couple brought with them a three-year-old daughter. So much for the RCMP marriage regulations. There was hardly any work to do at Cutknife. It was "break-up" time in the spring. Travel was difficult for me and for anyone wanting to make a complaint to the police. The only interesting thing that happened was that I sang at Roman Catholic, Anglican and United Church services on the same Sunday. I spent several hours the day before looking over a Protestant hymn book with the Catholic Priest, before finding something suitable for the Catholic church mass.

I also relieved a corporal at Maidstone detachment for three months when he went on a refresher course. He had left his wife and small daughter in the large house, which gave me no choice but to use a box-like room attached to the separate office building as a bedroom. But it worked well. The corporal's wife, with whom my fiancée stayed, was always glad to welcome her when she came to Maidstone on weekends. I used to make an evening patrol every Friday to my eastern boundary, which took me within twenty-six miles of North Battleford. I hurried into North Battleford, picked up my fiancée at the hospital, and dashed back to my detachment area. Then I would resume checking cars as my fiancée hid in the back seat. This arrangement continued without interruption for some time. But one morning, after an inspection by the C.O., he and I walked to the local hotel for lunch. On the way, without breaking step and looking straight ahead, the C.O. tapped me on my riding boot with his riding crop and said, "Police cars are for police business, young fellow." I knew exactly what he meant. I hadn't been as smart as I thought I was. I might well have landed in orderly room, charged with using a police car for other than police business. After that friendly warning my fiancée travelled to Maidstone by train.

I compared the work on these "southern" detachments with that at Goodsoil. The actual work wasn't much different, except for the way I travelled to get it done. On these detachments I had a police car and good roads, a luxury I had been denied the nearly three years I spent at Goodsoil detachment. I had to get into the habit of calling the sub/division office or a neighbouring detachment if I needed any advice, and the Inspector always arrived unexpectedly for an inspection. Cutknife and Maidstone were the nearest detachments to North Battleford, along different routes, and always the first detachments visited on a tour of inspection by the inspector. So I had no advance notice of his coming from someone who had just experienced an inspection. At Goodsoil he had to write me a letter telling me what date he was arriving to make sure I would be at home to greet him.

Back at North Battleford I investigated the theft of a herd of twenty horses from a nearby Indian reserve. The horses had been driven to Montana by the three thieves, who had been arrested by the Montana State troopers. The thieves had been returned to Canada as far as Swift Current where they were waiting for an escort to take them back to North Battleford for trial. The roly-poly sergeant and I went to Swift Current to bring them back. It was midsummer. It had rained for several days and continued to do so. It rained so heavily that the windshield wipers could not clear the rain as it fell on the car. The roads were heavily rutted and we made slow time. The car radiator kept boiling over and we continually refilled it from the water in the overflowing ditches.

The sergeant had been stationed at Swift Current and knew the district well. At one place he told me to drive into a farmyard. As we did so a naked four-year-old boy was running around the yard patting his head as the rain fell on it. A woman had come to the screen door to see who had arrived. The sergeant knew the woman, and in keeping with his generally tactless manner, he shouted to her, "Is that little bastard crazy?"

"You would act crazy, too," she answered, "if you were four years old and this was the first rain you had seen."

Before the rain came the crops had been dried out. The woman said, "but with a little bit of luck we'll get enough rain now to help us next year." I realized that we were in "next year" country. We had travelled 200 miles due south to Swift Current. On the way back the highway was so bad that, instead of travelling the last sixty miles due north from Rosetown, we took the hard-surfaced highway east to Saskatoon. The better-gravelled highway from there northwest to North Battleford, was an extra distance of about 130 miles. But this way we were sure of getting our three prisoners back without the police car breaking down.

Even though we had difficulties on this 400-mile return journey, I could not help but compare it, favourably, with some of the team patrols at Goodsoil detachment, over trails where sometimes the horses nearly had to swim to get through the deepest water-filled mudholes. On the journey to Swift Current and return we were never far from a telephone, or from a garage from which help could have been obtained if necessary. At Goodsoil I'd had neither.

At one point in our journey, I reminded the detective sergeant of our patrol a few years earlier, from Loon Lake to Beacon Hill by team and democrat. The only answer I received was, "Don't remind me."

1938, North Battleford. It was not all work at North Battleford.

TWENTY-NINE

I was enjoying my life at North Battleford. I found the work interesting and my social life enjoyable. I had met the girl whom I would marry. She was also my accompanist and singing coach. The current RCMP marriage regulations permitted marriage after six years of service, not seven, as had been the case until recently. This meant we could marry, if permission was granted, on July 6, 1939.

The only time I didn't enjoy my work was when the regular corporal in charge of the detachment was sent to relieve at another detachment for a few weeks. The corporal taking over from him had been recently transferred to North Battleford from eastern Saskatchewan. There was a mystery as to why he had been transferred. He was a married man but did not bring his wife, and the detachment strength did not call for an extra corporal. He was an unpleasant type. His nickname was "Windy", and we all supposed he had got into trouble of some kind. But he didn't interfere with our work until he became temporarily in charge of the detachment. Up to then he had been something of a fifth wheel.

By this time Bingham had been transferred to North Battleford, after a relatively short stay at Goodsoil, and between us we carried the major portion of criminal investigations. As a result we had been relieved of any routine duties, such as night patrols, and it was accepted that we should not be employed as night guards in detachment cells. Immediately the temporary corporal took over, he changed our routine and detailed us for night guard duties. This interrupted our investigations and court work, because having been up all night we were allowed to sleep in until twelve noon. But with court dates already set, several times we had to miss sleep in order to attend morning court.

There was no doubt why the corporal was doing this. Although there had been no open breach between us, we had experienced enough of his personality to know we had no use for his overbearing attitude. As the second corporal on the detachment we had had little official contact with him, partly because we avoided him. But after he had been in charge for a week we could no longer hide our opinion of him. We argued with him about the delays in our investigations and made it clear that they were piling up. The time came when a clash of some kind between the corporal and Bingham and me was inevitable.

One Saturday morning I was preparing to go on patrol when the corporal said he would accompany me, not giving any reason. We travelled east on a well-gravelled road, then turned north on a lesser road, then east again on a heavily rutted mud road, made much worse by a recent heavy rain. As was often the case on such prairie roads, cars kept to the centre of the road, in the ruts made by other vehicles. In fact that was the only way a driver could keep the car from sliding into the ditch.

At one point a steaming team of horses came toward us. I stopped the police car, and the team, hitched to a heavy wagon, pulled off the road into a very wide ditch, leaving the road clear for me to proceed. As the team passed us I started up the car, and immediately the team bolted. We watched until it galloped out of sight. Then the corporal snapped that I was responsible for causing the team to bolt. I told him it wasn't my fault, and before we finished we had quite a heated discussion, which included many references to my stupidity. He ended it by saying that when we got back to North Battleford he was going to take me into the Orderly Room on a charge of negligence in the operation of a police car.

I drove along to the next intersection and turned back the way we had come. He wanted to know why. I said I had taken the wrong road. Another round of abuse. Actually I wanted to catch up with the runaway team. I saw them a few miles farther on, at a farm where the farmer was having trouble unhitching the team.

I stopped the car and walked into the yard, helped the farmer unhitch his horses and led one of them into the barn. As the farmer was tying his horse to the manger I asked if the police car had scared the horses. He laughed and said it was the fourth or fifth time they had been scared that morning, once by some birds flying out of a tree. Then he explained that the horses had been in the barn most of the winter, and he had taken them out that morning to take some life out of them. What they needed, he said, was some hard work. In fact, when they started up he didn't even try to stop them. He wanted them, within reason, to "run themselves out".

I told him about the corporal and asked if he would give me a written statement about what he had told me. He agreed. With a signed statement in my pocket I returned to the car. The corporal wanted to know why I was so long and I told him I was gathering evidence to use in Orderly Room when he took me there. His manner changed immediately, "You don't think I would really lay a charge against you?" he asked.

I said that I didn't care whether he did or not. We'd be in Orderly Room because I was going to lay a charge against him for the manner in which he had treated a subordinate. With that I drove back to the detachment. Upon arrival I went to the typewriter, put the usual report form in it, and typed the report heading:

Re: Reg, No. 12001 Kelly, W.H. Const.

Complaint of: N. Battleford, Sask.

Then I left the typewriter and went upstairs to my room, knowing the corporal had been watching my every move from his small office, and would hurry to the typewriter to see what I had typed. Although there was no wording of complaint it was a sign that I intended to make a report on the morning's incident. He would not know until much later if I had done so, because I would not have put the report through him in the ordinary way, but directly to the C.O. through the sub/division office. At first I was upset enough to report the corporal, but I cooled off and didn't do it, although I told my friend Bingham about the incident. Meanwhile, the corporal continued to give Bingham and me night guard duties, and our investigations continued to accumulate.

A few days later the corporal ordered Bingham to get a pail and go with him to the railroad section house a mile away, to get some lime for the stones around the detachment property. Bingham had visions of whitewashing them. When they arrived at the section house and the section man began to fill the pail, he found a hole in the bottom. The corporal handed the pail back to Bingham with a large measure of uncontrolled abuse. Bingham dashed the pail to the ground, hitting the corporal on the ankle, and giving as much verbal abuse as he had received.

"Ha, ha," said the corporal, "I see you have been talking to Kelly." He didn't threaten to take Bingham to the Orderly Room knowing, perhaps, that it would give Bingham and me the opportunity to tell the inspector how the detachment was being operated. As he appeared to have come to North Battleford under mysterious circumstances this might not be in the corporal's best interests.

Eventually the regular corporal returned, and the first thing he did was check the complaint book. He saw how far Bingham and I were behind in our work. We were only too pleased to give him the reason. The corporal then called our antagonist to his office and closed the door. We got some idea of what went on when the duty detail was posted. The corporal was detailed as night guard. He remained on that duty until a week or two later when he was transferred to Edmonton, Alberta. It was the most unpleasant period in my thirty-seven years of service in the RCMP, so unpleasant that if it had been a permanent arrangement I would have applied for a transfer.

A few weeks after the corporal's transfer I met him in Edmonton where I had gone to escort a prisoner back to North Battleford. Because he knew me the corporal was detailed to meet me at the train. He greeted me as though I were an old friend. On the drive to the barracks he said, "I want to tell you something for your own good. They're a mean bunch here, Bill. Watch your step." I thought the only person I had to watch was the corporal, and that in the short time he had been in Edmonton the men there had taken his measure and acted accordingly.

My social life at this time consisted mainly of events associated with my singing. I had won first prize in the baritone class at the local festival. My fiancée suggested that I sing at the provincial festival in Saskatoon the next spring, as the win permitted me to do. If I won my class there, I would be allowed to sing a piece of my own choice in the open class for the winners of all voice categories. I plodded along with my fiancée's coaching and learned the *Prologue* from *Il Pagliacci*. Although I was the only contestant in my class in Saskatoon, my marks were high enough to allow me to compete later in the open competition.

Then I learned who else would be in that competition. For several years I had been listening to them over radio station CFQC in Saskatoon. I didn't think I was in their class at all. But win or lose there was the adjudication to be considered, always of some value to young singers. With my fiancée as my accompanist I sang the *Prologue*. The adjudicator spoke at some length about the singing of each of the others, beginning from the top with the sopranos, then the mezzo soprano, then the tenor. When he passed me and went on to criticize the bass singer, I was sure I wasn't good enough even for an adjudication. Then he said, "and now we come to the baritone – a clear winner." That was all the adjudication I received. This win was to change the direction of my career in the RCMP.

Unexpectedly as usual, soon afterwards I was transferred "permanently" from North Battleford to Maidstone detachment, sixty miles west on the Edmonton highway. It was a one-man detachment but important enough to have a corporal in charge, the one I had replaced for about three months the year before. He was transfered to Depot Division as a Criminal Code lecturer. The transfer itself was not a surprise, since I had grown used to being moved unexpectedly. It was a surprise, however, in view of my relatively limited service, to be transferred to a corporal's detachment with married quarters. Also, there were constables senior to me waiting for detachments, as well as those already in charge of constables' detachments who were in line for more senior detachments. My transfer indicated progress. I put it down to my earlier experiences in Goodsoil, and the fact that I would get married in a year's time. I wasn't to know the real reason for another ten years.

I was well acquainted with the Maidstone area. It was basically an English-speaking district with a long established French-speaking area and a negro settlement. The people in the detachment area were mainly law abiding. In addition to dealing with such minor criminal offences as thefts and assaults, and offences under the provincial Liquor and Motor Vehicles Acts, among others, I patrolled the highway by day checking on traffic, and by night I was on the alert for travelling criminals, particularly safeblowers.

There was only one lawyer in Maidstone, and I wondered how I would get along with him because of an incident when I had relieved the corporal the year before. I had arrested a farmer for being in charge of a car while intoxicated, and had placed him in the detachment cell. Soon afterwards the lawyer arrived, saying that he represented "Roly". I woke the sleeping Roly, telling him his lawyer was there to talk to him. Roly looked through the bars and said he didn't want a lawyer. To impress Roly the lawyer said he had been engaged by Roly's girlfriend. Again Roly said he didn't want a lawyer. When the lawyer persisted, Roly shouted at me, "Throw the bastard out."

After several further attempts by the lawyer to speak to the prisoner, and the latter's insistence that I "throw the bastard out," I asked the lawyer to leave as it had reached the stage where he was making a nuisance of himself. When he kept insisting that he had a right to remain in the detachment, I threatened to eject him. Up until then he had been standing at the cell door, but now he sat on a chair by my desk. I asked him again to leave. When he refused I opened the office door and dragged him outside. Before leaving he shouted that he would complain to my C.O. about the abuse he had received. He must have done so immediately, because in a short time my C.O. telephoned asking about the complaint. I told him the story, and he said that he would send a CIB man down to look into the matter. After all, a complaint of abuse of a lawyer who wanted to see a prisoner client was a serious matter.

I took a signed statement from Roly in great detail, in which he stated his reasons for not wanting his local lawyer to represent him. Some weeks before they had gone to North Battleford, where they became drunk. When he sobered up, Roly found his pocket watch was missing. He accused the lawyer of stealing it. Why would the lawyer steal his watch? Because they had run out of money and the lawyer wanted to buy more liquor. The CIB man investigated and submitted his report. The next I heard of the matter was when I received a copy of a memorandum from the C.O. of the Division in Regina, Deputy Commissioner Ryan. He said that if there was any complaint to be made against me, it was that I should have thrown the lawyer out of the office much sooner.

With this incident in mind I went to Maidstone, wondering what my relations with the lawyer would be. I had not been in Maidstone more than an hour before he came to the office and welcomed me, hoping to let "bygones be bygones". We became reasonably good friends and cooperated in putting on concerts for local charities. He was the first person I had ejected from a detachment office, but he was not to be the last. The next ejection was also at Maidstone.

My social life in Maidstone was very limited. I sang solos in the local United Church and participated in several local concerts. I occasionally went into North Battleford to sing in some church services there. At Maidstone I got to know both the Anglican minister and the local Catholic priest, a rotund, jolly French-Canadian, quite well. Both of them often visited the detachment after they had picked up their morning mail at the post office. One morning, with the Anglican minister present, Father Gauthier said he wanted to tell me about something which had happened recently in the community.

As though the Anglican minister was not present, he said that the "dean" of the black settlement, a man known to all as Virge, had asked the priest if it was possible for his "flock" to join the Roman Catholic church. The priest's answer had been that as the blacks were Protestants, they should try to link up with another Protestant denomination. He referred Virge to the Anglican minister. When he did, the answer Virge got was that he and the minister should pray for some guidance from the Lord. They met several times but neither had received any word from the Lord. But one day Virge told the minister that the Lord had spoken to him. "What did he say?" asked the minster. Hesitantly, Virge told the minister that the Lord said that he himself had been trying to get into the Maidstone Anglican church for years, and hadn't been able to do so. "Virge," the Lord said, "if I, the Lord, can't get into that church, what are the chances of a poor old negro like you getting in there?"

As he was ending the story the priest edged to the door. With a good belly laugh he finished his story and hurried out. Mr. Atkinson, the Anglican minister, who had sat through the story without saying a word, simply shook his head and said, "What next?"

One day I received a visit from two women who complained that the owner of a hotel in Waseca, a village a few miles west of Maidstone, was "running a card game" and their husbands were losing money there that should be going toward food and clothing. There wasn't much I could do alone. I made patrols to Waseca in the late evening, visited the hotel, and without a doubt disrupted whatever gambling was taking place. But this was no way to gather evidence on which to base a charge of "keeping a common gaming house" against the hotel owner. I reported the matter and requested that an undercover man be sent to Waseca, get involved in a gambling card game, and obtain the evidence required.

My nocturnal visits had some effect. The hotel owner visited the detachment. When I asked his business with me, he pulled a wad of bills from his pocket and laid it on the desk. I asked him what it was for. He said it was mine for *not* visiting his hotel. It took me a moment or two to realize that this was an attempt to bribe me to overlook his gambling game.

I should have played along with him and built up evidence on which to charge him. But my temper got the better of me. Before I realized what I was doing, I walked around the desk, grabbed him, and ejected him as forcefully as I could through the office door. I went back into the office, saw the wad of bills, and threw it out after him. The bills flew all over the place. As I watched him pick them up, I realized what I, stupidly, had done. The wad of bills could have been important evidence. This was poor policing, and I felt badly about the way I had handled the matter. Properly dealt with I would not only have stopped the gambling at the hotel, but might well have convicted him on a charge of attempted bribery. Later, not having counted the money he offered, I could only wonder how much he thought my cooperation was worth.

I continued to feel badly about the inept way I had handled the attempted bribery. I did feel somewhat better when two RCMP plainclothes investigators from Regina came into the detachment office one evening soon afterwards with the hotel owner in tow. They had joined in a card game in the hotel and obtained the required evidence. Helped by the local lawyer, he obtained bail that night and a week later he pleaded guilty of keeping a common gaming house. He was fined substantially. This ended the card games, but I continued to feel badly about my own ineptness.

It did amuse me, however, to think that the case had brought together the only two men I had ejected from a detachment office, at different times – the accused and his lawyer.

Not long after this I had occasion to go to North Battleford on police business. There I met the newly commissioned Inspector Metcalfe. He had come from Yorkton sub/division of the RCMP in eastern Saskatchewan to make inquiries of a confidential nature in a province-wide investigation. It was so confidential that only he could interview those concerned in the matter. One of the persons he wanted to interview lived in my detachment area – Maidstone. I was instructed by my commanding officer to drive him and his assistant, Constable Francis, to wherever they wanted to go in my area, and then to drive them back to North Battleford.

By the time they were ready to return to North Battleford that evening it was snowing. I suggested they might want to stay in Maidstone overnight, but the inspector insisted on going on to North Battleford, a distance of some sixty miles along a well-travelled highway in a straight easterly direction. By the time we started a strong westerly wind was blowing, sweeping the eastbound highway clear of snow. After travelling about thirty-five miles without any difficulty we passed the village of Delmas. After another couple of miles the windswept highway made a right-angled turn directly south, between open windswept fields. It was now dark.

The westerly wind had covered the slightly lower highway with more than a foot of snow, and had filled the ditches on both sides. Even worse, the blowing snow had cut down visibility to about 100 yards. We stopped to consider the situation. Then we decided that as we had only to go about four or five miles south before turning east, we should drive on.

After we had very slowly travelled an estimated one and a half miles, we found the snow on the road was deeper, the wind stronger. We encountered a near "whiteout". The car lights seemed to be hitting a cloud of fog. We decided to try to return to Delmas where we might stay the night. By this time we knew that the temperature must be well below zero Fahrenheit, and we became keenly aware that the police car had not been issued with a heater.

I tried to turn the car around while the others got out to guide me. But the snow and the danger of slipping into the ditch made us realize that our only hope lay in backing up the car until we reached the corner where we could head west to Delmas. I tried to back the car up but found it impossible to keep backing in the right direction. Because of the danger of landing in the ditch we considered abandoning the car, but had no idea where we could seek shelter. We had seen no farms on this stretch of highway. None of us were dressed for the weather we were facing. Francis and I wore everyday uniform and the Inspector was in civilian clothes. I started backing up again.

Francis volunteered to walk in front of the car to lead the way. But the poor visibility prevented this from being effective. I could not see him at all though the rear-view mirror on the 1934 Ford police car. The Inspector offered to get out and walk beside the car on the driver's side. He could then tell me, through the now open car window, which had been frozen in place until we managed to move it up and down, if I were not following in Francis's direction. We made slow headway. As the car driver I had some protection, but the inspector and Francis were in danger of freezing. A number of times we stopped so that they could get into the car to get warm. At one point Francis seemed utterly exhausted. But when I offered to take his place he said we had come so far he would continue to guide us.

Not the least of our worries was that we might run out of gasoline before we reached safety. We were also concerned that our over-worked engine might break down, leaving us stranded in the storm. But after several hours of stopping and starting we finally backed into the relatively clear road which led us westward to Delmas.

We had intended reaching North Battleford in time for supper, but it was 10 p.m. when we reached the village and its "hotel". We needed a warm bath more than a good meal, but there were no bathing facilities in the hotel. Because we had arrived so late, and so unexpectedly, the meal was one we might normally have complained about. That night we were just thankful to be eating anything in a warm, safe place.

We were also thankful to have extricated ourselves from a very dangerous situation, especially as we were ill-clad for the bitter winter cold. We realized that we could easily have been stranded in a snow-bound heaterless car, waiting for help which might not have come until the next day, perhaps too late.

By morning the snowstorm had abated. A grader had ploughed the southbound road and the sun was shining. Over breakfast the inspector and I agreed that Constable Francis had been mainly responsible for our being able to extricate ourselves from a potentially dangerous situation. The inspector promised to ensure he was suitably recognized for his part in the affair.

All three of us had learned a good lesson – don't take anything for granted when travelling in the wintertime in Saskatchewan, even on a normally well-travelled highway over a relatively short distance, even in a well-settled district. In winter one should dress appropriately for cold weather and possible worsening conditions. I had no contact with Inspector Metcalfe or Constable Francis after that incident. But within a few months Inspector Metcalfe had left the RCMP.

1938, Maidstone, Sask. Nora and me,
and the police car.

1938, Spruce Bluff, Sask. Visiting the farm of
Nora's relatives.

1938, Maidstone, Sask. At the detachment office door.

1937, Maidstone, Sask. Dog master Constable Lorne Cawsey and me with police dog Dale of Cawsalta.

1938, Maidstone, Sask. The future Mrs. Kelly and me.

1938, Maidstone, Sask. Police dog Dale of Cawsalta.

1938, Maidstone. Police dog Dale exercising on ladder.

1938, Maidstone. Dale and his pupil, Pilot.

1938, Maidstone. Experimental "snowplane", propeller-driven by a car engine on a high metal frame in the rear. Occasionally hired with driver to make a police patrol. It had insufficient power to be really practical.

1938, Maidstone. Rear view of experimental "snowplane" showing car engine with airplane propeller on high steel frame.

THIRTY

During my stay at Maidstone detachment I received a second man in the form of a dogmaster, with his famous charge, Dale of Cawsalta. Constable Lorne Cawsey was the dogmaster and the son of Dale's original owner, Sergeant J.N. Cawsey. The RCMP had purchased another tracking dog before him, Black Lux, Dale's son. Dale was, however, the first tracking dog used in the RCMP. Sergeant Jim Cawsey had used him in southern Alberta, where Dale had gained a great reputation for his tracking ability, particularly in regard to lost children. He was a magnificent-looking Alsatian.

With Dale, Lorne Cawsey brought to Maidstone a six-month-old pup named Pilot, which he wanted to train as a tracking dog. The RCMP authorized the building of a substantial kennel for Dale, but he never used it. Both dogs spent their nights lying between our two beds in our sleeping quarters.

Dale was both a help and a hindrance. All other work stopped at Maidstone when a request came in for the use of Dale at some distant point. I had to drive Dale and Cawsey to wherever the dog was required. But Dale helped considerably when I took him and his master on highway night patrols. Without him I would have had to walk around the dozen grain elevators in several small towns in my area, vigilant against safeblowers. Dale did this much more quickly and efficiently than I would have done. Only once did he find anyone – a drunken man asleep at the foot of an elevator. I gave Dale the credit for keeping my area free of travelling criminals. Word would get around that a police dog was stationed at Maidstone, and this probably kept them away.

This was in the mid-1930s when Bing Crosby's popularity began to rise, and Cawsey was a great Crosby fan. Whenever Bing sang on the radio, as he very often did, Dale would turn over on his back and give off a high-pitched whine. Cawsey was sure the dog was showing his appreciation of Crosby's dulcet tones, but I would say he must be suffering excruciating pain. Cawsey didn't think it much of a joke.

Now, some sixty years later, I seldom hear the word marijuana without thinking of an incident that took place when I was stationed at Maidstone detachment. I went to a farm to make a routine enquiry. I complimented the farmer on the fine windbreak he had grown on the west side of his house. It was about twelve feet high and fifty feet long, very bushy and green. In an area where the wind blew almost continuously windbreaks were a great asset.

As I looked at the windbreak it occurred to me that it was the Indian hemp (marijuana) that I had read about in my *CIB Instruction Book* at the office. Not being sure I said nothing, but snipped off a twig and left the farm. At the office I checked the instruction book. From the description and the illustrations, I concluded that the windbreak I had seen was made up of Indian hemp. Although not a narcotic, it had been designated as such by an international drug convention to which Canada was a signatory. The instructions were to cut down any Indian hemp forthwith, wherever it was found growing.

Within the next few weeks I had cut down several Indian hemp windbreaks, much to the disgust of, but with the help of the farmers concerned. They found it incomprehensible that such an attractive and useful plant could be harmful in any way. With what little knowledge I had of drugs I tended to agree with them. But the instructions were quite clear. The farmers knew that if they continued to let the plant grow they were liable to a charge under the Opium and Narcotics Drug Act, as the Drug Act was then named.

About a year later, as I was cutting down another Indian hemp windbreak at Hafford detachment, it occurred to me that I had not dug up the roots of the Indian hemp windbreaks in the Maidstone detachment area. I wondered if they had started to flourish again.

Maidstone, like other detachment areas, had its share of sudden deaths. As a result I got to know the coroner, Dr. Moran of Lashburn, very well. He was an elderly grey-haired man and looked exactly like the friendly and kindly family doctors portrayed in Hollywood. We spent a great deal of time together, travelling by car and sleigh, mainly to farms where sudden deaths had occurred. There were accidental deaths and suicides, but most deaths were caused by heart attacks.

One day, as we passed a farm, he mentioned that the woman who lived there thought he was the best doctor in the world. She had been complaining of stomach trouble for several years, but he could find nothing wrong with her. She insisted there was something wrong, and he told her that the only thing left to do was to have an operation to check. She agreed. The operation revealed that after an earlier operation, by another doctor, her innards had not been properly put back into place. Dr. Moran rearranged her innards and she had been well ever since.

Another story he told was about the visit of a Regina surgeon to North Battleford on the morning when a patient of Dr. Moran's was due to have a gall bladder removed. Dr. Moran, and the local surgeon who was assisting him, allowed the visitor to convince them that their diagnosis was wrong. Actually, the big city surgeon said the symptoms called for an appendectomy. He was invited to perform the operation. This he did, only to find a healthy appendix. Quite annoyed at being proved wrong, he proceeded to look for and remove the gall bladder, in a rather hasty and crude fashion, much to the disgust of Dr. Moran and his colleague. The patient required more than the usual time to get well, and Dr. Moran had to tell her that during the operation they had met with more difficulty than expected. But he never mentioned the actual difficulty.

This case led to the discussion of how doctors liked to "play God". This reminded him of a story that I initially heard from him but have heard from many other sources since. A doctor died and went to the gates of heaven. He gave his occupation to St. Peter and was told they were not taking in any doctors. "Try hell," said St. Peter. The doctor looked over St. Peter's shoulder and saw a man inside the gates in a white coat, with a stethoscope around his neck. "But," said the dead doctor, "you have a doctor in there, I can see him." "Oh, no," said St. Peter, "that's not a doctor, that's God. He likes to play doctor once in a while."

One thing I appreciated about this humorous doctor was that he always paid attention to the cause of death. There was nothing casual about the way he went about finding out. Often when we visited a farm he would open up the deceased person, usually on a door off a shed, to ascertain for certain the cause of death. It mattered not to me what was the cause of death, as long as it did not involve a criminal offence on the part of someone. His meticulous attitude arose from an experience he had had as a young doctor, when he had practiced in another district.

He and a member of the RCMP had concluded that the death of a farmer was by natural causes, until he received a call from the undertaker. He told Dr. Moran that when preparing the body for burial he had come across what looked like a bullet wound in the back. Dr. Moran and the policeman hurried to the undertaker's and found that the death had been caused by a .22 calibre bullet. A further police investigation led to the laying of a charge against the dead man's neighbour.

I learned a lot from Dr. Moran in dealing with sudden death cases, but even before meeting him I had gained considerable experience when I accompanied a Dr. Hamelin at North Battleford to check on sudden deaths. Sometimes it was necessary to obtain body samples for testing at the crime laboratory. Dr. Hamelin thought it great fun to hand me a pipette and tell me to suck into it liquid from around the kidney region. The doctor always gave me the job of opening up the skull so that he could take a brain sample. I then put everything back in place so that no one could see that the skull had been disturbed in any way. I used to tell the doctor that he only took me along to do the hard work. Actually, my presence was necessary in order to tell a court, if a prosecution resulted, that I had been present when the sample was taken from a specific body, and that I had carried it to the laboratory and handed it over to a specific scientist.

At North Battleford I had dealt with several suicides by mental patients at the provincial mental hospital. In each case it was necessary to conduct an inquest, but seldom was it necessary to have a post mortem. The provincial authorities rarely thought of appointing a lawyer to handle the inquest, and this became my job.

But on one occasion, because a well-known pathologist from Regina was taking treatment at the hospital for drug addiction, it was decided that he should conduct a post mortem for the edification of the local doctors. Dr. Hamelin suggested that I should open the skull because of "my experience". After the post mortem had been completed the visiting doctor congratulated me on the job I had done on the skull. Dr. Hamelin heard him and said, "He should be good, he's a student of mine."

I planned to get married on July 6, 1939, when I had completed six years of service. I looked forward to staying at Maidstone where there was a suitable house for a married member. But in April of that year, unexpectedly again, I was transferred to Hafford detachment, forty miles east of North Battleford on the Prince Albert highway. Hafford was a corporal's two-man detachment with both married and single quarters.

I would not have been surprised if I had been transferred to a constable's detachment without married quarters, but I was doubly surprised, after being at Maidstone for less than a year, to be transferred to another corporal's detachment where I had a second man. I had less than six years service. Obviously there was a message in these moves, but I failed to see that replacing a corporal with over twelve years of service meant anything more than that my C.O. felt I could do the job. About ten years later, after his retirement, he told me the reason for my surprisingly fast progressive transfers. He told me that he had hoped to see Constable Bingham and me achieve commissioned officer status. There wasn't the slightest suggestion at the time that he had this in mind. I did think that if I was able to handle the responsibility of a two-man detachment, I might expect a promotion in due course.

Two things of some slight significance took place in the RCMP while I was at Maidstone. Division headquarters in Regina sent out a memorandum to all detachments, saying that on a certain date we should listen to a Regina radio station which would begin broadcasting information of interest to detachment members, such as recent crimes and wanted criminals. The only problem was that Maidstone and other detachments in the North Battleford sub/division were beyond the range of the Regina radio station. But it was progress of a kind, the beginning of the RCMP's present-day countrywide communications network.

The other progressive step had to do with the comfort of RCMP members. Until then no RCMP car had been issued with a heater, although some members had purchased their own. When those members were transferred they took their heaters with them. Before this the story went that the supply officer in Ottawa was an old northern man who had travelled by dog team for many years. He could not see that there was any need for the luxury of heaters in police cars, and all applications for them were arbitrarily turned down. Things were about to change, but about that time police cars in the RCMP had only been in general use less than fifteen years. At Maidstone I was "issued" with a car heater.

There were many things that would change in the following few years. Later there would be no need to use an upended orange crate as a typewriter table, as I had to do when I took over temporary charge of Glaslyn detachment; or use a kitchen table as a desk as I had done at Goodsoil; or purchase a desk from the outgoing member, as some incoming members had to do. In Meadow Lake the sergeant had purchased a rolltop desk when he arrived there, to replace the table being used, and my typewriter table at Goodsoil had been made locally. Slowly, necessary office furniture was purchased, but then only grudgingly. Under these circumstances, supplying car heaters was a great step forward.

While I was still at Maidstone, I became engaged to be married, without a ring. There was no jeweller in Maidstone so I had to wait until I escorted a prisoner to Prince Albert.

THIRTY-ONE

I had not forgotten my singing success at the Saskatchewan Music Festival the previous year. By mid-1939, soon after I had been transferred to Hafford detachment, I had the idea that I would like to have my voice trained, with a view to becoming a professional singer. As far as I was concerned there was no place closer than Toronto, Ontario, where I could do so. I believed that I would have to leave the RCMP, but before doing that I went to Toronto in July 1939, to get an opinion on my voice from a vocal teacher. His view was favourable, and I returned to North Battleford with the intention of applying to purchase my discharge. My fiancée had accompanied me to Toronto, and because it was known that we had to postpone our marriage plans, because the six-year waiting period had been extended to seven years, I was kidded about the purpose of our going there together. My colleagues were not being facetious when they accused us, wrongly, of going there to get married.

On my way back to Hafford I asked to see the C.O. at North Battleford, to tell him what I intended to do. I felt rather badly about it because of what he had obviously done to further my career in the Force. I had it figured out that I would have to pay five dollars for every month of unexpired service, and as I had signed on for five years in July 1938, this meant a sum of $240. To my great surprise the C.O. was sympathetic to my plans. He said he had been in a similar position early in his career, and had always regretted not doing something about it. Rather than apply for discharge, he suggested that I should write a personal letter to the Divisional C.O. in Regina, telling him what I had in mind, and asking if it was at all possible to be transferred to Toronto. I should also tell him that I was writing to him personally on the advice of Inspector Spriggs, my C.O. This incident showed me something of the human side of the RCMP.

I followed the C.O.'s suggestion, and within a few days I received a personal letter from the divisional C.O., Assistant Commissioner C.D. LaNauze. He told me to make an official application for a transfer to Toronto, and that he would recommend it to the commissioner in Ottawa. A postscript said, "And good luck on your singing career."

What I didn't know until some years later was that the commissioner, with a probable war in mind, had asked western divisional commanding officers to recommend men with investigative experience for transfer to Eastern Canada. My application could not have been made at a more appropriate time. Within a couple of weeks my transfer had been authorized. I was instructed to clear up all my outstanding cases preparatory to leaving "F" Division (Saskatchewan), for "O" Division (Western Ontario) with headquarters in Toronto.

Meanwhile, I was attending to police work in the Hafford area. It was during my six months there that I encountered some events which gave support to the saying that truth is stranger than fiction. I received a call from a farm wife telling me there had been an accident. At the farm she led me to a field in which her husband had been ploughing. The horses were standing fastened to a gang plough. In a furrow immediately behind the plough her husband lay dead, with a shotgun near his body. He had been shot in the side and the ground nearby was saturated with blood.

A doctor arrived soon after I did and we listened to the wife's story. When her husband had not come in to lunch she went looking for him and found what I have described. He had always taken the shotgun with him to shoot crows, which were a great nuisance. In some way, she said, he must have accidentally shot himself. Although it might have been a case of suicide, after more questions there did not appear to be any reason for believing so. All I was really interested in was that no foul play was involved. The man's name was Peterson (not his real name).

A week or two later I received another call about an accidental death. A farmer and his wife and son, had been sitting down at the lunch table when a flock of crows landed in a field near the house. The seventeen-year-old son rushed out of the house, grabbing a shotgun as he left. Soon there was a shot and the mother and father thought that the son had fired at the crows. But when the son did not return the father went in search of him. On the way to the field the son had to take a very narrow path through some alder bushes. Apparently the cocked shotgun had caught on a branch, and the shot the father had heard was caused by an alder branch setting off the trigger. The boy had been shot in the side and had bled to death before his father reached him. The family name was the same as the one in the previous incident.

The third death I investigated, not long afterwards, was clearly suicide. A young man, known to have mental trouble, climbed a conical pile of split stovewood, put a rifle to his chin, and blew off most of his head. His name, too, was Peterson. Another feature of these deaths was that none of the dead persons was related, and the three families involved were the only ones in my whole area with the same surname.

Another case of interest occurred that summer. It had all the features of becoming an aborted case, immediately the police heard about it. One afternoon an elderly German bachelor farmer came to the detachment to make a complaint. He said that he lived about five miles east of Hafford, on the main road to the village of Krydor. That morning he had been in Hafford on business, and when he returned home he found that someone had broken into his house and had stolen three very valuable rifles. He valued them at $450, a large sum in those days. He gave me a description of the guns, and I entered all the facts in the complaint book.

By the time I was through writing I was anxious to go to his place to try to find any clues that would help me find the thief. I thought he might have left some tire tracks, or fingerprints, or even marks on the door frame where it might have been prised open. Also, I could check the area to see if any person had been seen around the farm that morning. When the complainant heard what I intended to do, he wanted none of it.

He said that such valuable guns could not be seen in the possession of anyone in the district without him being suspected of having stolen them. Then, said the old farmer, the police would be informed and only then should we take any action. I tried to point out the risk he was taking of the guns being disposed of without anything coming to police attention. Perhaps even as we spoke, I had said, the guns might be on their way out of the district. The longer we did nothing the more chance the thief had of getting away with his crime. Stopping police action, I told him, was simply assuring that he would never see his guns again.

But he still insisted that the police do nothing. His requirements were so strange that, for the first time, I had him as the complainant sign his name alongside my entry in the complaint book. When he left the office, my junior man, Constable Ted Burkmar, who had been listening to what had been taking place, shook his head and said something about "queer people". Whatever it was I agreed with him.

Early the next morning we received a visit from a very excited young man about eighteen years of age. He lived on a homestead north of the village of Krydor, he said, and his next words were, "Are you looking for some stolen guns?" I could honestly say that we were not. The night before, he continued, he had passed through the yard of a homestead on his way to visit a friend. From the yard he could see the homesteader in a shed. When he went to say hello, he saw that the homesteader was wrapping three beautiful guns in a gunny sack. Apparently caught unexpectedly, the homesteader said the guns had been left with him two days earlier by a stranger who asked him to deliver them to a friend down south. He planned to leave the next morning.

But before leaving for the south, he would first visit his brother about six miles west of his homestead, and go south from there. Before our conversation ended, I learned that the road he would take to get to his brother's place was an east-west road, about five miles north of the detachment. As he left, the young man said, "The guns I saw were pretty valuable. If no one has reported them missing yet, it won't be long before you hear about it." I thanked him for his information and soon Burkmar and I were on our way north to the east-west trail the homesteader was expected to take.

This trail rambled through a sixty-six-foot road allowance in heavy bush. I backed the car out of sight and waited. After an hour's wait, I was ready to return to the detachment and alert surrounding detachments to be on the lookout for the light delivery truck which the informant had described to us. Just then a light truck came along. Burkmar and I stepped out of the bush and stopped it. As I checked the driver's license Burkmar checked the back of the truck. In a gunny sack he found the three rifles. When asked what he was doing with them, the driver told us the same story as he had told the informant. A stranger had left the guns with him two days ago (one day before they were stolen) to take to an address down south. When asked for the address he couldn't remember it. I placed him under arrest.

Not being able to prove that he had stolen the guns, and remembering the lesson I had learned some years earlier on Loon Lake detachment in a theft of cattle case, I charged him with being in possession of stolen property valued at $450. Defended by a lawyer, he pleaded not guilty before a Police Magistrate. The prosecution evidence consisted only of that given by the elderly farmer and by myself and Burkmar about finding the guns. He was found guilty and sentenced to three years in the penitentiary. He signed a waiver of appeal which meant he would rather start serving his sentence than wait thirty days in the common jail for an appeal period to expire. It also meant that I could return the guns to their owner before he left for home.

After the owner had given me a receipt for the guns, he took fifty dollars from his wallet and offered it to me. I told him I couldn't take the money, but perhaps the informant would like it, and I would arrange for them to meet. I did so and I presume they met, as I never saw either of them again. Before he left I couldn't refrain from telling the old man how lucky he was to get his guns back. He wagged his finger at me and said, "I told you exactly the way it would work out." I had no answer to that.

About a week later, Burkmar and I were again in the same district. We were following a little-used trail when we came upon a young man sitting on the doorsill of the cabin he was building. Not knowing quite where we were I asked him for directions. In a high-pitched voice he told us. We had to turn back, he said, so we proceeded ahead a few yards to turn the car. Burkmar, who had a deep bass voice, said, "if he stood up his testicles might drop." As we were about to pass the cabin again the young man, now standing, stopped us to add to his directions. This time his voice was about two octaves lower. Burkmar and I couldn't help ourselves. We burst out laughing. Without saying a word we drove away, leaving the young man, I'm sure, wondering what had caused such an outburst of mirth.

In late August a date in October was set for my departure from Hafford. When World War II was declared early in September I wrote my C.O., suggesting that I could be of more use in an area that I knew well than in Toronto where I would be a stranger. Perhaps my transfer should be cancelled. He replied, saying that Corporal Spalding was on his way from the Eastern Townships in Quebec to replace me in the division. My transfer could not be changed.

Like many members of the RCMP, when war started I gave serious consideration to purchasing my discharge so that I could enlist in the armed services. Before I had a chance to do so, the commissioner stated in General Orders (G.O.s), that no discharges by purchase would be authorized. I had nearly four years to go on my current term of engagement, so there was little hope of enlisting for several years. In the following G.O.s, both the Commissioner and the Minister of Justice, the Hon. Ernest Lapointe, appealed to all of the members whose terms of engagement were about to expire, to consider staying in the Force for two main reasons. One, recruiting for the RCMP had been halted. Two, members of the Force would be expected to carry heavier loads in the future, not only enforcing the current laws, but also the new ones brought about by Canada's involvement in the war.

On October 12 my replacement arrived at Hafford and I left to stay overnight at North Battleford. I said goodbye to the C.O. and my friends the next morning. As I sat in the train the next day, waiting for it to leave, an RCMP member came aboard and handed me a letter from the C.O. In it he said some very nice things about my work and he ended by saying "Their gain is our loss." He could have said that to my face the day before, but didn't.

As I travelled east I had plenty of time to think over what I had done. My fiancée and I had set a date for our marriage the following July. Considering my police career, I could only think that I was giving up a fine opportunity by leaving the supervision of the officer who had done so much in such a short time to give me the opportunity to prove myself. I obviously left the sub/division with a good reputation. Now I would have to start building a reputation in the division I was going to. Any possible promotion would undoubtedly be delayed. But this was a penalty I would pay for doing something in my personal interest rather than in the interests of the RCMP.

What I hadn't counted on was the fact that the views held by my former C.O. on my work was recorded in the annual reports he had submitted on me. The original was sent to headquarters in Ottawa, and a copy was kept on my divisional file. I had no knowledge of what the reports contained, nor did I know that the latter would be forwarded to my new division. But Superintendent Schutz might have read them because he received me warmly. He was the officer in charge of the division's Criminal Investigation Branch.

He was also the 2 i/c of the division. We had met before under much different circumstances. He was the inspector at Regina who gave us the Criminal Code questions on Saturday mornings after the weekly inspection. I had failed to answer any of them. Now, however, he had told me he intended to make good use of my criminal investigation experience, and he was placing me in the CIB "down the hall". I couldn't quite believe it. I looked upon this as a promotion of sorts, since I had been in the division less than an hour.

It struck me as humorous that I had wanted to be a member of the CIB in North Battleford sub/division, with little chance of achieving that status. But now as a new member of "O" Division I had become a member of the divisional headquarters CIB, although only as